RENEGADE SISTERS

RENEGADE SISTERS
Girl Gangs On Film
by Bev Zalcock
ISBN 1 84068 071 7
© Bev Zalcock 1998, 2001
■ ■ ■ ■ ■
First published 1998 by:
Creation Books
www.creationbooks.com
New and updated edition published 2001
Design/layout/typesetting:
PCP International
Cover illustration:
"Charlie's Angels"
The Creation Cinema Collection – a periodical series.
A Butcherbest Production
■ ■ ■ ■ ■
Copyright acknowledgements:
New World Pictures, Deborah Twiss, Vivienne Dick, Dangerous To Know, BFI
Pictures & Stills, Film Makers Co-op, Allied Troma, for the reproduction of
stills. Stephanie Rothman stills by courtesy of Verena Mund at Feminale. All
other stills as credited, or from the Jack Hunter Collection, by courtesy of the
film distributors.
■ ■ ■ ■ ■
Author's acknowledgements
I wish to thank the following people, without whose help this book could not
have been written:
Bianca Adefarakan, Esther Aponte, Charlotte Baggins, Joan Bannon, Carol
Biggs, Pyllis Borden, Colin Burns, Sara Chambers, Ben Cook, Dave Couch, Laura
Hudson, Paula Graham, Helen de Witt, Carol Morley, Jocelyn Robson, John
Digance, Andrew Willie, Jack Sargeant, and the Centre for Extra Mural
Studies, Birkbeck College.
Dedicated to the gang: Sara, Bee and Maisie.
■ ■ ■ ■ ■
Creation Books
"Popular books for popular people"

CONTENTS

STAKING OUT THE TERRITORY

LOOKING back over a hundred years of cinema, across the spectrum of movie making, from the no-budget experimental short film to the mega bucks blockbuster, we can trace a small but rich vein of film making that features women as powerful and active agents instead of the usual passive objects.

In narrative cinema we find that there are three basic structures into which these active women fall: i) the central character who is solo; ii) the female duo in a buddy format; and iii) the girl gang. It is with this last and least common variation on the theme that this book will be concerned; exploring a range of girl gang representations down the years and across the genres.

SOLE SURVIVORS

As the ever-popular films of Alfred Hitchcock demonstrate, women characters, who assume male roles by taking on active agency, particularly if they are attractive and seductive, deserve to be punished. It was in fact Hitchcock's self-declared mission to 'punish the blonde' which he succeeded in doing very effectively, especially in his treatment of Tippi Hedren (Melanie Daniels in **The Birds**, 1963) both on screen and off. Melanie, who represents a personal (castration) threat to boyfriend Mitch and social destruction to the community at large, is brought to heel in a particularly sadistic way through wave after wave of aerial assaults by demented birds.

Hitchcock's perfection of cinematic misogyny continues to resonate in commercial film making as films like **Fatal Attraction** (1987), **Single White Female** (1992) and **Basic Instinct** (1992) (kill the bitches!) reveal, forming as they do part of a subgenre that can be described as 'the ambitious blonde punishment movie'.

There are films, however, where the central female character has endured so much punishment that she turns on her tormentors and blows them away! Rape-revenge dramas, for example, a staple of the low-budget horror cycle of the late 1970s and 1980s, show women staging a fightback – but only after a *lot* of violation. Carol J Clover, in her book *Men, Women And Chainsaws* examines the rape-revenge formula in discussions of films like **I Spit On Your Grave** (1977), **MS.45** (1981), **Positive ID** (1987) and **Lipstick** (1976), where she develops her notion of the 'final girl' who, to survive, has no other option than to take up arms.[1]

MS.45

Apart from the horror genre, there are other variants which feature central active females. These are the role reversal films in which the central role, normally associated with a male character, is played by a woman. Such films are often 'remakes' of movies where the original star was a man. For example, Brigitte Nielsen in **Red Sonja** (1985) reprises (loosely) the part played by Arnold Schwarzenegger in **Conan The Destroyer** (1984), both made, incidentally, by the same director, Richard Fleischer; and Jamie Lee Curtis who in **Blue Steel** (1990) takes up the role played by Clint Eastwood in **Dirty Harry** (1971). Stranger still is Pamela Anderson-Lee in **Barb Wire** (1996), who replays Humphrey Bogart's part as Rick in **Casablanca** (1942). Sadly none of the women are allowed the same *sang-froid* as their male counterparts, and invariably need a lot of support from the men to see them through.

DEADLY DUOS

More powerful than the single girl is the female double act; an image of friendship and fidelity along the lines of **Butch Cassidy And The Sundance Kid** (1969). In terms of resistance these girls are twice as tough and double trouble when it comes to 'kicking ass', which they do without much help from the boys.

   Thelma And Louise (1991) is one of the best and most popular examples of the female buddy film and while they (Thelma and Louise) are both endearing, they are also deadly; driven by a heady combination of righteous anger and irrepressible high spirits. But even if women are typically, if unconsciously, seen as a castration threat, they're not traditionally thought of as murderers, and female buddies who kill are still almost unthinkable in mainstream Hollywood. They do, however, crop up from time to time in European feature films, for example, in **Messidor** (Alain Tanner, 1978), **Butterfly Kiss** (Michael Winterbottom, 1994) and **La Ceremonie** (Claude Chabrol, 1995) as well as in exploitation cinema – as we shall see.

THREE'S A CROWD

For the purposes of the book, three or more female characters working together to resist oppression and fight back against injustice, constitute a girl gang. Because this female unit is a collective one, it is, in essence, more heroic than the solo female and more powerful than the duo. While acknowledging the importance of Hong Kong and other national cinemas[2] in the girl gang stakes, the discussions in this book will be confined to North American and European productions, simply because it is not possible to comment in detail on the impressive number of films coming out of the Far East without a specialist knowledge of the field.

BOYS' OWN

While the burden of this book is to explore the female gang set-up in cinema, gangs in Hollywood movies are almost invariably male and there is a range of genres that offer them as a matter of course. The war film proffers platoons and regiments (e.g. **The Big Red One**, 1980; **Platoon**, 1986), the western provides posses, good and bad (e.g. **The Magnificent Seven**, 1960; **The Wild Bunch**, 1969), and thrillers and action films supply an assortment of gangster groups from the Mafia (**The Godfather**, 1971) to homeboys (**A Rage In Harlem**, 1991). Male peer groups, as teams, can also be found in films about sport (**Bull Durham**, 1988), prison (**Escape From Alcatraz**, 1979) and the police (**Fort Apache The Bronx**, 1981). Such movies allow for both the display and demonstration of masculinity by male protagonists for essentially male audiences. Images of companionship and solidarity serve to legitimise the (patriarchal) codes that underpin 'desirable' behaviour both on an individual and social level. These include personal attributes like bravery, prowess and leadership as well as qualities of good citizenship like discipline, sacrifice and honour.

DIFFERENCE

Because the mainstream Hollywood films function to service a social hierarchy that is male dominated, female characters cast in central, active roles – be they solo, duo or gang narratives – are trapped in a double bind. As protagonists they must assume masculine attributes in order to drive the narrative forward but as women they are supposed to be feminine, recessive and passive – objects of the male gaze. In order to mediate this contradiction,

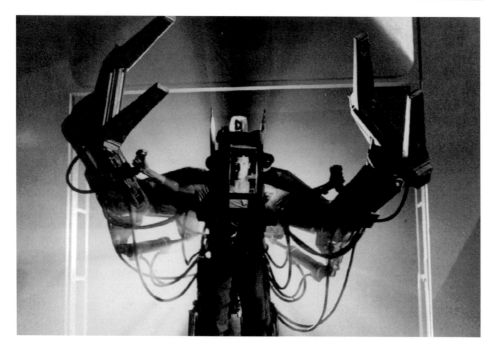

ALIENS

central female characters become honorary men, or to use the psychoanalytic jargon 'phallicised females'. It is this device that allows Ripley (Sigourney Weaver) in **Aliens** (1986) to function effectively. We see her defeat the alien monster mother (maternal/feminine) by borrowing male technology – the blowtorch, the automatic grenade launcher and the mechanical load suit (phallic apparatus) to defend her team and the organisation she works for.[3]

Another strategy of the role reversal movie is to invest the female lead(s) with only partial power, which means that there is a final man to bail the women out. Even Thelma and Louise, that redoubtable duo, need the help of Hal Slocombe (Harvey Keitel) who is not only trailing them but also supporting them; there is no female equivalent waiting in the wings for Butch and Sundance! Nevertheless, in spite of the constraints placed on active women in mainstream movies, there is always a subversive element at play, even if it is only the foregrounding of the mismatch between the male universe and the female subject. The spin offs include some degree of empowerment for the female audience and the inadvertent indication of a "wild zone" – the no-man's-land of female experience which goes with the territory.[4]

EXPLOITATION

So far, the focus of discussion has been with the Hollywood male genre movies which, taken collectively, can be seen to chart the journey from boyhood to manhood (rites of passage) to the final fulfilment – the attainment of patriarchal power. The films of Francis Ford Coppola clearly illustrate this project, taking us from adolescent (**Rumblefish**, 1983) to aged patriarch (**The Godfather Part 2**, 1974). As the poor relation to Hollywood, the exploitation movie, the low-budget, independent studio product, offers a slightly different, less respectful and respectable approach to gender representations. Exploitation films, many of which will be discussed in this book, traditionally produce many more dramas which feature strong and active female characters. These characters are more often than not wild and violent – and a lot of them move in packs!

These lawless gals seem to represent the norm rather than the exception (unlike Hollywood offerings) and because their drive comes from their sexuality, they are hot, heavy and extremely dangerous. This isn't to suggest that they ultimately fare any better than their Hollywood sisters. They are a threat and they have to be closed down, but since the niceties of narrative are stripped to the bare essentials – power in the raw – their potential seems that much greater. Greater too is the narrative requirement to restrain them. There are two basic choices in cinematic terms: i) physical confinement – chains, cages or even death; or ii) marginalisation. Since most of the exploitation films discussed in this book explore the first option, it is useful to see how the latter strategy works. To this end we will look briefly at a film that takes up the second option.

"THE WARRIORS"

The Warriors (Walter Hill, 1979) is basically a B-feature that got mainstream distribution. It is an adventure/sci-fi hybrid set in the twilight world of the New York subway system. It's about gang rivalries and features hundreds of different gangs: black, white, Latin, mixed. But with one exception they are all male fraternities. Visually it is an urban chic display against a tech-noir backdrop. The individual gangs are defined by clothes and rituals and there is a strong blaxploitation homage which includes brothers with afros carrying Uzis and plenty of action and suspense.

An hour into the picture it has been wall-to-wall boys apart from a newsreader on the radio and some guy's flaky girlfriend. The only girl gang – called The Lizzies! – are a tough exploitation-style bunch of chicks who dig power and one another. They lure the central good gang, The Warriors, back to their pad and proceed to seduce them using their feminine wiles plus some drugs and funky music. As the boys mellow out, The Lizzies set on them with an assortment of weapons. "The chicks are packed!" cries one of the guys as they beat a hasty retreat: a comment on their illicit phallic power. The Warriors make their escape and from then on it's back to the guys, so effecting the classic marginalising of female characters.

HIDDEN FROM HISTORY

The reluctance of most mainstream movies to depict women as armed and dangerous is a reflection of our culture as a whole. Public information about militant – or even military – women in news programmes and documentaries

SOLDIER GIRLS

is relatively rare and the fact that women play an active role in modern armies only comes to light when there is a problem; for instance the female fighter pilot recently sacked from the US Military for adultery.[5] Documentaries featuring women as soldiers are few and far between, with **Soldier Girls** (Nick Broomfield and Joan Churchill, 1980), a cinema verité film following three female recruits through basic training, providing a rare insight.

Not surprisingly there is even less film footage available depicting women's participation in armed liberation struggles. **Born In Flames** [see Chapter 5] does include some documentation of women training for combat in Western Sahara, and the North Vietnamese documentary **Vinh Linh, Steel Rampart** (Ngoc Quyunh, 1971) depicts women and men working together to resist 1,000 days of North American aerial bombardment, showing powerful images of women planting paddy, suckling infants and shooting down enemy planes as part of the day's routine.

In spite of the fact that women *do* fight, the prevailing mythology is that they can't or won't, and this feeds into the belief that those who do take up arms are unnatural, a notion that has been around since Joan of Arc. Ancient warrior queens excepted, there are very few historical female role models for fighting girls. Only the utopian epics of Ulrike Ottinger, **Madame X: An Absolute Ruler** (1977) and **Johanna D'Arc Of Mongolia** (1989) tap into that vein.

HIDDEN FROM THEORY

Academics and researchers have generally conspired to perpetuate the disavowal of active female groups, armed or otherwise. Even institutes whose brief is to study youth groups and subcultures, for example the Centre for Contemporary Cultural Studies in Birmingham (England) which was set up in the early '70s, generally excluded young girls from its frame of reference. Writing in 1975, Angela McRobbie and Jenny Garber observed: "Very little seems to have been written about the role of girls in youth cultural groupings. They are absent from the classical subcultural ethnographic studies, the pop histories, the personal accounts and the journalistic surveys of the field..."[6]

They suggest that female peer groups are rendered impassive and hence invisible by the sexist working of the subcultures themselves, an exclusion that academic research appears to have reinforced. While feminist writing in the '80s, and gender studies in the '90s, have served to begin to redress this imbalance (two notable examples being Lola Young's *Fear Of The Dark: Race, Gender And Sexuality In The Cinema* [1996] and Lynda Hart's *Fatal Women: Lesbian Sexuality And The Mark Of Aggression* [1994]), within cultural studies there continues to be a 'We Are The Lambeth Boys'/sub-cultures are male, approach to the subject.

As McRobbie and Garber remarked in their original article: "...girls negotiate a different leisure space and different personal spaces from those inhabited by boys," and suggest that "these in turn offer them different possibilities for resistance". These 'different possibilities' are something that this book will be concerned with, particularly with reference to girl gang films made by women themselves. Some of the films are low or no-budget shorts with minimal production values, but they come from the margins and speak from the wild zone and as such are both subversive and transgressive.

ON THE BORDERS

Two very different cinematic traditions where girls tend to gang up are the Hollywood musical and the American underground of the '60s and early '70s. For a number of reasons these areas fall outside the scope of the book, but they are definitely worth a mention.

GIRL GANGS AND MUSIC

One site of popular culture where girls are seen together and get to be heard is Pop Music. From the close harmony black girl groups of doo-wop and soul, to the all girl punk and rock bands and the currently ubiquitous Spice Girls phenomenon[7], pop music has traditionally offered a niche for the expression of youthful female solidarity. Hollywood too has tended to conflate female experience and music, with the musical and the melodrama as strongly female identified genres. Throughout the '30s, showgirls surviving was a popular subject in films like **The Wild Party** (Dorothy Arzner, 1929), **Goldiggers Of 33 and 35** (Mervyn LeRoy, 1993 and 1935), **Stage Door** (Gregory La Cava, 1937)

DANCE GIRL DANCE

and **Dance Girl Dance** (Dorothy Arzner, 1940). While it is certain that the studios were responding to the depression years with light, frothy and escapist products full of excess and euphoria – qualities regarded as typically feminine – the showgirls themselves, purveyors of the froth, were always depicted as struggling to put on the show in the context of grinding poverty and personal hardship. As such, the female representations in these films were always very tough – working class, organised and independent of men, whose function was often merely decorative.

With hindsight the musicals of this period are amazingly progressive and, although after the decline of the genre in the '50s, there were never quite such positive images again, they remain inspirational. Girl gangs reappeared a couple of times in the succeeding decades in **West Side Story** (1961) and in **Grease** (1978), but they are used in both films as feminine foils to the masculine aggressiveness of the boys. The Puerto Rican sisters in **West Side Story**, clearly more practical than their brothers, The Sharks, are, in the number "America", the mouthpieces for articulating the reactionary values of consumerism, integration and the all-American way.[8] Similarly in **Grease**, The Pink Ladies are the conservative element dreaming of romance and marriage, while their male counterparts are preoccupied with sex and fast cars. The number "Summer Nights" has Sandy recalling her romance with Danny. "He got friendly holding my hand", whereas Danny's version is lecherous: "We got friendly down in the sand!".

WEST SIDE STORY

Ascribing to the girl gangs the aspirations of nest-building and marriage is a far cry from the feisty females of **Stage Door**. Thankfully the two relatively commercial films made by John Waters, **Hairspray** (1988) and **Cry-Baby** (1990) go a long way to dispelling this stigma. These retro-musicals set in the early '60s and the '50s respectively, pay homage to rhythm and blues and rock and roll and the subversive power of both. They also both feature a girl gang of sorts. But most importantly they both provide images of extremely strong and independent women of all ages.

Cry-Baby celebrates Elvis-style music and is based in the Deep South around an extended, working class, and matriarchal family. Johnny Depp stars as the lead singer in a band called 'The Baby Combo' with a back-up group of funky young women called 'The Cry Baby Girls'. Described as "a sort of Grease II with balls" by Judy Rumbold in *The Guardian*, it features brilliant period detail – motorbikes, clothes, jukeboxes – and deals with class, conflict and female independence. The earlier **Hairspray** was made with Divine (Waters' favourite drag queen) and, like **Cry-Baby**, is Waters' homage to the teen pic exploitation films of the '50s. In it, Waters deals with racism and segregation in the music industry.

Whereas **Cry-Baby** is a pastiche with only occasional moments of classic John Waters travesty, **Hairspray** with Divine as a middle-aged Baltimore housewife is a full-blown parody. All the '60s artefacts – hairdos, clothes, décor and dance steps – are hugely exaggerated and fat Divine and her fat

STAGE DOOR

CRY-BABY

HAIRSPRAY

daughter Ricki Lake are pure camp. Cutting a swathe through racism and anti-fat prejudice, Ricki (I'm big, blonde and beautiful) with her girlfriends and their black friends in tow, leads the teenage demonstration down the street to the local radio station. But it is Divine, fat drag queen extraordinaire, who steals the show.

THE UNDERGROUND

Divine was no stranger to the underground, having appeared as the star in a number of John Waters' cult classics, including **Multiple Maniacs** (1970), **Pink Flamingos** (1972), **Female Trouble** (1974) and **Polyester** (1981). The subversive presence of the drag queen is also a feature of Andy Warhol's films in which there are gangs of girls but the girls are all boys and the boys are all junkies and gigolos. In the early '60s when Warhol was in control of his films, there was a minimalist aesthetic at play. Shot in grainy black and white with no sound, no editing, no camera movement and very little acting, films like **Sleep**, **Eat**, **Kiss** and **Couch** provided distantiated images of exotic characters ('the people are beautiful'). With **The Chelsea Girls** (1966), a double screen extravaganza, things had already begun to change; there was sound, colour, camera movement and self-conscious display (not exactly acting). There was still no plot to speak of but the people were still beautiful and as transgressive as ever, including the usual array of prostitutes, fetishists and drag queens.

FLAMING CREATURES

When Warhol got shot by Valerie Solanas, self-styled leader of SCUM (Society for Cutting Up Men), Paul Morrisey took over film productions and his narrativising tendency, already seen in the film **My Hustler** (1965), was realised in the production of full blown, trashy, semi-commercial dramas, starring Joe Dallesandro and an assortment of drag queens who were more than happy to 'walk on the wild side' for the camera. Most notable of these films were **Flesh** (1968) and **Women In Revolt** (1972), the latter starring the three (in)famous drag queens Candy Darling, Holly Woodlawn and Jackie Curtis. Whether these three constitute a girl gang is open to debate.[9]

Warhol had himself been inspired to take up film making after seeing a number of underground films at the New York Filmmakers Co-op in 1962. Many of the films of the period were made on a shoestring by homosexuals with a penchant for the tawdry glamour of the Hollywood B-movies of their childhood, among them low-budget melodramas. Jack Smith's **Flaming Creatures** (1963) and Ron Rice's **Chumlum** (1964) are famous examples of 'the transvestite orgy' genre, that gained critical acclaim and subcultural notoriety. Both films feature a bevy of demented drag queens and could be said to mark the most deviant strand in the girl gang representation.

The libidinal and liberational spirit of the 1960s underground continues to influence film making today and the gender play that was a feature of many of the films at that time provides an inspiration to many contemporary film makers working from the margins, and some of these are women, making films about girl gangs.

POSTSCRIPT

The following chapters will take one aspect of girl gang activity and look at how different kinds of film represent it. Additionally included are the transcripts of interviews given by American film directors Stephanie Rothman and Deborah Twiss, and by two London-based film makers, Vivienne Dick and Julie Jenkins, who have, in quite different ways, provided fresh and original representations of transgressive women in group situations. The book concludes with a consideration of the feature film of **Charlie's Angels**, a millennial celebration of the girl gang.

NOTES

1. *Men, Women And Chainsaws: Gender In The Modern Horror Film* by Carol J Clover. BFI: London, 1992.

2. See for example **Heroic Trio** (Johnny To, Hong Kong, 1993) and **Executioners** (Johnny To, Hong Kong, 1993) featuring "a kickass trio of gorgeous fighting femmes in action versus the forces of darkness". From *The Essential Guide To Hong Kong Movies* by Rick Baker and Toby Russell (Eastern Heroes). And in Japan, films range from the street-gang epics **Alleycat Rock** (1970) and **Naked Seven** (1974), and the Women In Prison series **Scorpion: Female Prisoner** (1972–77), through to **The V Madonna War** (1984) and the '90s trash films of Takao Nakano such as **Invasion Of Mu Empire** and **Playgirls**, which feature cat-fighting topless girl gangs and female sumo wrestlers (see *Eros In Hell: Sex, Blood & Madness In Japanese Cinema*, by Jack Hunter [Creation Books, 1998]).

3. See Barbara Creed: "From Here To Modernity – Feminism And Postmodernism" in *Screen* Vol 28, #2, Spring 1987, for a discussion of this strategy.

4. For an elaboration of the "wild zone", see "A Jury Of Their Peers" by Linda Williams in *Multiple Voices In Feminist Film Criticism*, Ed: Carson, Dittmar and Welsch. University of Minnesota Press: Minneapolis/London, 1994, in which Williams argues that the film **A Question Of Silence** represents that conceptual space closed off to men but which women share.

5. See the case of Kelly Quinn, which caused a scandal in the news in 1996.

6. "Girls And Subcultures" in *The Subcultural Reader*, Ed. Ken Gelder and Sarah Thornton. Routledge: London, 1997.

7. And of course the Spice Girls have now made their own "Girl Power" feature film, **Spice World – The Movie** (1997).

8. For example with lyrics like "I'd like a washing machine..." (girls). "What will you have not to keep clean?" (boys). "I'd like a house with a low rent..." (girls). "Better get rid of your accent..." (boys).

9. Hear in this connection Lou Reed's classic homage "Take A Walk On The Wild Side", on *Transformer* (RCA, 1972).

CHAPTER ONE

WOMEN IN PRISON

THERE has always been an enthusiastic audience for the lowly B-feature and for its subsequent metamorphosis into the exploitation picture. This enthusiasm has rarely been shared by film critics, although with the development of '50s exploitation films into sexploitation, blaxploitation and low-budget horror in the '70s, there developed in certain quarters a cultish celebration of what has been termed the 'incredibly strange' and the 'psychotronic'.[1]

Cinema's recent 100-year anniversary has seen a marked growth in interest in films which fall under the exploitation umbrella. Britain's centenary celebrations were marked in the summer of 1996 by two major retrospective festivals in London; the blaxploitation season at London's National Film Theatre and the Hammer Studio season at the Barbican. The quest for authorship in this field has also been a feature of popular culture since the '80s, with television profiles on the work of, among others, Roger Corman, Russ Meyer, Doris Wishman and Ted Mikels.[2] From the USA Tim Burton brought us the biopic **Ed Wood**[3], about the eponymous exploitation film maker *extraordinaire*, and in the autumn of 1996 the BBC screened a season of contemporary remakes of '50s teenage rebel films.[4]

All this activity has served to make more mainstream the pleasures of the exploitation flick, and reveal to a wider contemporary audience the enduring fascinations which are their focus: fetishism, taboo sexuality and transgression. Elements which in a sense constitute the appeal of cinema itself. This chapter will be concerned with one aspect of the huge exploitation field; a sub-genre known as the Women In Prison movie (WIP).

If you wanted to find images in commercial cinema of dangerous, sexually active and socially deviant groups of women, then the WIP movie would be the place to look. The female prison film was first conceived in Hollywood in the late '20s. For two decades it went through a period of gestation, until in 1950 it was delivered kicking and screaming to N. American audiences in the shape of the much-acclaimed **Caged** (John Cromwell, Warner Bros).[5] It was the watershed in the WIP movies' development, representing the end of the first phase of female prison movies with their mix of melodrama, social realism and a frisson of titillation, and the beginning of the next, the exploitation film with its formulaic plots, stock characters and erotically charged scenarios.

WIP's early history begins in 1929. Two films, Pathe's **The Godless Girl** directed by Cecil B de Mille, and First National's **Prisoners** were both released.

CAGED

The Godless Girl – released in both silent and sound versions – was by all accounts a run of the mill moralistic melodrama.[6] **Prisoners** was a murder mystery set in Hungary with Corinne Griffith billed by the studio as 'the world's most beautiful woman', as a waitress who gets seven months for stealing money to buy a dress. In the years that followed, the 'B' units of the major US studios began to explore the potential of the female prison thematic. Paramount kicked off in 1931/32 with **Ladies Of The Big House** starring Sylvia Sydney, made as a follow up to the male prison film **The Big House**. In the sister version, the leading lady (the new fish) is innocent, but ends up doing time for elbowing a gangster who then frames her. Both this film and Warner Bros' **Ladies They Talk About,** released a year later, provide hard-edged (for the time), socially concerned representations of conditions inside women's penitentiaries. They also provide an exotic array of convicts, including the gangster's moll, the upper class dame and the pregnant girl. There is also a hard-faced muscular matron. As the decade wears on the colourful inmates get tougher; in films with titles ripe for exploitation such as **Condemned Women** (1938, RKO), **Women In Prison** (1939, Columbia), **Prison Farm** (1938, Paramount) and **Girls On Probation** (1938, Warner Bros) we see the emergence of 'corrupt floozies' and 'mean top dogs'. All these features come out of the B-units and the films are generally no longer than an hour. The pattern is repeated throughout the '40s with new venues being added, such as the prison farm and the reform school, and with increasing amounts of corruption, torture and malaise within the walls. Notable too is the emergence of the independent low-budget studios as players in the WIP stakes. Two titles from the Producers Releasing Corporation – **Prison Girl**

CONDEMNED WOMEN

WHAT HAPPENS TO WOMEN WITHOUT MEN?

THE SHOCKING STORY OF ONE MAN AGAINST 1000 WOMEN!

GIRLS IN PRISON

RICHARD DENNING

starring

JOAN TAYLOR

ADELE JERGENS

LANCE FULLER

A
GOLDEN STATE
PRODUCTION

Executive Producer SAMUEL Z. ARKOFF · Directed by EDWARD L. CAHN

Produced by ALEX GORDON · Screenplay by LOU RUSOFF

(1942) and **Girls In Chains** (1943) – and one from Republic, **Girls Of The Big House** (1945) flag up developments to come with the dominance throughout the '50s of American International.[7] An indication of the level at which these films operated was provided by *Variety*, which described **Girls In Chains** as 'a handful of tough girls put on the leer effectively'.[8]

Looking back on these precursors of what was to become the lurid development of the WIP into a softcore exploitation product, it is staggering how innocent and how naive they seem. The prisons themselves are like strict boarding schools where the girls inside are supervised by matron. While often she, the prison administrator and at least one of the convicts is corrupt, they are shown as bad apples in a system which, though flawed, represents morality and justice. Lurking in the background is a good man, a priest or a doctor who believes fiercely in the innocence of our heroine, and restores confidence in patriarchal law and order. **Caged** changed all that.

The interesting thing about **Caged** is how unremitting it is and how hopeless is the system into which the women are locked. Warner Bros, the studio known for its social issues product, pulls no punches. The new fish Marie Allen (Eleanor Parker) arrives innocent and leaves a hardened criminal. In spite of the melodramatic trappings and the newsreel style social realist sequences, what emerges as memorable in this movie are the scenes of erotically charged power struggles between the prisoners themselves and between them and the sadistic matron. A kind of Mae West parody, the matron (Hope Emerson) rules the roost with a rod of iron. She is a caramel chewing sado-lesbian, who taunts the inmates with her power and crushes them with her cruelty. The bad con, a female ponce (Elvira Powell), recruits Marie and lines her up for a job soliciting when she's finally released. Sequences where matron dresses up to go out on a date, a con has her head shaved as a punishment and the inmates put on lipstick as a Christmas treat fairly crackle with repressed sexuality. So powerful were the images in this film that the plot and the character types are used again and again in the WIP films that followed. **House Of Women** (1962) and **Reform School Girls** (1986) are literally remakes, although the latter has its tongue firmly in its cheek.

The first notable development on the WIP scene in the '50s came with Columbia's remake of **Caged** in 1955 with the film **Women's Prison**, starring Ida Lupino as the repressed and wicked warden Amelia Van Zant. Described in the movie as 'a borderline psychotic', she doesn't seem able to get boyfriends. Though much less powerful than **Caged**, the lesbian subtext is much more overt; the corrupt craving for power by a woman finally had a signifier. Unfortunately the movie did not live up to its promotion – "Girls on the Rampage! Shock after Shock!" – but it did set the pattern for the '50s exploitation of the female prison theme. The unyielding matron reappeared a year later in Allied Artists' **Betrayed Women**. Ester Dale's memorable performance in this role was a reprise of her roles in **Condemned Women** and **Prison Farm**.

But 1956 was a crucial year for quite another reason. The low-budget independent studio American Releasing Corporation changed its name that year to American Independent Pictures and released the first of its notorious and lucrative double features: **Girls In Prison** and **Hot Rod Girl**. Geared to the

...what must a good girl say to "belong"?

THE FACTS ABOUT THE TABOO SORORITIES THAT GIVE THEM WHAT THEY WANT!

HIGH SCHOOL HELLCATS

Starring YVONNE LIME · BRET HALSEY · JANA LUND

Produced by CHARLES BUDDY ROGERS · Directed by EDWARD BERNDS · Story and Screenplay by MARK and JAY LOWE · A JAMES H. NICHOLSON and SAMUEL Z. ARKOFF Production · An AMERICAN INTERNATIONAL Picture

RUNNING WILD

TEEN-AGE...
TOUGH...
and TEMPTED
BY EASY MONEY

Hear the hit parade tune that's sweeping the country BILL HALEY and his COMETS' "RAZZLE-DAZZLE"

STARRING
WILLIAM CAMPBELL · MAMIE Van DOREN · KEENAN WYNN · KATHLEEN CASE

with Jan Merlin · John Saxon · Chris Randall · Walter Coy

DIRECTED BY ABNER BIBERMAN · SCREENPLAY BY LEO TOWNSEND · PRODUCED BY HOWARD PINE · A UNIVERSAL-INTERNATIONAL PICTURE

GIRLS ON THE LOOSE

teenage drive-in audience, AIP made no apologies for its sensationalist exploitation product. On the contrary, the studio thrived on teenage delinquency and rock'n'roll, with such entries as **Running Wild, Girls On The Loose, So Young, So Bad, Teenage Gang Debs, High School Hellcats** and **Sorority Girl**. Bad boys and girl gangs were their staple and from the mid '50s to the early '60s it produced a number of WIP films. **Girls In Prison** was followed in 1957 with **Reform School Girl**, released in a double feature with **Rock Around The World**. Addressing an affluent youth market was a perfect sales ploy. By this time TV was making inroads into mainstream cinema-going and, as the family cohered around the TV set, the disaffected teenagers, bristling with hormones and with their relatively new sub-cultural status, made for the drive-ins. The trappings of melodrama and high moral seriousness were gone from the female prison films and replaced with exuberant disorder and rock'n'roll music. The ad for **Reform School Girl** says it all: "Caged boy-hungry wild cats gone mad." The hunger for fantasy and desire to escape from stifling suburban conformity that teenagers felt was to keep AIP in business for years to come.

Cashing in on the youth market explosion and the current appetite for WIP films, Warner Bros and MGM released two B-features in the late '50s: **Untamed Youth** (1957, Warners) and **Girls Town** (MGM). The star of both films was Mamie van Doren, described by Warners as 'the girl built like a platinum powerhouse.' By the time **Girls Town** was made Van Doren was already an

UNTAMED YOUTH

icon of the exploitation picture, a blonde bombshell, the B-feature's Marilyn Monroe who, in 1959 alone, starred in five movies.[9]

The run-of-the-mill '50s WIP films ended with **Why Must I Die** (1960, working title **The Girl On Death Row**), another AIP production which was released as a double bill with **The House Of Usher**. There was also **House Of Women** (aka **Ladies Of The Mob**) another Warner Bros 'B', virtually a remake of **Caged** produced by Bryan Foy, who had produced **Women's Prison** for Columbia in 1955. At this point the WIP films petered out, although AIP continued to churn out exploitation pictures throughout the '60s, with Roger Corman at the company's helm.

It's worth noting that British productions dealing with WIP films retained throughout the changing decades a link with their earlier melodrama and social realist conventions and were often based on 'real life' stories. For example, **2000 Women** (Launder, Gainsborough Studio, 1944), **Yield To The Night** (J Lee Thompson, starring Diana Dors, 1956) and **Scrubbers** (Mai Zetterling, 1982).[10]

In spite of the lack of production of the WIP film on the N. American scene for a decade, throughout the '60s, the Eurotrash market ensured its continuity, in the form of serious sexploitation. Jesse Franco, Italian-based producer/director, was a key figure in the European development, directing **99 Women** (1969, with Mercedes McCambridge as warden and Herbert Lom as Governor). Franco's speciality – 'bondage, beatings, rape, humiliation and

SO YOUNG, SO BAD

2000 WOMEN

SCRUBBERS

sadism' – is characteristic of all his titles, which include such lascivious delights as **Women In Cell Block 9, Sadomania, Barbed Wire Dolls** and **Ilsa The Wicked Warden**.[11] Such pornographic offerings, cheaply made and poorly dubbed, were often produced in Germany and proved popular with 42nd Street audiences! While it's true to say they maintained the continuity of the WIP cycle, they are a far cry from the earlier examples of the genre, lacking even a hint of the social concerns that characterise the N. American product right up to the '60s. Jim Morton sums up the WIP picture thus far: "By the end of the '60s the archetypal roles of the WIP films had been established, i.e., The Queen Bee: dominant female prisoner who lords it over the others. The New Fish: usually the lead actress, in jail for the first time. The Sadistic Warden: more often than not the one who proves to be the root of all evil and unrest in the prison. The Hooker with the Heart of Gold: a street-smart dame who knows the ropes and befriends the New Fish for better of worse. The Dyke Guard: sometimes named 'Ruby'; no WIP film would be complete without one."[12]

With the European exploitation of the genre, by 1971 when New World released its first WIP picture, the stock characters had become crude stereotypes and the classic scenarios sado-masochistic (often lesbian) 'scenes'. Roger Corman, who owned and ran New World Pictures, was not slow to pick up on the potential of the WIP film, and throughout the '70s his Philippines-

SADOMANIA

BARBED WIRE DOLLS

based productions churned out a run of cheaply made movies containing lashings of sex, violence, nudity, sadism and excess, feeding male fantasies of highly sexed, wanton women. Because of the nature of production in the

THE HOT BOX

Philippines, the WIP films settings are most often an island penal colony and filmed in colour.

The two titles **The Big Doll House** (1971) and **The Big Bird Cage** (1972) share the same package with Corman producing, Jack Hill directing, and starring Pam Grier. Her presence in these films ensures a cross over into blaxploitation, which was a popular exploitation category of the time. Filming in the Philippines meant that the extras, cons, guards and revolutionary gangs tended to be Filipino and hence the cast was predominantly black. The nature of '70s WIP film is summed up by Addison Verril in *Variety*: "The women's prison epic is about as hardy a cinema chestnut as one can find these days but it's a perfect show case for the nudity, sex, violence, raw language and comic relief necessary in this type of exploitation programme."[13] Other notable Philippines-produced films include Gerry De Leon's **Women In Cages** (1971, again with Pam Grier), and Eddie Romero's **Savage Sisters** (1974).[14]

The Hot Box and Sweet Sugar, both made in 1972, reworked the prison farm theme established in the **Doll House** and **Bird Cage** duo. Women in skimpy tee shirts and hot pants toil in the plantation with brutal, sadistic, whip wielding guards overseeing them. This softcore fantasy-bondage format is usually spiced up with additional action from a revolutionary gang on the outside who link up with the prisoners and join in the concluding mayhem: the riot and the escape to freedom, a denouement, which is frequently bloody and almost always successful. **The Hot Box** is notable for Jonathan Demme's first credit as co-writer with director Joe Viola. **Sweet Sugar** (*aka*

BLACK MAMA, WHITE MAMA

CAGED HEAT

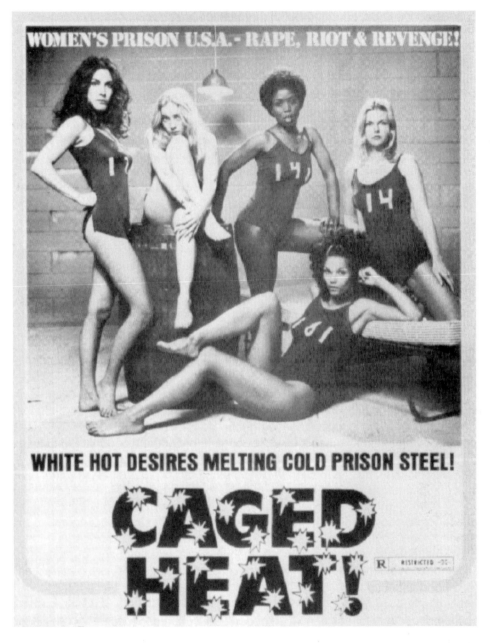

She-Devils In Chains, and scripted by Stephanie Rothman) is basically The Big Bird Cage remade but also features a mad scientist who is working within the prison camp with native drugs. The Hot Box was also remade by Eddie Romero as Black Mama, White Mama, a blaxploitation/prison picture (derived from Stanley Kramer's The Defiant Ones, 1958) which features Pam Grier as a black prostitute, chained together with a white revolutionary (Margaret Markov) and follows them in their attempt to escape from their island prison.

1972 was an action-packed year for the WIP film. As well as the

Philippino-based productions, the television company ABC produced the teledrama **Women In Chains** starring Ida Lupino, reprising her role as corrupt and sadistic head matron who refuses all promotion so the she can stay on the block because, as she says, "My girls are special"! Apart from Lupino's role, the film was average, although it did make a welcome change to be back inside a conventional prison.

In 1974 two crucial films were made which revived critical interest in the genre. **Renegade Girls** (*aka* **Caged Heat**) saw New World giving Jonathan Demme his directorial debut.[15] The two starring roles feature Juanita Brown as the top dog (she also appears in Jack Hill's blaxploitation/prison picture **Foxy Brown**, 1974) and Barbara Steele as the corrupt and crippled warden. It was generally acknowledged that **Caged Heat** was a cut above the rest, although the ad campaign places it firmly within the genre: "Women's Prison USA – Rape Riot and Revenge! White Hot Desire melting Cold Prison Steel". *Psychotronic* observes: "Audiences expecting another forgettable women's prison drive-in feature were a bit surprised to find politics and feminism mixed with the usual skin, shocks and lowbrow humour ...."[16]

The second important film of 1974 was **Terminal Island** (*aka* **The Knucklemen**) directed by a woman, Stephanie Rothman, who with husband Charles Swartz owned the production company Dimension Films (also responsible for **Sweet Sugar**). Rothman had gained directorial experience with New World, getting her screenwriting and directing debut in 1970 with **Student Nurses**[17] (a 'nurse genre' picture whose invention is attributed to Corman).

Pam Cook, a British film theorist and critic writing in the '70s, makes the case for **Terminal Island** being an oppositional film – oppositional, that is, to the prevailing patriarchal ideology of Hollywood and the Independent studios. Cook cites Rothman's own declared feminism and the fact that she as owner of the studio was able to exercise a great deal of control of the product, as making **Terminal Island** a likely candidate for countering the myths of male fantasies that underpin the exploitation film.

While there is no doubt that the target audience for the exploitation is young hormonal men, it has been argued that their hallmarks as 'trash movies' with bad acting, crude stereotypes and schematic narratives make them potentially subversive in that they denaturalise/make obvious the ideological structures which in more respectable films are concealed. Additionally, according to Cook, "the stereotype of the aggressive positive heroine obsessed with revenge"[18] is double-edged. In the WIP cycle women are caged and chained, menacing and monstrous, husband killers, dykes, violent, rowdy and sexually active. Their image as sex objects provides a wet dream for a male spectator but they are also always his worst nightmare, the castrating female.

While Cook's attempt to recouperate the exploitation picture for feminists exists in something of a political and critical vacuum, the links between the growth of feminism in the early '70s and the critical, feminist interest in **Caged Heat** and **Terminal Island** is instructive. The final part of this chapter will be concerned with notions of feminism and spectatorship, with reference to Rothman's film and to **Kali Filme**, a European underground film.

TERMINAL ISLAND

In **Terminal Island** convicted murderers are placed on an unguarded but impossible-to-escape-from prison island in lieu of capital punishment. When Carmen Sims, a black feisty convict is deposited there, she finds herself in a thoroughly brutalised regime. Bobby the top dog is psychotic and rules the convicts through his muscular sidekick Monk (the white boss and the black slave). The small group of women on the prison island are completely servile, doing farm labour, building work, all the cooking and cleaning as well as servicing the men sexually. While dishing out dinner to the male prisoners, one of the women observes, "I've got tits so I have to play Betty Crocker!". Soon afterwards the small female contingent are liberated by a splinter group of male convicts who have escaped from Bobby's tyrannical rule and live nomadically and collectively. In this more liberal set-up the women flourish, sharing activities, ideas and expertise and initiating plans to overthrow the oppressive regime using home made gunpowder and poison darts.

During this period sexual liaisons form but they are based on mutual desire and not always monogamous. One of the group, Dylan, is rather less progressive and tries to rape Joy. The other men chastise him saying "You've got to ask the women if they want to" and Joy gets her own back by pretending to seduce him, debagging him and rubbing his prick with royal jelly so that a nest of convenient angry bees sting him on the privates. Screaming, he leaps unceremoniously into the lake, much to the mirth of the onlooking group. Joy retorts "Now we're even".

This alternative set-up provides an idealised model of a world of sexual equality where tasks and risks are shared. Men show tenderness and women show strength. After giving one of their party a decent burial (unlike Bobby's camp who throw their dead over the cliff) two of the men reminisce about their biker days. One of the women observes "You men are fossils".

They finally overthrow Bobby's corrupt regime and Monk, the black bodyguard, is the only survivor. He is blinded by an explosion and the new regime lets him live with them. In the final sequences of the film we see images of the idyllic society they have built. Joy is pregnant, her man milks a goat and Monk warms himself by a communal fire. There is industry, harmony and peace. When a new prisoner is delivered to the island, she is greeted by a welcoming couple. The film has come full circle.

In affirming **Terminal Island** as oppositional, Cook argues that the bee episode "is a parodic reversal of normal strip-tease procedure"[19] and that while "many exploitation movies employ the positive heroine stereotype as a mirror of the male (i.e. as physically aggressive)" this film in its representation of an equal division of labour is in some way subverting or undermining the codes implicit in the WIP genre.

While **Terminal Island** is an exception to the rule in its structured feminism, the prevalence in '70s WIP films of images of women who are socially transgressive and active sexually and who must be chained and punished for violating patriarchal law and social order can, for the female spectator, be quite inspiring at certain moments. Those moments, for example, where we see raw images of highly charged powerful women working together to defy and destroy their masters. The power of this resistance is well illustrated in an underground film by Birgit and Wilhelm Hein called **The Frauenfilm** from their **Kali Filme** cycle (1987–88). The 12-minute 'Frauenfilme' ('Women's Film') is basically a montage of key moments in WIP and girl gang films taken from low-budget exploitation movies. Using the New World Symphony on the soundtrack, the film constructs the development of the female fightback in three movements from oppression through riot to the overthrow and castration of the oppressor. The Heins' comment: "Here you find women fighting, acting professionally with knives and guns and who 'take no shit from anybody'. They express their sexual desires without any reservation and they even use force to get them fulfilled".[20]

But what of the male spectator? It is clear from the above discussion that WIP films in particular and exploitation films generally present, in ways that Hollywood rarely does, images of active sexualised female characters for the pleasure of the male spectator.[21] The mechanisms that underpin these representations come from two impulses: voyeurism – the female as spectacle or sex object (in WIP movies women scantily clad or taking showers) – and fetishism – women armed and dangerous (the typical S/M regalia of the WIP film including boots, whips, chains and guns).

'70s feminist film theory argued that the strategies of voyeurism and fetishism are common to all Hollywood narrative cinema, serving as they do to reassert patriarchal power (the male gaze) by satisfying male fantasies of dominance while simultaneously allaying their (unconscious) fear of castration.[22] What separates the exploitation picture off from the more respectable, higher budget Hollywood movie, as Pam Cook has observed, is that its mechanisms are more overt – cruder and more obvious and, as such, function to reveal rather than conceal the underlying patriarchal codes,

KALI FILME

exposing in a sense the castration threat that the female representation carries. This, theoretically, at least opens up a space into which the female spectator may insert herself.

The pleasures available to the female spectator of the WIP film is noted in the Heins' **Kali Filme** (Frauenfilme) where sequence after sequence of female fury, using clips from a diverse selection of girl gang movies, are edited together untrammelled by the requirements of any one single narrative. This montage raids the most euphoric moments and functions to liberate them from the films' patriarchal framework and, in freeing them from the narrative constraints, renarrativises them into a different story. At a stroke the potential for an alternative, selective and very different spectatorship is realised.

CONCLUSION

The WIP film continued throughout the '80s and is still around today (Joel Siver's **Prison Heat** [1992] being one notable example). 1983, for instance, saw the release of the seminal **Chained Heat** (directed by Paul Nicolas), the first of several WIP movies to feature former **Exorcist** star Linda Blair (topless).[23] However, the constant reworking of the formula has resulted in a certain amount of parody, for example New World's **Reform School Girls** (Tom deSimone, 1986) was, according to producer Jack Cummins, tongue in cheek: "What we're attempting to do here is to exploit exploitation."[24] The song over the title sequence sums up the mood: 'So Young ...So Bad ...So What?'

CHAINED HEAT

and the advertising "They're tough and they take a LOT of showers!" confirms it. It would make a great double bill with **Caged**, of which it is a remake. Today the exploitation picture is something of a joke and it has also gone mainstream. Another great double bill would be **Barb Wire** (1996) with Pamela Anderson and **Chained Heat 2** (1993) with Brigitte Nielsen. One's an exploitation movie – but which one?

Dubious and prurient though it may be, the WIP cycle has consistently provided images of active women at the centre of its narratives. These images may not be positive but they are always dangerous and this is more than most other Hollywood genres can offer. Additionally, in its '70s incarnation, the WIP film was peopled with characters from groups marginalised or excluded by mainstream Hollywood, namely women of colour and lesbians. For these representations alone the WIP film is worth looking at.

NOTES

1. See *Incredibly Strange Films, The Incredibly Strange Film Book, The Psychotronic Encyclopaedia Of Film*, etc.

2. See the TV series entitled: *The Incredibly Strange Film Show*, shown in Britain in 1988, director Andy Harris.

3. As well as directing the Howco International crime production **Jail Bait** (1954), Ed Wood also scripted A C Stevens' delirious softcore WIP epic **Fugitive Girls** (1973).

4. Including **Girls In Prison** (1994).

5. Oscar nominations: Best Actress (Eleanor Parker), Best Supporting Actress (Hope Emerson), and Best Story and Screenplay.

6. According to *Variety*, "Cecil B de Mille had his tongue in his cheek when he directed this hack yarn with religious undercurrents".

7. The renamed Producers Releasing Corporation.

8. See *Prison Pictures From Hollywood: Plots, Critiques, Casts And Credits For 293 Theatrical And Made-for-Television Releases*, by James Robert Parish. McFarland & Company, Inc. Publishers (Jefferson, North Carolina and London: 1991).

9. Including **Beat Generation**, **The Big Operator**, **Girls Town** and **Vice Raid**.

10. A notable exception being **House Of Whipcord** (Peter Walker, 1974), a pure exploitation picture concerning an illicit correctional institution for 'wanton' girls.

11. Other notable examples of ultra-sleazy European WIP fare include Bruno Mattei's **Caged Women** (1982) and **Women's Prison Massacre** (*aka* **Blade Violent**, 1983). Sergio Garrone's **The Big Bust-Out** (1973) features a sadistic dwarf guard amongst its attractions. Both directors graduated to the most abominated "refinement" of the prison film, the Nazi/SS Concentration Camp genre, with Mattei's **SS Extermination Camp** (1976) and Garrone's **SS Camp 5** (1976) among the most atrocious. Perhaps the most brutal, misogynistic film in the WIP genre is, however, a Hong Kong production; **Bamboo House Of Dolls** (Kuei Chih-Hung, 1977), was even banned – in its uncut form – from domestic release for ten years, in a market where just about anything goes.

12. In *Incredibly Strange Films*, ed by V Vale and Andrea Juno; Plexus, London: 1986, p152.

13. For further details on the critical reaction, see *Prison Pictures From Hollywood*. Op cit. p26, 27.

14. Later Philippines WIP productions have included Kurt Raab's **Escape From Blood Plantation** (1987, with Udo Kier and three horny dwarfs), and Cirio H Santiago's **Caged Heat II: Stripped Of Freedom** (1994, not much like Demme's original). Santiago previously directed the likes of **Ebony, Ivory And Jade** (1976), about three American women ("3 Foxy Mama's Turned Loose") in a kidnapping adventure.

15. Demme also wrote the screenplay and his wife Evelyn Purcell is the producer.

16. *The Psychotronic Encyclopaedia Of Film*, p98.

17. Rothman had previously helped complete Corman's **Blood Bath** (1966), a film begun by Jack Hill. Her other projects include **It's A Bikini World** (1967), **The Velvet Vampire** (1971), **Group Marriage** (1972), and **The Working Girls** (1974) – see Chapters 9 and 10 for more details.

18. In British film journal *Screen* (1976).

19. *The Cinema Book*, ed Pam Cook. BFI, 1982, p200.

20. London Film Makers Co-op Catalogue, 1993, p61.

21. Examples of WIP films which incorporate hardcore sex include: **Prison Babes** (Ted Roter, 1976), **Bare Behind Bars** (Osvaldo De Oliveira, 1987), and **Women In Prison** (Michel Ricaud, 1989); more softcore entries include **Caged Desires** (Don Davis, 1970) and **Caged Women** (Leandro Luchetti, 1991).

22. For an elaboration of the theoretical approach see "Visual Pleasure And Narrative Cinema" by Laura Mulvey in *Screen* 16 No 3, Autumn 1975.

23. Other Blair WIP vehicles include: **Savage Island** (1985, actually a film shot as **Escape From Hell** with 10-minutes of additional Blair inserts) and **Red Heat** (Robert Collector, 1985, also featuring **Emmanuelle** star Sylvia Kristel).

24. See *Prison Pictures From Hollywood*. Op cit. p353.

CHAPTER TWO

GIRLS' SCHOOLS

INTRODUCTION

WHILE the WIP movie, with some notable deviations, is identified with the US exploitation genre, the "Girls' Boarding School" (GBS) picture has a distinctly European pedigree. This isn't to suggest that the GBS has been completely absent from the Hollywood horizon – as early as 1905 the Edison Studio produced a short called **Boarding School Girls** – but that the potential of the context was never really exploited, most probably because the private school system, with its status as a conduit for the ruling classes, is a singularly un-American cultural phenomenon. In US cinema boarding facilities for girls are more likely to be correctional than educational institutions.[1]

This chapter will be focusing on two distinct types of GBS films, in a sense typical of the national cinemas from which they emerge; the serious and the humorous. The serious strand of the GBS tradition can be characterised as melodrama, not surprisingly since traditionally films about females (women and girls) which are located around the domestic and the emotional, fall under this generic umbrella. We will be looking at two such melodramas, one from Germany, **Mädchen In Uniform** (1931) and the other from France, **Olivia** (1953). In both cases these particular films were written and directed by women and both are concerned to explore the developing relationship between the new girl (adolescent pupil) and her schoolmistress (adult woman). As such the narrative follows the movement from the crush through collective desire to unrequited love. Such intense and overt representations of lesbian love have ensured a continuing cult following for the films in question. While it was the impulse of the women's movement of the 1970s to place female-identified narratives centre frame, it has been Gay and Lesbian Film Studies that has sustained and developed that interest.[2]

Since the girls boarding school, like the women's prison, provides an obvious site for a bondage scenario[3] – heavy manners, strict discipline and lashings of lesbian sex – it's no surprise that the GBS has been a candidate for the softcore market, and titles including (sex in the church pews) **Theresa And Isabel** (Radley Metzger, France, 1968) and (sex in the dorms) **Lust For A Vampire** (Jimmy Sangster, GB, 1971) are indicative.[4] And Dario Argento notably utilised the GBS genre for his visually excessive horror classic **Suspiria** (Italy, 1976), in which a residential girls ballet school turns out to be built over a door to Hell. Bloody murders, a rain of maggots, and a coven of witches are

SUSPIRIA

just some of the girls' problems.

British Cinema is the focus of interest for the second part of this chapter but the films to be discussed are neither melodrama not softcore porn/horror, but comedies. These are the GBS cycle known as the **St Trinian's** films, the memorable creation of writer-director team Frank Launder and Sidney Gilliat, which lasted three decades from 1954 to 1980. Although the films in this quintessentially British comedy cycle do not involve obvious feminist or lesbian interest, they do nevertheless provide a radical representation of anarchy, disorder and riot. In fact, at their best, the films are positively (and euphorically) carnivalesque.[5] It is hard in other cinemas – national or Hollywood – to conjure up any images as powerful, memorable and enjoyable as those the **St Trinian's** films provide – gangs of girls taking up arms – lacrosse sticks and tennis racquets to repel all invaders – including rival hockey teams, the police and the army. In fact, the closest visual and ideological influence in this respect is Jean Vigo's famous surrealist diatribe against the French establishment, **Zero De Conduite** (1933)[6], reprised in 1967 by Lindsay Anderson's **If** which dealt with revolution at a boy's boarding school. Because of its obviously serious intent, **If** caused something of a national sensation, whereas the **St Trinian's** films – actually much more liberational, and with violent girls to boot – because they are comedies were received with affection by British audiences and continue to inform a small but powerful part of the national psyche. Timely in this respect is Julie Jenkins' lesbian comedy **MUFF Match** (1996) based around a hockey tournament in an (unspecified) girls school and drawing heavily on the **St Trinian's** comic tradition – although much more explicitly sexually deviant. [See Appendix for Julie Jenkins interview]

PART 1: THE EUROPEAN MELODRAMA

Mädchen In Uniform (Leontine Sagan, 1931)

While quite unique for its time with its strong female production and all female cast, it is useful to place **Mädchen In Uniform** within the context of German National Cinema which throughout the '20s was acclaimed for its silent feature films. Renowned for the stylistic influence known as Expressionism, which in the films took the form of low-key lighting and strangely angled compositions, the *mise-en-scène* constructed a heightened and often bizarre emotionality and strange psychology, which impacted on the representations of sexuality. This is evident in early classics which include the manic **Cabinet Of Dr Caligari** (Robert Wiene, 1919), the vampirish **Nosferatu** (Murnau, 1923) and the sexually simmering **Blue Angel** (Von Sternberg, 1930). But perhaps the key influence on **Mädchen In Uniform** are two films which deal explicitly with female sexuality: **Pandora's Box** (1929) and **The Diary Of A Lost Girl** (1930), both directed by GW Pabst. These two films construct strong and dangerous female sexuality, particularly through their central female characters played by Louise Brooks.

Pabst, during a visit to the United States, had seen Louise Brooks in a couple of movies, **A Girl In Every Port** (Howard Hawks, 1928) and **Beggars Of Life** (William Wellman, 1928) in which she cross-dresses. Brooks took up Pabst's invitation to work with him and resituated to the decadent Berlin of the Weimar Republic. Brooks, whose sexual appeal, as a star, crossed genders, was by all accounts very at home among the polymorphous perversity that dominated the cultural scene in the Berlin of the early '30s. She cites the nightclub Eldorado as offering "collar and tie lesbians" and thrived in the sub-cultural life which was seen as a signifier of the state in crisis.[7] This was also the scene in which the playwright Christa Winsloe thrived. She wrote the play on which **Mädchen** is based and was herself an "out" lesbian.[8]

In the film **Pandora's Box**, Louise Brooks plays the character Lulu who in one memorable sequence does a seductive tango with the predatory lesbian character the Countess Geschwitch, decked out in tweed suit and bow tie. In **The Diary Of A Lost Girl** Brooks plays Thymian, a young girl who is seduced by the local chemist and subsequently sent away to a private school by her respectable parents in order to avoid the public shame of her pregnancy. This school is an institution for delinquent girls and is a hybrid of a boarding school and a reform school. It is here that Thymian encounters girls with attitude; with regulation tunic and short hair cuts. The regime is sparse and regimental. Like the WIP scenarios there is a predatory matron who polices the girls, especially in the dormitories, and a sadistic governor with no hair. In this segment of the film there is a strong visual and ideological resonance with **Mädchen**, made a year later; but in Pabst's film the girls are badder – harder probably because they are less individualised. In their

PANDORA'S BOX

free time they do not discuss poetry or art but rather sit around smoking, playing cards and eyeing one another up.

The cinematic highlight of this narrative segment is the callisthenics class led by matron, where the rigorous work-out routines cause girls to drop with exertion and exhaustion; while matron's eyes blaze with sadistic glee. Pabst's films, famous for their fast cutting, find their apotheosis here as the cuts from matron to the victims get faster and closer. This spatial and temporal effect of pace and distance (ie speeding up and moving closer up) is a sublimely realised sequence, which links power and pain, repression and arousal. The relentless regime of the school is punctuated by moments of recreation and relief. We see the girls putting on make-up and close-dancing together, and in collective resistance – which recalls the final sequences of **Mädchen** – they gang up against matron (who is trying to get her hands on Thymian's diary) in an exciting ruck.

Thus a number of threads connect Pabst's last silent classic with **Mädchen**, an early example of German sound cinema. In **Mädchen** the school provides the sole site of the drama which like the school in **The Diary Of A Lost Girl** is run on military lines and where the headmistress tyrannises

MÄDCHEN IN UNIFORM

teachers and pupils alike, ruling them with a rod of iron. The film's implicit critique of the authoritarian state, based in masculine brute force and patriarchal repression, did not go unnoticed by the Nazi Party who banned it on coming to power. It was censored in the USA for another reason, namely its explicit plea for lesbian recognition, and for American release a number of key exotic moments were excised.

The imagery of **Mädchen** is very effective – based in Expressionism there are starkly angled compositions, hard-edged and off kilter, lit by shafts of light which fall in on vast empty hallways constructing a *mise-en-scène* of cold and emotionlessness oppression. The headmistress is a paranoid control freak and the crushing regime conducive of an atmosphere of near hysteria, recalls the twisted madness of **Caligari**. Against this backdrop is played the central drama of forbidden desire – the love that dare not speak its name. The girls form close, physical and emotional bonds with one another and focus the collective force of their adolescent desire upon their liberal form teacher, Fraulein von Bernberg. She, like any matron in a WIP movie, is responsible for the dorm at night and settling the girls down. Her kisses goodnight to each girl in turn have the converse effect however. The girls are aroused and excited by this nightly ritual, especially Manuela – the new girl – with whom the teacher goes much too far – kissing her on the lips and loaning her (shock horror!) her own underwear, a silk slip. Public exposure of the private passion comes out after a riotous party where the girls get drunk and somewhat disorderly. Manuela in the garb of Don Carlos (she has been performing in the school play) declares her love for Fraulein von Bernberg; to a shocked and stunned audience. This ends the fun and frolic which has preceded it, where the girls have danced together and been uninhibited – gesturing, posturing and touching. Manuela, distraught at the prospect of never seeing von Bernberg again, climbs to the top of the hall staircase and threatens to throw herself off. The girls, as one, move across the hall and climb the stairs in a desperate and determined wave to stop her. Their support and solidarity saves her life. The final message being that collective resistance can stem the tide of destruction. The systematic and stark sadism of the boarding school regime in **Mädchen In Uniform** has rarely, if ever, been equalled.

Olivia (Jacqueline Audry, 1951)

Olivia is a classic costume melodrama set at the turn of the century which relies on music and *mise-en-scène* to construct its mood of aestheticised desire. Based on an autobiographical novel of an English girls' boarding school by Dorothy Strachey Bussy, it was for it time a rare film in French cinema, being one on the very few films directed by a woman. The silent period, by contrast, boasted two crucial female directors Alice Guy and Germaine Dulac[9], but thereafter film production in France was a male enterprise.

    Olivia, in terms of both style and content, is much more soft-centred than **Mädchen In Uniform** and, as such, has elicited less scandal and less attention; but because they share so much content, narrative, structure and dramatic moments they make an interesting comparison – the one stark, the other decorative. As with **Mädchen**, the film begins with the new girl arriving at the school. Olivia is English and has come to this elegant finishing establishment to perfect her feminine attributes. For this is not the regimental regime of **Mädchen**; on the contrary, the young women dress in *haute couture* and drift in a languorous manner through rococo spaces (that only barely resemble classrooms) reading Racine and gazing at the moonlight. Richard Dyer, commenting on the predominating curve at the centre of the film's composition, refers to the feminine aesthetic of the place.[10]

    Central to this sophisticated set-up is Mlle Julie who teaches literature and seems emotionally and domestically bound to Mlle Carla, who is a hypochondriac. Carla is petulant, demanding and suffers. She holds court reclining on a *chaise-longue* where sensitive, ardent students minister to her every need. There is a tense unspoken rivalry between these two central women for the girls' love and loyalty. Since Mlle Carla is the passive aggressive *femme* of the duo, her popularity wanes as Mlle Julie's waxes. Mlle Julie, the butch with the masochistic streak (a kind of Joan Crawford type) is in deep denial, although she recites tragic poetry at the drop of a hat and singles out Olivia for special attentions, including a cosy cultural outing to Paris. There is rather less solidarity among the girls than in **Mädchen In Uniform** and jealousies erupt periodically when favourites of Mlle Julie, for example Mlle Carla and Olivia herself, feel they are being replaced. Olivia, the innocent,

OLIVIA

suffers tears and fainting fits, whereas the manipulative minx Mlle Carla conspires to make Mlle Julie's life a misery by innuendo and guilt trip. Most of the passion and illicit emotion is unexpressed or sublimated into music and poetry. There is very little actual physical contact between the characters and no mention of underwear, but the undercurrents ripple and are lyrically expressed through subtle exchanges of words and glances, with the emphasis compositionally on groups of girls talking about their feelings.

As in **Mädchen** it is the masquerade that marks the turning point of the story and concludes the respective heroine's rites of passage. In **Mädchen** it is the performance of Schiller's *Don Carlos* that precipitates the dressing up and emotional exposure. In **Olivia** it is the Christmas costume ball which liberates the girls out of bustles and bows and into more exotic attire, e.g., Olivia wears a sari. By the end of the night Mlle Carla has been poisoned (an overdose of medicine) and in the inquest that follows the dubious goings-on at the school are blown wide open. Then there is tragic disarray, much reciting of poetry and final departures. Olivia's love, like Manuela's, is unrequited but in a sense it was fun while it lasted; an overwrought fantasy no doubt, but girls cannot live by geometry alone!

The importance of **Mädchen In Uniform** and **Olivia** for a contemporary female, and specifically lesbian, audience cannot be overestimated, providing as they both do rivetting representations of the love that dare not speak its name. Over the years these films have gained international acclaim as landmarks of lesbian cinema. They also represent a critique of the respective repressive periods during which they were made; **Mädchen** holds a mirror up to fascism, while **Olivia** constructs an image of conservatism and privilege in

OLIVIA

the post-war years. We do not return to the female produced, lesbian feature film until the early 1990s, with **Claire Of The Moon** (1992) and **Go Fish** (1993), both of which come out of the growth of 'queer' cultural production in the United States.

PART 2: THE BRITISH EXPERIENCE

In complete contrast to the films discussed above, the British GBS comedy film cycle seems positively upbeat. Four of the titles were the collaborations of Frank Launder and Sidney Gilliat. They are the commercially successful **The Belles Of St Trinian's** (1954), **Blue Murder at St Trinian's** (1957), **The Pure Hell Of St Trinian's** (1960) and **The Great St Trinian's Train Robbery** (1966)[11]. The final film in the cycle was written and directed solely by Frank Launder, called **The Wildcats Of St Trinian's** (1980), and was in a sense too late historically to do well at the box office. It is the first two films – made in the '50s, and arguably the best – that this chapter's discussion will focus on.

Apart from the riotously anti-social behaviour of the girls themselves, there is an interesting range of deviant female representations provided by the teaching staff and a fine example of female impersonation provided by Alistair Sim as the headmistress Miss Fritton; Sim also plays the role of Clarence Fritton, her brother, a dodgy bookmaker. The sense of sexual anarchy and teenage delinquency that the films provide, highlights the conflict in the strict sexual roles available to women in '50s Britain and makes for, albeit light-heartedly, a strong social critique of the post-war era.

THE BELLES OF ST TRINIAN'S

The idea for the films came from the cartoons of Ronald Searle, which were circulated in magazines throughout the '40s. From 1947–1952 they were so popular that they were collected into books, e.g., *Hurrah For St Trinian's* (1948) and *Back To The Slaughterhouse* (1951). Launder describes how his daughter provided the inspiration: "She brought home a book of them from school, and said all the girls were mad about them. Sidney agreed that it sounded like a good basis for a comedy, and we negotiated the rights with Ronald Searle, including an agreement on his part to provide the background to credits and the posters."

Comedy had from the early period of silent cinema been one of the most commercially successful genres of British Cinema. The films of The Hepworth Manufacturing Company, based in the Walton Studios are a case in point. Popular in the company's repertoire was a tomboy team series with leading ladies Alma Taylor and Chrissie White who became the 'Tilly Girls'. The best film, **Tilly The Tomboy Visits The Poor** (made in 1910) is described as 'pure screen anarchy'[12]. Subsequent titles including **Tilly's Party** (1911) and **Tilly And The Fire Engines** (1911) developed the hilarious high jinx of the two tomboys and were popular with the British audience. This strand of bad girls re-emerges in popular British children's comics from the '40s with characters like Minnie the Minx and Beryl the Peril, which feed into the naughtiness of St Trinian's 4th years.[13] Active girls with pluck are also to be found in girls' Annuals which have their roots in publications for girls in the late 19th century.

The Girls Own Annual (1885) is typical – a collection of stories from *The Girls Own Papers* made into a book. For the first half of the 20th century the girls' Annual was an important part of popular culture.[14] Many of the stories are set in girls schools with a strong emphasis on active sports and problem solving; from map reading to foiling diamond heists and above all, the forging of links and loyalties among groups of girls. Visuals frequently featured girls in uniform playing team sports, tobogganing and even riding motorbikes. The girls school, with its fostering of autonomy and activeness among its pupils has obvious potential as a site from which patriarchal power could be challenged – a potential that the **St Trinian's** films exploit to the full.

Another popular cultural influence on the **St Trinian's** cycle and (British) film comedy in general is the Music Hall tradition. Like the girls' literature, the halls have their roots in 19th century Victorian Britain. Funny 'men', clowns and comics crossed over from music hall to cinema almost as a matter of course and in the '30s and '40s film comedies, which incorporated music hall turns, were popular. Will Hay, a jester of the boards, appeared in a number of films, two of which are set in boys boarding schools: **Boys Will Be Boys** (1935) and **Good Morning Boys** (1937). The plot of the latter is reprised in **Blue Murder At St Trinian's**.[15]

In the next decade, the boarding school was establishing itself as a prime site for juvenile high jinx. Launder and Gilliat's comedy **The Happiest Days Of Your Life** (1950) is an unmistakable precursor, pointing the way to the **St Trinian's** development. In this film, as Marcia Landy observes: "...the comedy is based on the question, 'What would happen if a group of girls was introduced into a boys school?'. The answer is: 'Chaos'." Sound familiar? Additionally in **The Happiest Days** the Ministry of Education is a target of satire. The school teaching staff are devious and/or eccentric, played by a team of comic actors many of who reappear in **St Trinian's**. The headmaster is played by Alistair Sim and there are two wonderful performances by Margaret Rutherford as the headmistress and Joyce Grenfell as Miss Gossage ("Call me Sausage") the gawky games mistress – a role that she recreates in **The Belles Of St Trinian's** where she plays Miss Crawley ("Creepy Crawley") working undercover for the Barchester Constabulary. **The Happiest Days Of Your Life** has all the hallmarks of a Launder and Gilliat comedy; verbal wit, wonderful slapstick, individual characterisation and the merciless satirising of those rigid institutions which represent the British Establishment: Public Schools, The Ministry of Education, the Police Force and the Army.[16]

Launder and Gilliat's comedies also seem quite specifically preoccupied with exploring a range of female roles and while this in a sense makes them quite unique in the annals of British film comedy, there are precedents within the Music Hall tradition for such preoccupations – particularly at the point where gender and class intersect.

A Music Hall comic duo the Waters Sisters, Elsie and Doris, provide a strong example of the stereotype of resilient British working class womanhood[17] in their film **Gert And Daisy's Weekend** (1941) in which they play two sisters who volunteer to take a group of unruly town kids (evacuees) to a country estate. While class distinction is at the heart of the comedy, gender difference is also a crucial component. Another example of gender

OLD MOTHER RILEY'S NEW VENTURE (1949)

play comes from the music hall act which featured Arthur Lucan's female impersonation as "Old Mother Riley", a shrewd Cockney washerwoman, a role that plays on working class and female stereotypes to a populist effect.[18] While Old Mother Riley is literally a travesty of working class womanhood, Millicent Fritton, Alistair Sim's female character in **The Belles Of St Trinian's** is upper class and flakily genteel, representing the fading values of Edwardian England.[19]

Another obvious Music Hall legacy is the presence in British film comedy of recurring teams of comic characters. For example, in popular cycles like **The Doctor (In The House)** films, the **St Trinian's** films and the **Carry On** films[20], the comic actors will reprise their original roles across a number of titles. Such actors included Terry-Thomas, Joyce Grenfell, Margaret Rutherford, Hatti Jacques, Alistair Sim and Sid James.[21] Again this resonates with acts in Music Hall like The Crazy Gang whose members, six in all – three pairs – are distinguished by type (as in **The Frozen Limits**, 1939) not unlike the Marx Brothers or The Three Stooges.

LAUNDER, GILLIAT AND THE ST TRINIAN'S FILMS

Together the team of Launder and Gilliat scripted and directed 26 feature films; their first collaboration being a wartime movie **Millions Like Us** (1943). Their cinematic careers actually started in 1928 working at the script department of British International Studios, but because of the state of the

British Film Industry which was hidebound by a dressing-room concept of 'theatre' and the constraints of the quota system, it took them some years to gain overall control of their scripts. Their idiosyncratic productions were characterised by a distinctive approach to plot and characterisation and Gilliat in particular was a fanatic for precise detail – as one can note in the use of décor, for example in headmistress Miss Fritton's study-cum-drawing room which is fantastically detailed. In terms of their comedies it was Launder who assumed control and he directed all their films. In 1950, after the success of **The Happiest Days Of Your Life**, they founded a new company – Launder and Gilliat Production Limited.

THE BELLES OF ST TRINIAN'S

In the pre-credit sequence of the film we see the school name board, a ramshackle wooden affair being peppered with bullets and the sound of machine gun fire. The subsequent titles are illustrated by Ronald Searle with an upbeat musical accompaniment. In a memorable early sequence we see the steam train carrying the St Trinian's pupils pull into the station. This is followed by a montage: station guards scarpering, shopkeepers pulling down shutters, streets emptying, hens running down the coop back into the henhouse, banks padlocked up, cars reversing down roads and police securing their stations and locking themselves in their cells; suggesting that no living creature in the vicinity of the school is safe. As the screaming girls arrive we can identify two distinct groups. One, the terrible 4th formers with their long tunics, plaits sticking out from under battered panamas, scarves and socks in disarray, clutching an assortment of dangerous weapons – hockey sticks and lacrosse sticks and tennis racquets. These are the little monsters who distil gin in the chemistry class and cause explosions in the lab. By the time they have bundled through the school entrance, their defenceless coach driver has been debagged.

The second group of girls are the sophisticated 6th formers. They sport mini-skirts, black stockings with suspenders and high-heeled shoes. They chew gum and backcomb their hair. These are the minxes who kidnap visiting men from the Ministry of Education for their harem where they play pop records, smoke cigarettes and sip Hawaiian cocktails through straws. No man is immune to their charms. This heady combination of riot and seduction sums up the tenor of the school. The girls are a menace to decent society.

The headmistress Miss Fritton is benignly indifferent to the goings-on among her pupils. Her sole preoccupation is to balance the books. The staff haven't been paid for a term and they are virtually without food and heating. One of the new girls is a Sultan's daughter called Fatima. She has £300 pocket money. Miss Fritton takes the money – for safekeeping – issuing Fatima with an IOU and hiding it in the safe behind three elaborate locking systems! In the all-female staff room we find an equally bizarre group. An upper class alcoholic, a golf player with a tweed jacket and a monocle, a teacher in leather bondage who is on the run from the law, and a bohemian painter with palette and brushes – who is not the art mistress! All these characters are signally unsuited to their professed subjects and collectively represent the

THE BELLES OF ST TRINIAN'S

flotsam of a decaying aristocracy. Others are simply misplaced, like Miss Gale, the literature mistress (played by Irene Handl), a chirpy character, who greets the pupils with a broad cockney "'ello ducks!".

The sense of farcical chaos and pervading anarchy is, in fact, carefully crafted. Highlights include the 4th year's foiling a bookmaking scam by kidnapping a racehorse and stabling it in the dormitory. There is also the statutory hockey tournament in which the entire team from a neighbouring school are carried off on stretchers. The gymnasium has already been burnt down and by the end of the film all the school's sporting trophies have disappeared as well. Meanwhile the sexy 6th formers are organising orgies and consorting with crooks and petty criminals.

While their subversive potential is more fully realised in the second film of the cycle, **Blue Murder At St Trinian's**, the girls' ability to ride roughshod through all sections of the British Establishment was hugely popular from the start and on **The Belles'** opening night in London, the queues stretched from the Haymarket through to Lower Regent Street. In **Blue Murder** the film opens with the school under army occupation. The headmistress (Alistair Sim in a cameo appearance), meanwhile, is doing a stretch in prison and a replacement head is expected. The Army retreat, with heavy casualties and losses of personnel and trousers, and the police force are drafted in to ensure the safe arrival of the new head.

There are two unlikely intertwining strands to the preposterous plot.

The 6th formers are harbouring a wanted jewel thief in the dorm – he's the father of one of the girls. They force him into women's clothes and pass him off as the new headmistress, the genuine article having been kidnapped and left bound and gagged in the school bell tower. Simultaneously, the 6th formers are planning an elaborate scam, which involves entering a beauty contest in order to seduce a rich Italian bachelor. To get to Italy the class enter the UNESCO Cultural Competition, the first prize being a European trip culminating in a visit to Rome for an inter-schools water polo match. The girls stage a moonlight raid of the Ministry of Education where they substitute their dismal attempts at answering the UNESCO quiz with a complete set of correct answers. Working with the 4th formers they pull off a precision break-in with stop watches, drills and chain saws. The 6th formers are materialists, motivated by greed and desire; their 4th form sisters, however, are anarchists, who challenge authority wherever they find it. When they all finally get to Rome there is complete mayhem and the final sequences are pure slapstick. Commenting on filming in Rome, Launder observes: "The location in Rome had Italian schoolgirls playing St Trinian's girls and their uninhibited behaviour matched that of our British girls. We got permission to shoot a chase with the girls through the Forum and Coliseum on the grounds that the film was a 'cultural documentary'."[22]

As we have remarked, all the films discussed in this chapter depict, in quite different ways, 'girl gangs' within the boarding school milieu. The films in question also typify the elements of the respective national cinemas from which they emerge.

Mädchen In Uniform with its expressionist style and psychodramatic content is reminiscent of many films made in Germany during the silent and early sound period, with their almost exclusive focus on individual suffering and institutional repression.

Olivia which is a lyrical and elegant costume drama, is characteristically French, echoing the fascination in French culture with Romanticism in both art and literature. This romantic sensibility has proved an enduring element of the French film industry, as the continuing box office appeal of the costume (melo)drama suggests.[23]

The **St Trinian's** films are finally, quintessentially British, based in comic traditions which cross over from Music Hall to the cinema. The humour (which combines visual elements – travesty and slapstick – as well as verbal wit) is based both in clowning and class difference and its impact on contemporary situational comedy is still being felt to this day, particularly in television.

NOTES

1. See for example **Reform School Girls** (1986). The sorority and summer camp is a more all-American venue for groups of girls. See for example **Slumber Party Massacre** (Amy Jones, 1982) and Cairo Cannon's short film **True Blue Camper** (1996).

2. See in particular discussion in *Now You See It*, Richard Dyer. Routledge, London & New York: 1990; and *Vampires And Violets*, Andrea Weiss. Jonathan Cape, London: 1992.

3. Phantasy as the *mise-en-scène* of desire is exploited in porno vampire films like **Satan's School For Girls** (1973) and **Daughters Of Dracula** (*aka* **Vampyres**, 1975).

4. In fact, the lesbian vampire film has proved something of a staple for the British studio, Hammer; memorable films include **The Vampire Lovers** (1970), **Countess Dracula** (1970), and **Twins Of Evil** (1971).

5. See discussion on Bakhtin's notion of 'the masquerade' in *British Genres: Cinema And Society 1930–1960*, by Marcia Landy. Princeton University Press: 1991, p332.

6. See the slow-motion pillow fight in **The Belles Of St Trinian's**, which is a homage to Jean Vigo.

7. For further discussion see *Vampires And Violets: Lesbians In The Cinema* by Andrea Weiss. Jonathan Cape, London: 1992, p22–23.

8. For further details see *Now You See It: Studies On Lesbian And Gay Film* by Richard Dyer. Routledge, London & New York: 1990, p30.

9. See **A House Divided** (Alice Guy, 1913) and **The Smiling Madame Beudet** (Germaine Dulac, 1922) as examples of the early melodrama directed by women.

10. For details see Richard Dyer, *Now You See It*. Op cit. p31.

11. See *Lauder And Gilliat* by Geoff Brown (BFI: 1977), for detailed discussion.

12. BFI/NFT programme notes.

13. See *The Dandy*, *The Beano* and *The Beezer*.

14. For example *The Oxford Annual For Girls* (1928), *The Great Book Of School Stories For Girls* (1932), and *The Champion Book For Girls* (1948).

15. Not surprising since Will Hay and The Crazy Gang worked for Gainsborough studio, where Launder too worked as a script editor in the late 1930s.

16. Holding a crazy mirror up to British post-war reconstruction: "One can almost regard **The Happiest Days Of Your Life** as a picture of Britain in the years of post-war reconstruction, seen through a crazy mirror." (*Launder And Gilliat*, p19.)

17. As was Gracie Fields in **Sing As We Go** (Basil Dean, GB, 1934).

18. See **Old Mother Riley's New Venture** (1949) and **Old Mother Riley, Headmistress** (1950).

19. Miss Fritton says: "When poor Freda and I started this school during the General Strike of 1926 we vowed to make it the happiest, most carefree establishment in the whole of Britain – and what a gay Arcadia of girlhood it was until the war broke out. " (From **The Belles Of St Trinian's**.)

20. Key titles include **Carry On Cruising, Carry On Camping, Carry On Abroad, Carry On Matron** and **Carry On Up The Khyber**.

21. These comic actors should be distinguished from clowns or naturals like Sid Field, Norman Wisdom and Benny Hill, whose comedy is based in individual persona (The Cheeky Chappie) rather than situation of type/role.

22. *Launder And Gilliat* by Geoff Brown, p142.

23. See 1997's **Marquise** (Vera Belmont), set in the court of Louis XIV.

Patsy
KELLY
Mary
BRIAN

Danger!
WOMEN
AT
WORK

DRAG STRIP SHOCKS!   PISTON-HARD DRAMA! ROCK 'N ROLL LOVE!

ALLIED ARTISTS presents

Scorching st
the Slick Chi
who Fire Up
Big Wheels!

HOT
ROD
RUMBLE

LEIGH SNOWDEN   RICHARD HARTUNIAN

WRIGHT KING with JOEY FORMAN · BRETT HALSEY

CHAPTER THREE

WOMEN ON WHEELS

INTRODUCTION

THIS chapter is divided into two parts. Part One consists of a spin down the exploitation road, glancing en route at films which feature female hot rod racers and motorcycle riders. We will be taking a longer look at one of the most critically acclaimed of the exploitation pictures, Russ Meyer's **Faster, Pussycat! Kill! Kill!** (1965) whose subject matter falls within what I've termed the 'Women On Wheels' (WOW) sub-genre.

All the films mentioned in Part One were produced and directed by men for the adolescent male drive-in (double bill) audience. From about the middle of the '50s, the Juvenile Delinquent (JD) film, of which WOW movies form a sub-category, came into being.[1] Spearheaded by American International Pictures (AIP) with Roger Corman at the helm, the small independent studios began to niche-market the new and affluent post-war teenage consumers and produce low-budget exploitation quickies on the subjects of youth rebellion and rock'n'roll.

Influential in this respect was MGM's 1955 release **The Blackboard Jungle** (Richard Brooks) which starred Glenn Ford as the school master known as Daddy-O and had as its theme song Bill Haley and the Comets' hit "Rock Around The Clock". This very successful movie provided the prototype of the JD exploitation cycle which lasted for the rest of the decade. AIP's first double bill, **Girls In Prison** and **Hot Rod Girl** (both 1956) and, four months later, **Shake, Rattle And Rock** and **Runaway Daughters** led the way in providing teenage audiences with a diet of hot cars, teen gangs, bad girls and rock'n'roll. Other small independents followed suit, Republic's **Juvenile Jungle** and **Young And Wild** (double bill, 1958) being typical. The cool of rock'n'roll culture and the heat of teen gang violence with sexy girls on the side proved an irresistible combination for the white youth of middle America, and AIP's title **The Cool And The Crazy** (1958) sums up this winning formula.

The rise of Elvis Presley in delivering rock'n'roll music to a white audience was an important factor in the popularity of the JD exploitation cycle. Many of the low-budget films that came off the production line were little more than vehicles for musical numbers. Roger Corman's **Carnival Rock** (1958) is a case in point with its minimal plot and lots of numbers from obscure rockabilly bands and a cameo appearance from The Platters. The motor car, a popular commodity among middle-class teenagers, was also a crucial focus. Car racing – hot rodding and the 'chicken run'[2] – frequently provided the dramatic thrills that the exploitation film banked on. Young women – bad girls and girl gangs – were also centre frame and the image of girls, as well as boys, 'burning rubber' was another aspect of these films' appeal.

With the '60s came a shift of emphasis from cars to motorcycles and this represented a shift also from delinquency to deviancy. Generally with the development in the '60s to a much more graphic 'sexploitation', the image of 'Women On Wheels' takes on a much harder edge. In the motorcycle movies of the '60s it is the notorious Hell's Angels chapters that provide the inspiration for the sex and violence. Because of the misogyny of the Angels and their sexist ethos there are fewer images of women burning rubber than in the previous decade. There are, however, some notable exceptions, as we shall see. At all events, movies that featured cycle gangs at the centre of their narratives were all but burnt out by the early '70s. Girl bike gangs ride off into the sunset, only to be seen in re-runs or retro-chic excursions like **Dark Town Strutters** (William Whitney, 1975), an earlier blaxploitation/WOW film, or Troma's **Chopper Chicks In Zombietown** (1996, see below).

In Part Two we will explore how women film makers coming out of feminism and the new 'transgressive' underground[3] have used images from the exploitation movie to re-work the girl gang for a female audience. The woman behind the wheel of a racing car or astride her hog is recuperated to become a powerful image and role model for the female spectator as a rebel outlaw with lashings of power and oodles of sexuality.

Made on minuscule budgets, the films discussed in Part Two are mostly short, often experimental and frequently concerned with desire and gender trespass. Produced outside of the studio system, these films tend to circulate via the international film and video festival route, especially at Super-8, alternative, Lesbian, Gay and Women's festivals. They are definitely not commercial products and their production values are often extremely limited. That said, it would be hard to find a more home-made looking film than Herschell Gordon Lewis' exploitation classic **She-Devils On Wheels** (1968), which is discussed below.

PART ONE: EXPLOITS AND SEXPLOITS

"Ladies and Gentlemen, welcome to violence. The word and the act. While violence cloaks itself a plethora of disguises, its favourite mantle still remains – sex. Yet violence doesn't only destroy. It creates and moulds as well. Let's examine closely then this dangerously evil creation, this new breed encased and contained within the supple skin of woman. The softness is there, the unmistakable smell of female. The surface shiny and silken. The body yielding yet wanton. But a word of caution: handle with care and don't drop your guard. This rapacious new breed prowls alone and in packs. Operating at any level, at any time, anywhere and with anybody. Who are they? One might be your secretary, your doctor's receptionist or a dancer in a go-go club."

(Voiceover in the opening sequence of **Faster, Pussycat! Kill! Kill!**)

FASTER, PUSSYCAT! KILL! KILL!

We have noted in the discussion so far how at the heart of the exploitation movie is the issue of the destructive nature of female sexuality. And how such films almost deliberately reveal what the more respectable Hollywood genres seek to conceal, the castration anxiety which underpins voyeurism and male spectatorship, almost as a contrary desire to take the audience to the edge. We will also suggest that in the exploitation product the female characters are fetishised to such an outrageous degree that the representations become (almost) a parody of the cinematic process whereby the castration threat is traditionally played. Women in s/exploitation movies are wild and, because they are so extreme, reside on the sharper edge of male fantasy, invoking a kind of masochism in the male spectator – as the opening statement in **Faster, Pussycat! Kill! Kill!** indicates.[4] We have already seen with the WIP cycle how female protagonists shift from being passive objects – of the camera, the narrative and the gaze – to becoming active agents. Such a shift, with its potential for role reversal, is even more marked in the WOW movies for, unlike their sisters in prison, these babes are at large – unchained and hence more dangerous – burning rubber on an octane high of sex, drugs and rock'n'roll.

In the exploitation films of the '50s, hot rods and, to a lesser extent motorcycles, represent both individual desire and social resistance. Images of fast cars, souped-up Porsches and Chevvies and chopped bikes like the

SCORPIO RISING

Bonnevilles and the Harleys were instantly recognised as symbols of personal expression and group rebellion. Initially these objects become central in the testing ground of the adolescent male rites of passage movie, as the site for both bonding and battle. Two films, **The Wild One** (Laslo Benedek, 1953) and **Rebel Without A Cause** (Nicholas Ray, 1955) provide the benchmark for such youth rituals of brotherhood and cool display, with stars to die for in Marlon Brando and James Dean respectively. The pattern is repeated in hundreds of drive-in movies with titles like **Running Wild** (1955), **Hot Rod Gang** (1958), **Joy Ride** (1968), **Teenage Thunder** (1958) and **The Hot Angel** (1958).

   The homo-erotic sub-text of such films is uncovered in Kenneth Anger's underground classic **Scorpio Rising** (1963). Intercut with sequences of the biker gang in **The Wild One**, Anger provides images of Coney Island Hell's Angels preparing their bikes and themselves for a burn-up. Shot seductively with the eyeline at crotch level and with a soundtrack from the current pop charts, including "Blue Velvet", "My Boyfriend's Back" and "Devil In Disguise", Anger's film is a paean to homosexual desire. Similarly, in **Kustom Kar Kommandos** (1965), Anger plays with the ambiguity of boys bonding around a customised, chromed-up driving machine. Two young men in immaculate white tee shirts and sharply pressed blue jeans shine the car's bodywork to perfection with a pink powder puff, to the whisperingly erotic soundtrack of the Parris Sisters' "Dream Lover": "'Cos I want/A boy/To call/My own..wn..wn".

THE '50s: BACKGROUND AND FOREGROUND

With the commercial success of the teenager-centred movies in the Hollywood mainstream the small independent studios, as we have seen, not only followed suit, but additionally placed teenage girls – especially *bad* ones – centre frame. A clutch of late '50s AIP productions give the flavour: **Untamed Youth** (1957), **Girls On The Loose** (1958) and **High School Hellcats** (1958) are notable examples, complete with torrid by-lines and lurid publicity visuals. Notable too is the emergence of exploitation star Yvonne Lime whose bad girl role in **Untamed Youth** and **High School Hellcats** is reprised in **Dragstrip Riot** and **Speed Crazy**. Her roles reveal that girls could be bad, not only in sororities and on street corners, but also behind the wheel of a fast car.

Precursors of the WOW sub-genre can be found in the '40s with PRC's **Blonde Comet** (1941), which stars Virginia Vale as a racing driver (remade in the '80s as **Heart Like A Wheel**). Another offering, **Danger Women At Work** (1943), has Patsy Kelly as an ace car mechanic. Films like this mark the shift in demographics in the USA of the '40s, with women moving into hitherto male-dominated jobs while the men are off to war. So, for a short while, women enjoy social and cinematic parity with men.[5]

It wasn't to last though, and in the post-war '50s the bad, freewheeling, economically independent 'femmes fatales' are reined in. In a decade where women were under strict orders to relinquish their newfound freedoms and get home, stay married and raise families, mainstream media (TV and Hollywood) proffered two basic representations of women – the unmarried 'bimbo' looking for a husband (e.g. Marilyn Monroe in **How To Marry A Millionaire**, 1953) and the married woman and mother (e.g. Lauren Bacall, long-suffering wife in **Written On The Wind** 1956).

In the context of repression on the home front and the Cold War on the international front, it is not surprising that women were consigned to the margins. In cinematic terms women who aspire to power or control over their own lives are depicted as at best damaged, at worst deranged. Girls who are as bad as boys are by virtue of their gender, adjudged to be much worse. In the exploitation films they are out of control, wreaking havoc at home and on the streets.[6] Inevitably by the end of the movie they are reformed and ready to settle down. In spite of titles that promise female passion and power, **Hot Rod Girl** (1956), **Drag Strip Girl** (1957) and **Hot Car Girl** (1958)[7], the films always fail to deliver.[8] The drive, race and ride sequences where the girls show that they are every bit as hot and heavy as the boys are all too brief. Before long our heroines are dragged down by the romantic undertow that is a feature of the genre. They are tamed because they are soft inside – emotional. They fall in love. It is their downfall because it means they must hang up their goggles and get into a frock. Just like their mainstream relative, the Hollywood melodrama, these exploitation pictures and their female characters are soft centred.[9]

"WHY MUST I BE A TEENAGER IN LOVE"

Just as film studios both large and small were focusing on the misunderstood teenager (the boy with the hormones, the girl with the emotions), the music industry, that other strong force in the production of Youth Culture, was exploiting the new affluent market. Along with the rise of Elvis Presley and the explosion of rock'n'roll, another strand with a particularly female slant was developing. In the late '50s a black girl group called The Chantels was pioneering a new sound that brought to contemporary pop music the emotional intensity of the teenage girl experience by taking doo-wop and giving it a female address. As Charlotte Greig observes in her book about Girl Groups from the '50s *Will You Still Love Me Tomorrow*: "The Chantels' style, a blend of devotional love lyrics and simple rhythm and blues backing with youthful yet heartfelt wailing from the girl lead singer and cooing sweet harmonies from the chorus, formed the basis of the girl group sound that was to hit America and Britain in the sixties."[10] Their lead was followed by another black all-girl group called The Shirelles, who mark a transition from the fluid emotionality of the '50s to the harder-edged chic of the '60s. Hits like "Tonight's The Night" and "Will You Still Love Me Tomorrow" balance sexuality with vulnerability and mark the beginning of the girl group explosion that was to dominate popular music in the '60s. Then, in 1962, another black girl group, The Crystals, have a hit with "He's A Rebel", which expresses a new female confidence. This new mood is picked up by The Ronettes, the 'bad girls with beehives' whose 1963 hit "Be My Baby" takes a step from the emotional to the seductive. As with teenage music, so with teenage films. The '60s herald a new mood. The romantic undertow so characteristic of female representations in the '50s begins to recede. As John Waters' two retro films **Hairspray** (1988) and **Cry-Baby** (1990) (set in the late '50s and early '60s and dealing with pop music and girl gangs) reveal, female teenagers in the next decade are becoming more demanding and more sexually active than their '50s sisters. By the middle of the decade, exploitation films have become sexploitation films and the bike gangs ride into frame.

THE '60s

"Biker movies were good to a lot of producers, distributors and actors. They were quick to make, required minimal scripting and made few demands on anyone's talent."[11]

The '60s was definitely the decade of the US motorcycle picture, which reached its apotheosis in 1966 with AIP's release of Roger Corman's epic **The Wild Angels**. While most of the films focus on a male chapter with girls confined to riding pillion at best, or as casual sex objects at worst, there were a handful of films produced which featured an all-girl bike gang.[12] Produced in the late '60s, the cycle chicks movie was an attempt on the part of the small studios to take the motorbike genre as far as it would go. Notable titles include **Teenage Gang Debs** (Sande Johnsen) which was filmed in Brooklyn and returns to the format of the bad kids film of the '50s, although there is a lot more graphic sex and violence as the film's publicity suggests: "They all talk, fight and love just one way... DIRTY!".

CRY-BABY

The Mini-Skirt Mob (Maury Dexter, 1968) is an AIP release promising 'hog straggling female animals on the prowl'. Billed as *the* big summer draw for the drive-in trade, its highlights are sadistic violence, a catfight between the two female leads and some exciting motorcycle footage. The title, though, is something of a giveaway and the girls spend more time on their appearance than on their bikes; and, horror of horrors, the pack travel with their boyfriends! Two tougher titles – The Hellcats (Robert F Slater, 1968) and Sisters In Leather (Zaltan G Spencer, 1969) – feature a drug smuggling girl pack and a gang of lesbo-motorcycle chicks respectively. The gals in The Hellcats do get to kill a cop but this is their finest hour and they never really burn enough rubber to create a smell, while the girls in Sisters In Leather have a ball initiating the wife of a businessman into the pack. There is a wild champagne-drinking and nude-riding orgy which is fun while it lasts – that is, until the bike boys arrive to close it down.

By far the best of the girl biker batch is Herschell Gordon Lewis' She-Devils On Wheels (1968) in which an all-female motorcycle gang called 'The Man Eaters' show who's on top and effect something of a genuine role reversal. Their refrain is not an empty boast: "We don't owe nobody/And we don't make no deals/We're swinging chicks on motors/We're man eaters on wheels!". Lewis, who as a director is renowned for his penchant for gore, is relatively restrained in She-Devils On Wheels, with only three serious gore scenarios: a bashing, a flaying and a decapitation.[13] In all other respects, the hallmarks of Lewis' work are present; for example, the amateur approach to film making, including the tactic of filming silent and post synching the sound, basic one camera set ups, non-professional acting (most of the cycle gang are

See! The Authentic Initiation Ritual Never Before Dared On Film. See! Female Hellcats Ruling Their Men With Tire-Irons As Their Instruments of Passion.

members of the real-life cycle gang 'The Cut Throats'), laboured dialogue and soporific editing. On the other hand, **She-Devils On Wheels** has a lot to recommend it and remains one of Lewis' most popular films, with only **Blood Feast** making more money.

The female characters who dominate the drama are distinctive and relatively well drawn. They include Queenie, the mouthy dykish leader of the pack, Whitey her sidekick, a large Valkyrie-like diesel with a penchant for rhyming couplets, Karen, a good girl on weekdays (when she lives at home) and a goer at the weekends, and Honeypot, the scooter-riding young novice and innocent who is desperate to get initiated as a full member of the gang. The gals prove to be as hot and heavy as their male counterparts in terms of the genre. They terrorise towns, intimidate citizens, break the law and beat up their rivals. At one point in the movie, a group of hot rod boys trespass on their turf and The Man Eaters dispatch them with gusto. They prove superior in strength and fighting skills to their male rivals. Another aspect of the gender role reversal of this film is the way in which the female pack use men

casually for their own sexual gratification. For example, after a race, the winning girl gang member has the privilege of selecting the stud of her choice. As such, men are around to service the females' desires; the publicity boasts: "See! Female Hellcats ruling their Men with Tire-Irons as their Instruments of Passion". Queenie rules the pack with an iron fist: "Guts As Hard As The Steel Of Their Hogs". She is ruthless, and, when Honeypot is kidnapped and beaten up by the Hot Rod gang, the revenge is swift and devastating – their leader Joe Boy is decapitated by being lured headlong into neck-high steel wire stretched across the road. Even Karen, the weak link in the gang because she is romantically inclined and prone to get emotionally involved with men – first Bill who she gets too fond of and later her ex-boyfriend Ted who wants her to abandon the gang – is ultimately loyal to her sisters and drives off into the sunset with them at the end in celebratory mood.

She-Devils On Wheels provides a glimmer of how truly subversive the exploitation picture can be. The film sustains the reversal of gender roles throughout the narrative right to the end. There is no cop out, no compromise – the girls stay together, ditch the men and dodge the law. It's good – but Russ Meyer's **Faster, Pussycat! Kill! Kill!** is even better.

FASTER, PUSSYCAT! KILL! KILL!

A lot of ink has been spilt on the subject of Russ Meyer's cult movie. Much of the discussion has focused on its superbly camp depiction of the exploits of three hot rod girls with more than their fair share of cleavage and attitude. But in a sense, **Faster Pussycat** is much more than a camp classic. It is a radical exposé of the repressiveness which typifies both mainstream American society and mainstream American cinema. Meyer's critique is effected through a satirising of the melodramatic mode that dominated teenage dramas throughout the '50s, both in the big budget and the small budget film studios. **Faster Pussycat** serves to expose the sentimentalism and conservatism that lies at the heart of the Hollywood melodrama, with its emphasis on family values, traditional gender roles and heterosexual relationships.
This project re-emerges in Meyer's **Beyond The Valley Of The Dolls** (1970) when the studio, 20th Century Fox, somewhat misguidedly hired Russ Meyer to make the sequel to **Valley Of The Dolls** (Mark Robson, 1967). In their article *Russ Meyer, Biography*, J Morton, Vale and H Cross sum up the film as follows: "If there is such a thing as a perfect motion picture, **Beyond The Valley Of The Dolls** is it. In a world of Hollywood glitz it combines elements of sexploitation with experimental camera work and narration worthy of the best educational film with the bouncy good nature of a Beach Party movie. It has sex and violence, rock'n'roll, drugs, Nazis, hermaphrodites, lesbians, cripples, blacks, pathos, bathos and a woman giving head to a .45 automatic...."[14]

Meyer's project in **Faster, Pussycat! Kill! Kill!** is like that of **Beyond The Valley Of The Dolls**, but his earlier film is much less convoluted and as a result much more deadly. His hyperbolic play with the already exaggerated codes of the '50s exploitation movies, his outrageous rendering of narrative, character and visuals, effects a critique of the denial that resides in such movies, particularly in terms of female representations. For example, in **Faster, Pussycat! Kill! Kill!** it is the men who are ultimately the emotional subjects and who are situated in the traditionally assigned female space – the home, the domestic heart of family life – while the women freewheel around them in a strutting posse, occupying the traditional male terrain – the great outdoors.

From the film's opening title sequence (a semi-experimental affair with white sound waves visualised on a black frame and a male voiceover warning

BEYOND THE VALLEY OF THE DOLLS

of the dangers of violent women in groups), Meyer gives notice of his intention to override the safety mechanisms which are normally released in the exploitation genre to close down the female threat and keep the women in check. These mechanisms, typically the exploitation of the emotional weakness of the female character towards her eventual narrative taming, appear not to exist in **Faster Pussycat**. Only at the beginning of the film, in the Go Go Club sequence, do we see the female gang in anything that resembles a traditional role. Even then the aggressive nature of the editing and the accompanying sound track serve to subvert the image of the stripper as a passive object of the male gaze. On the contrary, the threat of the near-naked female is emphasised and their power as castrating she-devils underlined with the jump cut on maniacal female laughter to the image of Varla, gang leader, racing her Porsche in the desert.[15] Varla (Tura Satana) is mean, violent and takes no prisoners. She is the statuesque embodiment of the female threat and she, and the other two gang members, are shown to be in their element burning rubber in the desert. All three are presented as active, tough and combative, engaging in the kind of horseplay and bonding more usually associated with the male gang.

Meyer's female characters and their hard-edged dialogue are striking aspects of **Faster Pussycat** and the first half of the film concentrates exclusively on presenting the gang. Varla is clearly the most powerful – fearless, intimidating, and with the deepest cleavage. Like Doris Wishman's films with Chesty Morgan (**Deadly Weapons** and **Double Agent 73**, 1974), the

FASTER, PUSSYCAT! KILL! KILL!

iconography of the female breast is reversed to represent not the maternal and the reassuring but the seductive and the lethal. Varla typically wears a lowcut black jumpsuit with black leather accoutrements – boots, belt and gloves. She smokes a black cigarillo and drives a black sports car. Tura Satana, who plays the role, is an Oriental-American (part Japanese, part Cherokee) and her long, sleek, black hair sets her character off to perfection.[16]

The willowy Haji (who also plays in **Beyond The Valley Of The Dolls**) is Rosie, Varla's adoring sidekick. Her role as femme to Varla's butch is noted

FASTER, PUSSYCAT! KILL! KILL!

by Billie (Lori Williams), the third gang member who says: "Jack and Jill, they make the Mafia look like Brownies!". While Rosie loves Varla, Varla loves no-one but herself and the 'long greens' (money). And it is precisely because she lacks emotions that Varla is so powerful. She remarks: "I like a man with a big appetite – but I could never find one to match mine!".

Billie, the all-American blonde, a Barbie doll with attitude, is clearly the most heterosexually defined and it is her interest in men that proves the weak link. She is not reliable, and the fact that she doesn't desire Varla means that she is unwilling to acquiesce unconditionally to her leadership. Her attire also marks her as different. She wears whites and pale colours – hipster jeans with a white belt and a tight short tank top exposing acres of midriff. She's the one we see taking a shower (although shot discreetly from behind)[17] and she's the only one of the three to change her outfit – relinquishing her jeans for white hot pants and knee-length white boots. Billie betrays the gang for a man who she approaches, Mae West-fashion, when she sees him training with weights: "I don't know what you're in training for but as far as I'm concerned, you're ready!". Consequently Billie is the first one to die at the hands of her leader, with a switchblade in her back.

DIALOGUE AND ATTITUDE

The gang's initial encounter is with a couple of nerdish squares, a young couple – the 'good guy' casually dressed in shorts and a loose shirt and the

'good girl', known as 'the playmate' who is clad (absurdly) in a bikini throughout. The gang's attitude to all-American values is revealed during this encounter. The ensuing conversation, while the gang plan a car race with the couple, is instructive.

Good girl:	*Do you want a soft drink?*
Rosie:	*Honey, we don't want nothing soft!*
Good boy:	*Do you beat the clock?*
Varla:	*I don't beat clocks, just people!*
Good girl:	*Is everybody ready?*
Billie:	*Honey, I'm always ready!*

After the race there is an altercation in which Varla kills the boy with her bare hands by breaking his neck.

NARRATIVE DEVELOPMENT

The second half of the film is located in and around a desolate farmstead run by a wheelchair-bound patriarch who rules his two sons, The Bookworm (all brains) and The Vegetable (all brawn) with a rod of iron. It is into this all-male household that the gang venture with the 'good girl' as their prisoner. They

FASTER, PUSSYCAT! KILL! KILL!

need somewhere to hole out after the murder and they've learnt from a local garage attendant that the old man is sitting on a fortune. Driven by need and greed they appear, rather like a reversal of the 'gentlemen callers' in a Tennessee Williams' play!

The domestic space is repressive and full of impotent and inadequate men. Varla is undeterred; she's after the money and ready to use all her powers (seduction, intimidation and violence) to get it. Recognising her almost as a kindred spirit (in her ruthlessness) the old man observers: "She's more stallion than filly!".

After various encounters involving all the men, Varla in frustration unleashes an orgy of violence with karate, switchblade and even her Porsche as deadly weapons. In the manic scenes that ensue every character comes to a violent end, with the exception of The Bookworm and the 'good girl' who become a kind of replacement heterosexual couple. This absurd finale, as they walk (unconvincingly) towards the horizon, sets the satirical seal on Meyer's film. It is of course the traditional Hollywood ending but in Russ Meyer's universe it is pure kitsch, absolutely off the wall.

With **Faster, Pussycat! Kill! Kill!** the girl gang/WOW movie reaches sublime heights and shows Russ Meyer at the pinnacle of his film making talent. His subsequent attempts to reprise the female thematic and send up the melodramatic nature of American values are enjoyable, but never attain

FASTER, PUSSYCAT! KILL! KILL!

the casual deranged genius of **Faster Pussycat!**.

THE '70s AND EARLY '80s

Angels' Wild Women (1972) was exploitation's 'Women On Bikes' swansong. Made by Al Adamson – who gained notoriety with Hell's Angels titles including **Satan's Sadists** (1969) and earlier what Steve Puchalski in "Attack Of The Cycle Pyschos"[18] describes as the 'indescribably incoherent' **Hell's Bloody Devils** (shot in 1967 and released in 1970) – it features four biker women, who split from the guys and start their own gang. Starring Regina Carroll (Adamson's wife) and Vicki Volante, the poster publicity is perhaps its best feature: "HOT, HARD AND MEAN ...Too Tough for any Man!! They'll BEAT 'em, TREAT 'em and EAT 'em alive!". Filming at the Spahn ranch, where Charles Manson and his followers had lived, was no doubt a tacky attempt to give the film a greater commercial appeal. At around the same time Adamson directed **The Female Bunch**, the tale of five women who "...dare to do what other women only dream about... their law is the whip – their trade mark a branding iron!" A violent, sexy, trashy female version of Peckinpah's **Wild Bunch**, starring Regina Carroll, Lon Chaney Jr and Russ Tamblyn amongst other B-movie notables. Adamson's other 'western' was **Five Bloody Graves** (1969).

EPILOGUE: CHOPPER CHICKS IN ZOMBIETOWN

Things went downhill from the early '70s, as the image of strong women astride hogs pretty much disappeared from view – until it resurfaced, briefly, in Troma's recent **Chopper Chicks In Zombietown**. This video release, written and directed by Dan Hoskins, is in many respects strongly reminiscent of H G Lewis' **She-Devils On Wheels**, featuring strong bike riding footage, an authoritarian leader, a small town backdrop and a range of gang members including the soft girl who rekindles things with an ex-boyfriend and threatens gang unity. Troma's titles – including such gems as **Surf Nazis Must Die, A Nymphoid Barbarian In Dinosaur Hell, Macho Woman, Femme Fontaine: Killer Babe For The CIA, Ferocious Female Freedom Fighters** and **Teenage Cat Girls On Heat** – certainly recall the heady days of the drive-in, with dubious subject matter and production values to match. Reminiscent too of early '70s biker-horror hybrids like Michel Levesque's **Werewolves On Wheels** and Don Sharp's **Psychomania, Chopper Chicks In Zombietown** combines burning rubber with mashing monsters, adding a dash of the morality tale that has characterised zombie movies from **Invasion Of The Body Snatchers** (Don Siegel, 1956) to **Dawn Of The Dead** (George Romero, 1979) in the good versus evil stakes.

The film opens with 'The Cycle Sluts' driving into town to a funky rock'n'roll soundtrack. "Eight broads on the rag!" the leader of the pack comments as the throbbing chrome hogs screech to a halt. What they don't know is that the hostile redneck town hides a dirty secret. In a back room at

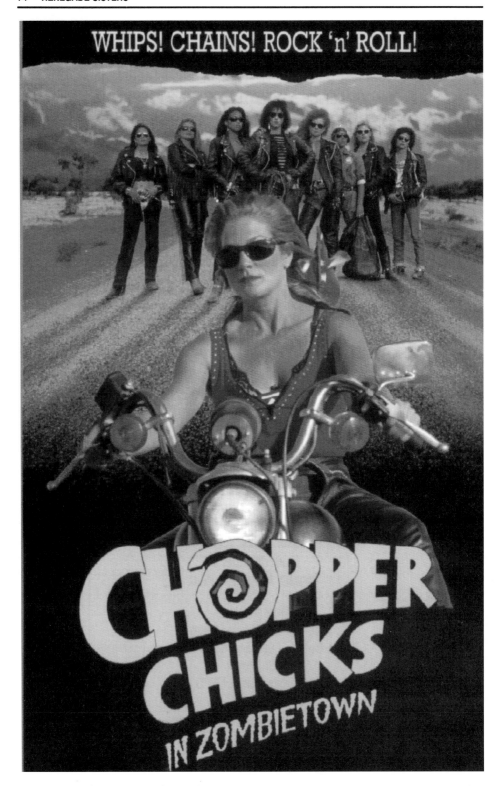

CHOPPER CHICKS IN ZOMBIETOWN

the local Funeral Home the deranged proprietor spends his days draining blood from his murder victims and experimenting on their corpses. Meanwhile on the outskirts of town a scarecrow army of zombies gather. At another location the school for blind orphans prepare for a coach outing.

The Sluts split up. One gets laid; another checks out her ex, another gets murdered. Oblivious to all this, the leader of the pack in a heart to heart with one of the gang girls who can't speak, explains why she's so hard on them all. "You guys are all I've got, kid. For the record, I'm a dyke." Her mission is to protect the girls from 'doom in normalsville' and to keep them together. When they discover that one of their number is dead, the Sluts regroup and after rescuing a baby from a zombie attack and saving the blind orphans on the bus from a similar fate, they prepare for the denouement. It comes in the form of luring the zombies into the local church and blowing them away. During the final mopping up operation, where they zap the remaining zombie stragglers, the surviving townspeople warm to them and give them a vote of thanks. To smiles and applause the Sluts hightail it out of town with a local lad or two riding pillion. The girl with the husband dispatches him with the words: "Husbands are for normals. I'm not normal!". A fitting epitaph to the deviant potential of the WOW cycle.

PART TWO: WOMEN CHART THE ROUTE

As we have seen, powerful images of women behind the wheel of a fast car or astride a throbbing motorcycle are part of the exploitation films' repertoire. Their potential for expressing deviance and desire, rebellion and resistance is picked up by women film makers working from the low- and no-budget margins of independent production. Blazing the trail in Europe are two sub-cultural, queer classics, Derek Jarman's **Jubilee** (Britain, 1978) and

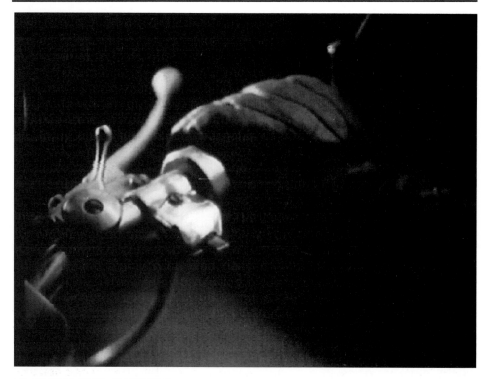

AN INVITATION TO MARILYN C

Monika Treut's **The Virgin Machine** (Germany, 1988), both of which provide images of female gangs on motorcycles as markers of danger and deviancy.[19] In the following discussion we'll look at a number of films that resoundingly reject the notion of the woman as passenger or pillion rider and place her firmly in the driving seat.

The first three films to be discussed use one central female character and her vehicle to represent a group or even a movement. They are **An Invitation To Marilyn C** (Jacqui Duckworth, Britain, 1983), **Desire Drives Her Car** (Kathleen Maitland-Carter, Toronto/London, 1989) and **It Wasn't Love** (Sadie Benning, USA, 1992). They are all short, semi-experimental dramas made on a shoestring budget and in each of them it is lesbian desire that powers the motor of the narrative. The central protagonists are all confident, even swaggering characters, in each case representing the preoccupations of the period in which the films were made. Collectively, the films allow us to chart the development of the lesbian sub-culture from the early '80s onwards; from feminism, through lesbian visibility to transgenderism.

The central character in **An Invitation To Marilyn C** is Roxanne who is sexually exploited by her husband, pornographic film director, Paul. Roxanne, with the help of Paul's female assistant Connie, succeeds in liberating herself, punishing Paul and running off with Connie, while taking time out to mount a one-woman attack on a Soho cinema showing porn movies. The film connects up with feminist activism in the early '80s referencing two powerful campaigns of the period – 'Reclaim The Night' and 'Y B A Wife'.[20]

The title of the film and its subject matter also refers directly to Marilyn Chambers, star of the celebrated and hugely popular softcore movie **Behind The Green Door**. Jacqui Duckworth's film is an invitation to all female workers who are victims of the sex industry to break their chains and escape – preferably with a woman!

Roxanne reaches a point where she can no longer bear to be humiliated by the roles she has to play in her lecherous husband's films, and, in sheer frustration, rides her motorbike down to Soho, London's red light district. Parking it outside the entrance of a tacky sex cinema, she opens up the throttle and revs the engine until the smoke from the exhaust literally drives the male punters out of the screening – choking and gagging onto the street.

Since 'the personal is political' is the slogan of the day, Roxanne needs to save herself, as well as cleaning up the streets of London. Early in the film she has been depicted within the confines of the film frame or the field of the view finder; trapped as an object on sexual display. Roxanne's revenge, aided by Connie, is to reverse the role and imprison Paul the pornographer. The plot is hatched and after much mathematical calculations of focal lengths, the two of them who by now appear to be lovers, put their plan into action.

Shot throughout in moody night-time *noir*, the film's climax involves handcuffing Paul to the bed and then confining him in a purpose-built and meticulously measured box in which he is forced to stand naked and helpless. Revenge is sweet and, as the film suggests, relatively easy to implement. Its message is a feminist rallying cry: The Power of Men is the Patience of Women.

Kathleen Maitland-Carter's **Desire Drives Her Car** focuses, as the title suggests, on the seductively powerful image of the car in American cinema, culture and society. In this film, the car promises the possibility of the fulfilment of sexual fantasy – it is visualised as both a site of narcissistic desire and a means for seeking sex – 'cruising women'.

In the opening sequence – a montage of close-up shots; a hand turns the ignition key, an arm and hand shift the gear stick, a booted foot presses down on the accelerator pedal, accompanied by the rev of the engine and the beat of a Patti Smith rock'n'roll sound track – the mood of sexy rebellion is established.

The camera pulls back to middle distance, frames a gorgeous young dyke ('80s lesbian boy) with regulation short back and sides haircut – greased back to a sleek shine – sporting US Air Force shades, white tee shirt, black leather jacket and faded blue jeans holing at the knee; every inch as cool and sharp as James Dean.[21]

Cut to a long shot of the car as our hero slow-drives her way along the strip and round the block in a cream limo, moving desultorily, lazily checking for action; glancing out the side window and at the rear view mirror, lighting a cigarette, taking a long draw, stopping at lights. A few point of view shots next as she drives around the city but mostly it's us looking at her. The music on the soundtrack is intermittent, creating a sense of edgy anticipation.

DESIRE DRIVES HER CAR

Then there's a cut, possibly a flashback or a flashforward or even a fantasy and the car is parked while the driver and another woman make out. As so much of the film's desire has been located around the lone protagonist in terms both of her narcissistic desire and the audience's desire for her, it's a shock. With the stripped down narrative drive of the film, her role in looking for action mirrors our role (as audience) in looking for action at her. Apart from the brief insert with the other character, she *is* the action; she *is* the ride.

Desire Drives Her Car is clearly located in the late '80s when the debates around lesbian visibility constructed the dyke who was young, cool and very, very sexy. A period in which fantasy, desire and sexual pleasure was at the forefront of the sub-culture and it was cutting edge to put out and pose in leather. When girls wore coloured hankies to indicate their sexual preferences and young women were confident and cruisey. The film captures perfectly the social moment and demonstrates the power of the woman with wheels to provide its fitting image.

Getting it on in a car is also the subject of the third film in this discussion. If **Desire Drives Her Car** gives us James Dean retro, then Sadie Benning's bravura performance in **It Wasn't Love** delivers us River Phoenix. Filmed in grainy black and white on a Fisher Price toy camera ('Pixelvision') mainly in her bedroom, Benning's much acclaimed 'queer' video tells the story of an unravelling fantasy in which two outlaw babes take off in a car together looking for adventure. Using snatches of pop songs, including "You Go To My Head", "I Put a Spell On You", "Blueberry Hill" and "I Love Rock and Roll", to create a mood of timelessness and a sense of personal history,

Benning also uses deadpan voiceover to narrate the fantasy, utilising fragments of her diary entries and extracts of half-remembered conversations. This semi-free association style is underscored by words like 'faggot' and 'tomboy' scrawled over the images, setting a scene of youthful and forbidden desire.

The scenes are filmed in shaky hand-held close up and through them Benning explores the inner world of a young woman drawn to deviancy and transgression. She confesses: "I worship girls who make girl power, creatin' sexy girl sweat and pumping girly sounds." Her home movie footage is intercut with scenes from TV soaps, Hollywood dramas and gangster movies to provide the backdrop for the incident she is recounting where she drives off in a car with a hot date. The journey to Hollywood is constructed by using a toy car, some street footage shot from her bedroom window and a funky blaxploitation music track. Her voice intones, "She said get in the car we're going to Hollywood."

Like a kid playing with a dressing-up box and using some old makeup and a burnt cork, Benning plays out the various roles of outlaw, bad girl and innocent in a series of charades. First the vamp in dressing gown and blonde wig, then the gangster with a moustache, greased back hair and a big cigar – cue the '40s classic **The St Valentine's Day Massacre** in the background. Then the voiceover rebel monotone: "So I played it cool... permission, I forgot all about it. Trouble, I got a lot of that." She explains that they never made it to Hollywood but pulled up in the car park of a fried chicken outlet just outside town and made out in the back of the car. Cue some very close-up sexy thumb sucking. "It wasn't love, but it was something," says the voice.

This amazingly original appropriation of the male rites of passage film, from **East Of Eden** to **Rumblefish** to **Running On Empty**, so apparently simple yet so incredibly layered, is an inspiration for girl outlaws and dreamers. The video is dedicated to girls everywhere and manages to be cool and tender as well as hip and hot, giving the sharp '80s image of the lesbian boy a depth and range of imaginative possibilities and personas. In terms of providing a new twist to the WOW theme, Benning's quirky reworking of the tradition – a Dinky toy and an account of dyke sex in the back seat – works as both a homage and recouperation of the '50s teenage drive-in scene. The power of the image and its continuing influence on youthful imaginations – it is, after all, the *idea* of the car that counts in this video – demonstrates that the car is both the motor and the repository of desire in teen-orientated cinema, irrespective of budget and genre.

SLANTS AND SLIDES

Sadie Benning provides an even quirkier variant to the WOW imagery in her music video **German Song** (1995), with its central image of a young woman on roller skates. The eye-catching intimate low budget quality of her 'Pixelvision' videos are transferred in this later work to produce an atmospheric image of moody girl-grunge. With more sophisticated production values, this video is set in a derelict downtown district of Boston. Filmed in black and white, there are a succession of closed down images – a deserted

FIREWORKS REVISITED

fairground with silent carousels, an abandoned dog pound with one lone dog behind the wire, decaying graffiti-ridden buildings and bridges – against which backdrop a young girl in scruffy jeans and tee shirt whirls past on her wheels.

The romantic desolation of the scene, emphasised by the writing on the walls, "Fuck the Police" and "Beat It", produce a kind of road movie reverie. Then, imperceptibly, the mood shifts from stasis to movement and then follows a series of cuts matched to the motion of twirling carousels, a blizzard, tracking shots from a car, fires burning and a woman dancing in the snow. Evoking a range of elemental emotions from childhood memories to wish fulfilments, the effect is reminiscent of the film poetry of Tarkovsky.[22] The earlier meandering nature of the character on skates is taken up by the wandering, almost aimless, progression of the video itself, ending as it does on a shot of a plane flying through the clouds – at which point the moody rock song fades and the film ends.

The romantic angst of the '60s underground reworked by contemporary dyke film makers, shooting from the hip so to speak, is reprised in my own short film **Fireworks Revisited** (Zalcock, Britain, 1995) which is a homage to Kenneth Anger and a remake of Anger's subversive classic **Fireworks** (USA, 1947). Borrowing too from the style of Anger's **Scorpio Rising**, **Fireworks Revisited** is basically a girl gang bike fantasy. Where Anger's film visualises the dream desire in terms of a group of sailors, his masochistic fantasy made flesh, **Fireworks Revisited** has a girl biker gang to personify pleasure and pain. Featuring real life members of the London-based female bike pack, The Black Widows, the group appear in riding formation half way through the film at the moment of transition from black and white/silent to colour and sound.

Dismounting from their bikes and playing with an assortment of whips and chains, the gang march menacingly towards the central female character – the dreamer. A montage of booted feet marching in formation down a rake of steep steps recalls the 'Odessa Steps' sequence in **Battleship Potemkin**.[23] The dreamer, lying helplessly at their feet, looks up at their faces – a subjective, low angle silhouette shot that whirls wildly round the circle of heads. But their threat of destructive power is dispersed at the last minute when the bikers tie the dreamer to the central cone of an electricity cable and rotate her in a heady spin. The circular movement is the crucial motif of the film, corresponding to the image of the spiralling Catherine Wheel that opens and closes the film; a kind of female version of Anger's Roman Candle, the firework of his title.

Reclaiming and reinventing the past, and stealing and adapting the iconography of the cinematic tradition, has been a feature of all the films discussed in this section. The requirement to trespass into the male terrain and appropriate its rituals and images is no more clearly expressed than in Kadet Kuhne and Sophie Constantinous' seven-minute video **Impact Zone** (USA, 1996) which boasts 'Hot Wheels, Hot Girls, Hot Cars, Hot Crashes!'.[24]

Built around the adrenaline high of a car race video game, **Impact Zone** uses a mix of home movie documentary race footage, digital computer graphics and video to create its excitement, against a wall of hi-energy music and computer-generated sound effects. In locating the car as exclusively the site of female activity and desire, it is the ultimate WOW gender trespass movie. All the women in the film play with cars in one form or another, from the racing car game in the bedroom through to the video game and the car chases (real and imagined) to the women (solo and duo) making out both in and on cars. The car ride as the metaphor for having sex, with traffic lights and road signs (hill/yield/slow/etc) charting the progress, crosses over into the sexual buzz of the high energy car chase itself and is intercut with images (documentary and computer generated) of heart-stopping overtaking manoeuvres, cars leaping over bridges and dramatic smashes and crashes. Punctuating the relentless drive is black and white Super-8 shots of kids playing on swings and roundabouts, a woman gassing up her car at a petrol station, another humping the body of her Volkswagen and two dykes making out in an open sports car.

The images come thick and fast, creating the excitement and anxiety of a computer game in digitalised dissolves and saturated colour. The film never pauses for breath and the cuts are fast and furious. It is completely sensational – but never mindless. It takes the stream of imagery associated with the fast car in American culture – the car as the object of male desire – and refocuses it for the female spectator. Young women in this film use the car to their own particular ends; they and it together become the symbol of hi-energy, pro-active power. The message is clear: young women will take

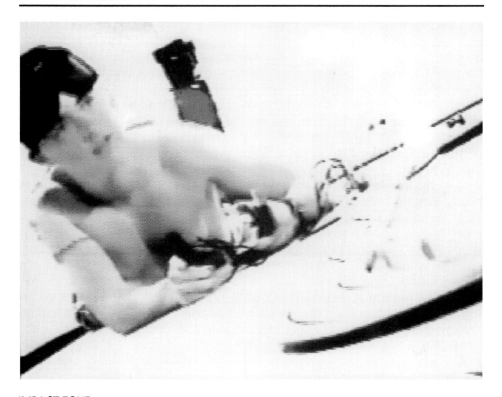

IMPACT ZONE

their pleasure in themselves, in each other and in their wheels. And nobody is going to stop them.

NOTES

1. For detailed discussion see "Juvenile Delinquency Films" by Jim Morton in *Incredibly Strange Films*, ed. V. Vale and A Juno. Plexus, London: 1986.

2. As featured most notably in Nicholas Ray's **Rebel Without A Cause** (1955).

3. For further details about The Cinema of Transgression see Jack Sargeant's *Deathtripping* (Creation Books, London: 1995).

4. For further discussion on spectatorship and masochism see "Masochism, Masquerade And The Erotic Metamorphoses Of Marlene Dietrich" by Gaylyn Studlar in *Fabrications: Costume And The Female Body* ed. Jane Gaines and Charlotte Herzog. AFI Film readers. Routledge, New York & London: 1990.

5. For further insight see Connie Field's documentary *The Life And Times Of Rosie The Riveter* (1980).

6. See also the first example of the genre in **So Young So Bad** (Bernard Vorhaus, 1950), a JD classic'.

7. See also **Hot Rod Rumble** (1957) and **Motorcycle Gang** (1957) for female interest.

8. Female JD literature of the time was harder-edged, with gang-rapes and sex initiations amidst the ghetto violence; classic pulp publishers like Avon, Beacon and Gold Medal produced luridly-jacketed Girl Gang books such as *Gutter Gang*, *Gang Girl*, *Rebels In The Streets*, *Angels In The Gutter*, and Hal Ellson's *Tomboy*; epics of flaming she-youth whose covers screamed by-lines like "the clubhouse was her bridal suite", "I am queen of a schoolgirl wolf pack", and "they came from filthy slums – where even their dreams were dirty!".

9. See for example Natalie Wood in **Rebel Without A Cause** (1955) move from bad girl to substitute mother.

10. *Will You Still Love Me Tomorrow: Girl Groups From The '50s On* by Charlotte Greig. Virago Press, London: 1989.

11. "Biker Films" by Jim Morton from *Incredibly Strange Films*. Op cit.

12. The UK's sole treatment of the female biker was Jack Cardiff's **Girl On A Motorcycle** (1968), a dreary film notable only for the sight of Marianne Faithfull dressed from head to toe in black leather (and nothing underneath).

13. H G Lewis' gore films include **Blood Feast** (1963), **Color Me Blood Red** (1965), **The Gruesome Twosome** (1967), and **Wizard Of Gore** (1970).

14. From *Incredibly Strange Films*. Op cit.

15. This is reprised in the opening of **Barb Wire** where Pamela Anderson, during her striptease performance, uses the stiletto heels of her shoes as a deadly weapon, unleashed on the male spectators.

16. All three gang girls have long hair, which may be read as representing an alternative lifestyle rather than as a typical fetish.

17. It's a shock to discover that there is actually no nudity in this Meyer film!

18. In *Shock Express*, Winter 1988/89, Vol 2, Issue 5.

19. In **Jubilee** an anarcha-punk gang burn off through London's underpasses at night time. For further discussion of the film see Chapter 5. In **The Virgin Machine** Treut uses footage of real life San Francisco female bikers to represent sexual outlaws.

20. 'Reclaim The Night' involved women-led anti-porn rallies through notorious red light districts. The 'Y B A Wife' campaign was spearheaded by radical and revolutionary feminists in their challenge to hetero-patriarchy.

21. For discussion on James Dean as a lesbian icon see Sue Golding's article "James Dean: The Almost Perfect Lesbian Hermaphrodite" in *Stolen Glances: Lesbians Take Photographs* ed Tessa Boffin and Jean Fraser. Pandora Press: 1991.

22. See particularly **The Mirror** (Andrei Tarkovsky, 1974).

23. Anger was crucially influenced by Eisenstein, in particular the Russian director's theories of montage (for a complete analysis, see "Blue Velvet" in **Rapid Eye 3**, ed Simon Dwyer, Creation Books 1995). He saw **Fireworks** as his "American **Potemkin**".

24. Mix NY Festival Programme.

CHAPTER FOUR

GIRL GANGS IN SF/FANTASY FILM

THE GENRE

GENERICALLY the most obvious place for a girl gang in popular cinema is in the science fiction movie and its close relative, the fantasy film. These two forms, one connected with providing an image of the future, the other with a pictorial reconstruction of the past, are underpinned by notions of the utopia and dystopia of human destiny. In written fiction, these preoccupations typically range across a spectrum from the serious (adult) novel at one end, the (kids) fantasy comic at the other. There is no such span in cinema. Science fiction in the movies has tended to occupy the adolescent comic-book end of the market – with one or two notable exceptions including Kubrick's **2001: A Space Odyssey** (1968) and Tarkovsky's **Solaris** (1971).

In the '50s, the sci-fi/fantasy movie was colonised by exploitation cinema. Low budget schlock poured out of the majors' B-feature studios and the small independents had a field day with creature features which were lurid monster pics, that mixed sci-fi and horror. Whereas the literature of the period explored womens' roles in different societies in a relatively serious way[1], the sci-fi movies of the '50s translated ideas of matriarchal rule, female separatism and gender reorganisation into a male wish fulfilment. In the British-made **Fire Maidens From Outer Space** (1956) which is absolutely typical, three astronauts landing on Jupiter are confronted with a bevy of girls in bathing suits and high heels who seem more likely contenders for a Miss World contest than the all-female civilisation of Jupiter.

THE ISSUES

Science fiction cinema is most critically acclaimed for its ability to hold a mirror up to contemporary society. In the '50s the reflection was predominantly that of the USA in the grip of cold war paranoia. Monster-alien invasion (the Soviet Union) **It Came From Outer Space** (1953) and the enemy within (communism) **Invasion Of The Body Snatchers** (1956) were high points in a rake of low-budget releases with similar themes throughout the decade. Women's position in American society was never seriously addressed, although the idea of women in control was frequently parodied. It was, after all, an anxiety experienced by American manhood, along with the fear of nuclear war and losing the space race.

COBRA WOMAN

THE ECONOMIC BACKDROP

In the '50s the spread of television became a factor that commercial cinema had to reckon with. TV increasingly took over the role of the News Reel and began to poach from melodrama, comedy and the western for its shows. Fighting back, cinema made wide-screen extravaganzas and special effects films which, in terms of genre, translated into historical epics, musicals and fantasy features. So while TV occupied the prosaic middle ground of news and small time drama, film pushed further into the world of fantasy – the uncanny and the unconscious.

THE '40s

In popular cinema, the world of the unconscious, repression and sexual drive was often located within the (so called) Dark Continent. And women were, from silent cinema onward, represented as the exotic other, savages of the jungle, beautiful, wild and seductive. The fantasy female of '40s cinema was Maria Montez, who starred in two films, Universal's **Cobra Woman** (1944) and United Artists' **Siren Of Atlantis** (1948) that set the tone for the prehistoric exploitation fantasy film of the '50s. The jungle goddess thematic was a

strand running through all the Tarzan films (from the '30s), adding sexism to the film cycle's innate racism. In **Tarzan And The Amazons** (1945) for example, there is a lost tribe of white women discovered in darkest Africa! **Jungle Goddess** (1948) continued the trend – a lost heiress in a leopardskin bikini – and two films from 1950, **Prehistoric Women** (beauties in animal skin drapes and lipstick) and **Untamed Women** ("savage beauties who feared no animal") confirmed the prototype for girl gangs in sci-fi cinema.

THE '50s

In '50s exploitation, as we have seen, the castration threat, implicit in female representation, is allayed by portraying its women as loud, lurid and larger than life. This is true of the 'Juvenile Delinquent' girl gang films and the 'Women In Prison' sub-genre. In science fiction and fantasy however, a somewhat different strategy is employed. The women are rarely shown as a serious threat because they are represented as absurd, incongruous and fetishised in the extreme. An early example of the approach is shown in **Cat Women Of The Moon** (1953), made in 3-D, which gives us beautiful telepathic women in tights. In **The Mesa Of Lost Women** (1952) a mad scientist creates super women with long fingernails and in AIP's **She Gods Of The Shark Reef** (1956) we are treated to a tropical island inhabited exclusively by pearl-diving women in print swimming costumes. **Cat Women Of The Moon** was remade in 1959, by Richard E Cunha, as **Missile To The Moon**. The previous year Cunha made **She Demons**, in which a group of bikini-clad women on an island are made into ugly monsters by a deranged Nazi war criminal, who keeps them in bamboo cages.

The production values on such movies are often as far-fetched as their female imagery. **Queen Of Outer Space** (1958), which starred Miss Hungary, Zsa Zsa Gabor, was a relatively lavish affair – filmed in colour and Deluxe Cinemascope. Even so, costumes came courtesy of **Forbidden Planet** (1956), sets and a spider from **World Without End** and the rocket from **Flight To Mars**! And, of the fantasy film **Viking Women And The Sea Serpent** (1958), director Roger Corman boasts shooting seventy-eight camera set-ups in a single day, to make ends meet.

In so far as sexual politics was ever explored in '50s sci-fi, it was most likely to focus around a solo female rather than a girl gang. In **She Devil** (1950), Blanchard the heroine goes on a murder spree after testing a serum for the cure of TB. In the British independent **Devil Girl From Mars** (1954) a woman arrives from planet Mars to capture men for breeding purposes. A similarly sexy alien arrives on earth in AIP's **The Astounding She-Monster** (1958), and in the celebrated **Attack Of The 50-Foot Woman** (1957) a woman who has been turned into a giant by an alien goes on the rampage and murders her cheating husband – squeezing him to death in a bar where he's canoodling with his girlfriend! Apart from the violent sexuality of these women, they are strongly fetishised. The female alien in **Devil Girl From Mars** power dresses in boots, padded shoulders, black tights and a cape. In **The Astounding She-Monster** the female alien is blonde and clad in a skin tight metallic suit and high heels. This image of the seductive, sadistic and

SHE DEMONS

fetishised female would find its apotheosis in the sexploitation sci-fi offerings of the '60s.

Ironically the alien girl group prove to be much less effective than their solo counterparts. The all-female matriarchy which is characteristic of so many of the '50s sci-fi exploitation films, almost invariably fails to deliver. In both the prehistoric (fantasy) and extra terrestrial (sci-fi) settings the formula is the same. An all-female civilisation, often controlled by a man-hating dominatrix, is desperate for men to breed with. This is the basic plot in **Love Slaves Of The Amazon** (1957), **Queen Of Outer Space** and **Wild Women Of Wongo** (1958).

Given the attire of the gals in question it's not hard to see that the films' central appeal is prurient. The wild or alien beauties are a fashion parade for male spectators, frequently doing (synchronised) ritual dances, often in the briefest of animal skin bikinis.[2] The only redeeming feature of such movies is that they are hysterically funny; so that although they don't offer anything in the way of strong female images, they do provide a laugh.

"QUEEN OF OUTER SPACE"

One of the best of the '50s crop is **Queen Of Outer Space** which is so wonderfully camp it warrants a bit more than a mere mention. In the very long pre-title sequence, four astronauts in the future (the '80s) set off for Venus. Captain Turner, the best looking of a bad bunch, lingers over a final embrace with his platinum blonde girlfriend, who has a voice like Marilyn Monroe and a cleavage to match! Earth girls are certainly easy compared with what is in store. As she stands gazing up at the rocket blowing kisses in a

QUEEN OF OUTER SPACE

lime-green taffeta evening dress and ruby red diamante evening gloves, the men think that they are looking their last on the classic curvaceous '50s female. But not for long. On Venus, they observe "Twenty million miles from earth and the little dolls are just the same!"

After a bumpy ride, they are met by a coterie of mini-skirted babes in low-cut tops and high-heeled shoes. They wear red with gold crossover holster braces and sport '50s earth girl hairstyles. The man-hating leader Queen Ilyana wears trousers and a spangled mask to hide the scars she's sustained in their war with men. "Men caused the ruin of this world," she observes ominously. We first see Zsa Zsa Gabor in the lab wearing a tight-fitting white silk dress with a side slit to the thigh. She plays Talia, one of the rebel Venusians, who actually likes men and wants to overthrow the separatist regime. She is inevitably the central character and the main focus.

The backdrop and settings are garish and tacky with a 'vapour disintegrator' as the centrepiece. It looks like it's made of cardboard and probably is. While Talia plots to free the men, the Queen is beginning to fall for the captain's charms. Despite holding men responsible for her radiation burns, she is bound to admit that "A woman needs a man's love".

Meanwhile, Zsa Zsa Gabor, in yet another slit-skirted outfit, this time in red, foments subversion and joins ranks with the men, saying "We have no life here without love and children!". In the artex-walled atrium, a swirling mix of oranges, browns, blues and pinks, the men and the small group of

FIRE MAIDENS FROM OUTER SPACE

female rebels plan their escape. The astronauts greet their liberators with the words: "Hiya dolls! It's good to have you on our side!". As they pair off and make for the caves, the hardcore man-haters, those in the masks, begin a manhunt. In the cave, Zsa Zsa, the Venusians and the earth men get into some heavy petting, punctuating the action with such gems as: "Peace is not enough. Women can't be happy without men." In the denouement, the Queen is defeated and unmasked. We realise that she's not a man-hating tyrant at all, merely a woman who has been hurt very badly. The men fly back to earth with the rebel girls on their knees and plan a wholesale colonisation programme. Zsa Zsa wears a black and gold slit skirt and plans to initiate a new civilisation on Venus. The film ends on a note of freedom and happiness.

Queen Of Outer Space is hard to top, although scenes from the black and white British offering **Fire Maidens From Outer Space** come close. The female survivors of Atlantis, resituated on Jupiter, receive the attentions of three male astronauts who have lost their way. Dressed in gym slips with graeco-roman piping, toga-style veils and thong sandals, the girls treat their newly arrived guests to a floor show. Against a tackily painted Minoan background, they dance to the strains of "A Stranger In Paradise" in an attempt to lure the men into some desperately needed breeding action. It's all rather coy and unthreatening and the men are unimpressed. They need a Zsa Zsa Gabor to spice things up.

DR GOLDFOOT

THE '60s

By the '60s any semblance of seriousness has disappeared. The girls are simply sex objects; the films are simply spoofs. Two AIP titles **Dr Goldfoot And The Bikini Machine** (1965) and **Dr Goldfoot And The Girl Bombs** (1966, Italy) mark the shift. In a parody of the James Bond movies, the films feature a gang of female robots controlled by a mad doctor (the wicked Dr Goldfoot, played by Vincent Price) who in the first film seduce rich and powerful men and in the sequel lure NATO Generals into love making, during which they spontaneously combust due to a bomb implanted in their navel. In Antonio Margheriti's **Wild Wild Planet** (Italy, 1965) a female gang in leather pants are sent to Earth, where they shrink human beings and carry them off to a city full of dwarves and mutants.

Throughout the '60s, the sexually explicit comedy in an exotic setting is the dominant form. Films like **Invasion Of The Star Creatures** (1962), **Voyage To The Planet Of Prehistoric Women** (1966) – starring Mamie van Doren who leads an alien female tribe clad only in clam shell bikinis – and **Some Girls Do** (1969) in which an army of female robots try to conquer the world – make fantasy subservient to sexual content.

This progression can also be seen in a sequence of prehistoric dramas produced in England by Hammer Films, starting with **Slave Girls** (1966), in which Martine Beswick is the ferocious leader of a tribe of dark-haired amazons who clash with the local blonde tribe in a classic jurassic rumble. By

WHEN DINOSAURS RULED THE EARTH

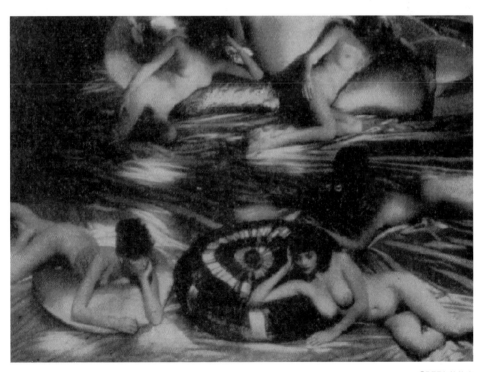

SPERMULA

the time **When Dinosaurs Ruled The Earth** (1970) and **Creatures The World Forgot** (1971) were released, female nudity had become completely paramount over plot.[3]

Harder-edged films like Ted V Mikel's **The Astro Zombies** (1968) and **Brides Of Blood** (1968) move from sci-fi/fantasy to erotic horror. Sexploitation along these lines continues through the '70s with films like **Flesh Gordon** (1974), **Invasion Of The Love Drones** (1975) and **Spermula** (1976), the last being an erotic horror about female vampires in outer space who feed on sperm rather than blood.

During this period, director George Lucas was reworking the science fiction genre and in 1977 released the first of his big budget, family entertainment, space opera cycle, **Star Wars**. At this juncture, girl gang interest, such as it was, disappeared from view. The extra-terrestrial, all female fighting force remains consigned to the bargain basement of film history. It was revisited briefly in Juliet John's excellent Australian short **Retro Sheilas – Space Aliens Are Tooling Our Sheilas!** (1996) in which a supergirl gang, the Retro Sheilas, embark on a mission to defend the earth against alien invasion. The rest is silence; in space no one can hear us scream!

NOTES

1. See for example the novels of Ursula K Le Guin and Issac Asimov.

2. As in **Horror Of Spider Island** (W. Germany, 1959), in which a gang of eight exotic dancers are stranded on a remote atoll. This trend reached its logical conclusion in Doris Wishman's early "nudie" film **Nude On The Moon** (1960), in which two astronauts land on the moon only to find it populated by topless women (with antennae)!

3. True to form, the Italians took this formula to its logical – exploitative – conclusion, with **When Women Had Tails** (1970).

CHAPTER FIVE

OUTLAWS

OUTSIDE OF SOCIETY

THIS chapter will look at a range of films that deal with the female as outsider or 'other' to the classic female representations of mainstream cinema. The films discussed are not confined to one particular genre or style of film making. On the contrary, they are selected from the spectrum of film production with Hollywood big budget features at one end to 'no-budget' Super-8 short films at the other and all types of films in between, including art house, independent, underground, new wave and docudrama.

What all the films share is their focus on women who are consistently marginalised because of what they are or what they do and, because of the social positions assigned to them, these female characters become, by definition, undesirable – subversive and dangerous. They are typically sexual 'deviants', often lesbians or prostitutes, or just plain promiscuous. Frequently they are set apart from the normal on the grounds of their race or ethnicity; women of colour, who are African, Latin or Asian in origin. They may also defy or fall outside the feminine norm because they do not defer to men or they are violent, rebellious, or no longer 'young and beautiful'. For whatever reason the women in these films are renegades and live outside of society or on the sub-cultural margins. They are the antithesis of 'Stepford Wives' and provide audiences with fresh, original and inspirational role models of female being. The chapter is divided into four sections:

QUEERCORE GIRLS

The films in this section focus on young women in the punk/bad girl mould. The spirit of these characters and the films themselves coincide with the 'Queercore' movement of low-budget magazines produced in the United States that reject the values of mainstream society and the straight world.[1] The films are generally short, low-budget, underground and female produced. Their characters present an array of transgressive styles – punks, dykes, sado-masochists and dragkings. Films to be discussed include:

Jubilee (Derek Jarman, Britain, 1978)
Superdyke (Barbara Hammer, USA, 1975)
Mano Destra (Cleo Uebelmann, Switzerland, 1986)

Our Us We Bone One So Naked Known (Anie Stanley, USA, 1994)
The Adventures Of White Trash Girl (Jennifer Reeder, USA, 1995)

BUFFALO GIRLS

This section features movies that take the 'Western' and turn it on its head by making the central cowboys female. Establishing itself as a commercial sub-genre in the '80s and early '90s, the films discussed are mainly studio productions directed by men with big stars and big budgets. They provide an interesting assortment of female characters including prostitutes, dykes, dragkings and rebel rousers. Films to be discussed include:

Buffalo Girls (Rod Hardy, USA, 1995. TV mini-series)
Bad Girls (Jonathan Kaplan, USA, 1994)
The Ballad Of Little Jo (Maggie Greenwald, USA, 1993)
Hours Of The Idolite (Anie Stanley, USA, 1995)

FEMALE BONDS

The films in this section are female directed, independently produced narratives, located within a semi-realist, semi-experimental tradition. They address particular and often under-represented female subjectivities and deal with groups of women who are located outside the mainstream; including lesbians, prostitutes, women of colour and older women. Films to be discussed include:

Liberty's Booty (Vivienne Dick, USA, 1980)
Mi Vida Loca (My Crazy Life) (Allison Anders, USA, 1993)
The Company Of Strangers (Cynthia Scott, Canada, 1990)
Daughters Of The Dust (Julie Dash, USA, 1991)

UP AGAINST THE STATE

A range of genres from the feminist new narrative through documentary to blaxploitation are referenced in the films discussed here, towards a consideration of strategies for a female fightback. As such, the films collectively represent a critique of the state and of sexist representations as well as a celebration of women's struggle, both personal and political. Films to be discussed include:

A Question Of Silence (Marleen Gorris, Holland, 1982)
Born In Flames (Lizzie Borden, USA, 1983)
Set It Off (F Gary Gray, USA, 1996)

SECTION ONE: QUEERCORE GIRLS

HAMMER HITS

While **Jubilee** and **Mano Destra** provide the archetypes of '70s and '80s versions respectively of the sexual outlaw, representing as they do the twin legacies of the trashy and the transgressive, it is underground lesbian film maker Barbara Hammer's short films that definitively frame the bad girl tradition. Hammer's films favour sisters doing it for themselves in titles like **Dyketactics** (1974), **Menses** (1974), **Women's Rites** or **Daughter Is The Truth Of Time** (1974), and **Multiple Orgasm** (1977). Representing lesbian activists with a comic edge her film **Superdyke** (1975) follows a group of shield-bearing Amazons (prototypes of the contemporary Lesbian Avengers) around San Francisco and subsequently into the countryside where they romp and play *au naturelle*.

In the city, the female warriors rampage good-humouredly through City Hall and race around Macy's department store clutching cardboard shields. On motorbikes and on foot, sporting 'superdyke' and Superman tee shirts, the crazy posse emerge from the shopping mall in zany high spirits, waving dildoes and saucepans. Onlookers at street corners and bus stops appear astonished but also amused by these antics. Just before leaving town the women invade a local 'erotic' art exhibition where they stand in front of an array of vaginal images, clutching their crotches and groaning.

Hammer's frenetic hand-held style gives the film its pace, energy and a raunchy 'in your face' feel. The home movie quality is, in fact, extremely accomplished, for example the sequence filmed in Macy's is pixillated to create a pastiche of silent film comedy, as the piano accompaniment suggests.

In the countryside the mood shifts from audacious and outrageous to sensual and spiritual. The film's overall effect – to combine humour and joy – is only a small part of Hammer's opus, which provides an amazing document and insight into the lesbian sub-culture of the '70s, while proffering representations that make much of the later so-called 'transgressive' imagery appear tame by comparison.

JARMAN'S "JUBILEE"

Gay British film maker, Derek Jarman's **Jubilee** explores the sub-cultural life of London at the time of Queen Elizabeth II's Silver Jubilee (1977), a period of activism and the blossoming of the Underground in terms of politics and alternative culture. The film begins with a flashback to the 16th century when the Tudor monarch Elizabeth I was on the throne and uses the perspective of England's glorious past as the starting point for looking at its dismal present – a preoccupation which Jarman pursues in his later film **The Last Of England** (1987).

The main action of **Jubilee** is based in a squalid squat in SE London inhabited by a motley mix of characters that form an anarchic punk girl gang. This female crew consists of Mad (Toyah Wilcox), a pyromaniac who thinks she's a revolutionary and sports a bright red crew cut, Crabs (Little Nell), a sex-

JUBILEE

mad actress with too much libido and too little brain, Bod (Jenny Runacre), leader of the pack who is confident, upper class, bossy and sadistic and claims 'love snuffed it with the hippies' (Mad thinks sex is for geriatrics), Viv (Linda Spurrier), an artist, Chaos (Hermine Demoriane), a French au pair and Amyl Nitrate (Jordan), a punk historian and philosopher of art, desire and fantasy. All the key female characters are played by sub-cultural personalities and there is a fine line between the characters, their real life personalities and their roles in the film. For example, punk singer Jordan, who plays Amyl, is in a sense simply expressing her alter ego. "She's our heroine," remarks one of the gang and the musical numbers she sings in the film as part of Britain's entry to the Eurovision Song Contest were released at the time on record by another of Jordan's personas, Suzi Pinns.[2] The Slits, a British female punk band of the period, also make an appearance in the film as a gang of delinquent street girls.

In a typical scene, early in the film, the gang are together in the living room of their derelict squat with its graffiti-lined walls and broken windows. In the foreground is a television set droning out the news, with Mad and Bod lying on the bed next to it. Bod takes off her shirt and strokes Mad's spiky red hair. Mad reciprocates by carving the word 'Love' into Bod's back with a flick-knife. In the middle distance Amyl sits on a bed reading aloud from her book *The Condensed Complete History Of Human Rights*. In the background, Chaos does the ironing.

In narrative terms, the film consists of a series of violent set pieces, loosely connected. Both the content and the style of **Jubilee** are strongly influenced by the Underground. It's shot on grainy Super-8 and uses the primitive tropes associated with '60s underground films including the long take, jump cuts and glitch edits. Similarly, the plot and the characters, while much more rounded than most underground offerings are basically just that, more dramatically developed than the films of, say, Warhol. It is additionally one of the few films of Jarman's in which the central focus is female. It is also more politicised than the average underground offering.

In one scene, Viv the painter discusses the devaluation of meaning under late capitalism and references the work of Situationist Guy Debord's *The Society Of The Spectacle*.[3] In this connection we are introduced to Borgia Gins, a sleazy, greedy impresario who is preoccupied with profit and producing the Eurovision Song Contest winner and who is the personification of Debord's theory of late capitalist logic. Meanwhile, Crabs is picking up men and finds "a real cute sex object in a café". As opponents of both sex and love, Bod and Mad feel the need to dispose of the man which they do by asphyxiating him – Bod, naked and wearing a crown and Mad in a clown suit. They wrap the body in a black bin bag and dump it unceremoniously into the River Thames. At the same time they lecture Crabs about her romantic attachment to the outdated notion of love; Mad remarks: "Your mind's like a faded collage of *Penthouse* and *True Romance*."

In another episode the girls are playing 'Monopoly'. Crabs in a bikini, Amyl wearing a twinset, Mad sporting a Batman mask, Bod in a smart black suit and Chaos in leather. As the game progresses they discuss plans to kill a transvestite rocker called 'Lounge Lizard'. Later, when Bod strangles him with her bare hands, she says, "The world won't miss his missing chromosome." Mad sits close by, playing with a metronome while Crabs reads the magazine *Beauty* and drinks a Coke. Amyl, sitting on the sofa looking bored, shakes a desultory tambourine.

Later, outside a decadent gay club called 'The Palace of Earthly Delights', a disaffected street gang (The Slits) dressed in leather and big boots, trash a car. As the film proceeds the violence accelerates and when the women learn of the death of two acquaintances, The Deptford Boys, at the hands of the police, they organise for ultimate action. Bod stands on the stairs with a machine gun saying, "Don't cry – crying's a negative reaction. Come and make some firebombs instead, it will help you feel better!". Mad responds with jubilation, "It's party time; let's liberate the zoo!". In the next sequence, with Amyl's help they capture a cop, cut him open and firebomb his house. The backdrop graffiti reads "No Future".

Jubilee ends on a negative note with the women working for Borgia Gin in a girl group called 'The Daughters of God'. Having been co-opted by capitalism they observe, "It's a tragedy that socialism and freedom weren't compatible". Holding up a mirror to contemporary British society, Jarman's film is an indictment of greed and anarchic violence. Like Anger's **Scorpio Rising** over a decade earlier, it's a fascinated but also horrified gaze at the street culture of disaffected youth. Again like Anger's film, it foregrounds a sub-culture; in **Scorpio Rising** it was male bikers, in **Jubilee** it is an angry, violent and deviant group of young women who seem to represent the malaise of a society in crisis.

"MANO DESTRA"

Transgressive women who are threatening and powerful is also the subject of the avant-garde, art-house film **Mano Destra** (1986). Real violence is sublimated via ritual and taboo into what appears as sado-masochistic performance art. All action in the film takes place in the cellar of a female S/M collective known as The DOMINAS. As the film opens we see the women involved dressed in black leather leaning against a white Mercedes, holding a banner on which their name is inscribed.

The central female focus (star, dominatrix, director and performance artiste *extraordinaire*), Cleo Uebelmann, plays on the ambiguous cusp of documentary and fantasy – posing and pouting her way through a series of bondage scenes. She is always in black leather fetish gear – (shiny, shiny, shiny) boots of leather, jodhpurs, jacket, cap and framed centrally in a film, whose imagery recalls black and white glossy photographs for coffee table consumption.

The art-house moody noir style – low-key lights, door frames, bar motifs and a sense of entrapment – constructs a chic aestheticised distance. This is accompanied by intermittent soundtrack provided by The Wyllies (Diamanda Galas meet Siouxsie Sioux). The audience is disorientated in terms of character (how many?), plot (what is happening?) and intention (is this seriously scary or an elaborately constructed confidence trick?).

The character/s who play the bottom – victim, masochist, zeitgeist, alter ego – she/they of the sheer black tights, the low-cut high strut lycra leotard, the high spiky heels – all in black, recall Allen Jones' '70s phallic females which caused such a stir in feminist circles (graphics and domestic sculptures) and which prompted Laura Mulvey to write her first Freudian-based article on representation, "You Don't Know What Is Happening, Do You Mr Jones?"[4] Are we supposed to take these images seriously, without a grain of irony, the ghost of a smile?

One thing is certain. The film is emblematic. The aetheticisation of power is typically of the '80s. Power is sexy and so are its trappings: handcuffs, ropes, cages, whips. This is a female-only fantasy zone where power relations are not informed by gender privilege but by mutual and consensual power games. The images presented often in long takes as photographic stills are black and white and in high definition and sharp focus. Compositionally careful, the stark-stripped images of vertical and horizontal bars meet at right angles, just as the thigh does the shin when lashed into an immovable relationship.

Much is made of preparation. The knots, the ropes, the techniques, the anticipation and the deferred gratification. We are given images, surfaces, e.g., use of photographic exhibition within the film using stills taken from the film itself to emphasise the voyeurist relay that underpins our fascination and then, invariably, the emptiness. A cut to black. We are given a promise – the adrenaline of the soundtrack, the marching boots in the early sequences – but there is no action of any kind in the film. It eschews involvement and denies development.

As we proceed into the depth of the underworld, windowless and set apart – only plumbing and bondage paraphernalia – we begin to long for that squat in Deptford we moved on from a decade ago.[5] It's definitely too clean and too corrupt here; a stylised camera of slow pans and very long takes; a ritualised heroine posing, posturing and preparing to tie another woman precariously on to yet another set of parallel bars. Or is there a gang? Is there more than one woman? Is this the elaborate playing out of one woman's fantasy? And what a woman!

Shot from slightly low angle, an almost static figure resplendent in black leather with cunningly embossed straps and slashes and zips and studs recalling the dispassionate concentration of a camp commandante as she almost casually, yet fluently, lashes her victim to a metal contraption. For everything is in stainless steel. All shining surfaces. No depth. The perfect postmodern girl gang drama. Just when it seems that the film will be interminable (it feels unremitting and relentless) with a shot of yet another masochist (or the same one – we never see the face) lashed to yet another contraption while the star controller (sadist) waits in the wings, there's a jump cut, dazzling in its stark contrast. Outside, the Merc seen at the opening drives past an arabesque scene of building (lighthouse) with palm trees and intense daylight throwing it into relief. On the soundtrack there's classical cello music.

On our return to the dominant world, the murky dark interiors, the dominatrix-cum-curator is mounting a photographic exhibition in an empty white gallery. The images are stills, moments we have witnessed in the film already; bondage! We hear on the soundtrack noises that suggest a launch party. The dominatrix sits at a desk in front of huge photos. The scene hints at what we suspected. The images that comprise the film are the currency of art (images within images/a relay of images). At the end there's a short sequence in which we are privy to a relaxed moment – the only physical contact between two characters – a cigarette and a neck massage.

The film is memorably self-reflexive, exploring as it does the power of the image and the image of power. It also puts a spin on notions of deferred anticipation/gratification, both in terms of narrative and physical climax. Waiting and watching are crucial components of pornography and voyeurism and this becomes the subject of the film itself and the experience of the spectator.

SHORT 'GIRL GANG' FILMS OF THE '90s

Coming up from the tradition of '70s underground, so-called transgressive films, Anie Stanley's **Our Us We Bone One So Naked Known** (1994)[6] is a Super-8 film that combines the high dyke spirits of Barbara Hammer's films, the anarcha-punk elements of **Jubilee** and the heavier female sexual threat of **Mano Destra**. Shot in black and white using shaky hand-held camera, the film deals with notions of voyeurism and gender role reversal. It opens with a shot under a bridge and a pan to a fire, then a shot to an old Nickelodeon-style jukebox with a coin being placed in the slot.

Then a sequence with a woman clad only in a stetson, cowboy boots and a holster belt approaching the middle distance – shot from behind the windscreen of a car. As the gunslinging gal moves into close-up, the

OUR US WE BONE ONE SO NAKED KNOWN

windscreen wipers flap nervously. The camera position and the spectator's point of view is lookout from the car. As the woman takes out her six-gun and twirls it, there's a cut to a close-up of the gun barrel and the car headlamp. The sequence that follows is an abstract play of movement and light. After which we return to the position behind the windscreen as a gang of dishevelled young women – four in all, scantily clad in hot pants, cut off tee shirts, low-necked tops, torn tights and boots – mount a sexual assault on the car and hence the subject inside the car. As there is no visible character, we, the audience, are the victims of the scam – the objects of the abuse. With the gleeful high jinks of Beryl and the Perils, the girls proceed to make out lasciviously. To a fractured soundtrack from '30s and '40s musical numbers including "Shuffle Off To Buffalo" and "My Forgotten Man" the antics are shot in in-your-face, grainy close-up. We hear Peggy Lee crooning "Wrap up some red roses for a blue lady!" and the sound of bullets ricocheting and girls giggling as the delinquent gang commit unspeakable acts with the car and with one another, intercut with both explicit and arty close ups of boots, spurs, gun barrels, bare buttocks and breasts – the iconography of female power fantasies. This orgy of activity is the central part of the film, punctuated by big grainy close shots of spurs on nipples and gun barrels penetrating various orifices. The overall effect is of attitude rather than erotica; it's funny and scary, as well as having the occasional artistic distance of abstract shots of reflected light playing on textured surfaces.

THE DEVIL INSIDE

Throughout this mayhem of lusty enjoyment and deviant threat, the subject of the assault is the audience, occupying the point of view of the unseen character within the car. As the original cowgirl walks away into long distance, the delinquents invade the car waving and whooping and in long shot they drive off. They have succeeded in reversing the usual spectator-subject position structure of Hollywood cinema and are profiled individually over the end credits.

POST SCRIPT

On the subject of the thoroughly scurrilous female comeback film with a country and western flavour, Miss Jennifer Reeder's **The Devil Inside From Clit O Matic – The Adventures Of White Trash Girl** is worth a mention. Set in the redneck zone of the deep south and including Sadie Benning among its credits, this video (coming to do some damage at a trailer park near you) recalls early John Waters and is funny, irreverent and outrageous. (White Trash Girl says suck my dick!) This warped melodrama opens with Ruby, a sluttish teenager polishing her nails in big close-up. Uncle Bruce, a gross slob, rapes her and when the unwanted baby is born, Ruby flushes her infant/doll down the toilet. In the sewer, the child survives and emerges fully formed as superbaby Angel – Miss Debbie – the White Trash Girl. A southern voiceover describes her as angry and out of control, "If you cross her you're fucked",

THE LAW OF DESIRE

and soon enough White Trash Girl is on the rampage assembling a gang of motley misfits around her, including Mental Girl and Ron, a no-hope boy – he ain't dangerous, he's just gross! With its crude effects, low production values, hand-held camera and lurid colour, the film is irresistible.

Jennifer Reeder's **White Trash Girl Part 2: The Law Of Desire** continues the revenge structure of the original film and utilises deliberately low-budget effects. Made on video it raids film and TV footage and uses rock music samples for its sporadic – and ironic – soundtrack. The central character here is Trailita, a working-class Mexican woman, who has been driven already to murder a violent boyfriend. Alone and poor, Trailita drifts into casual work for the North American sex industry, first as a topless dancer and later for a fantasy phone line.

To underline Trailita's exploitation by the state, her image is intercut with footage of Mexican farm labourers. She spirals into deep depression and seems to be resigned to her fate, when suddenly she has a chance encounter with White Trash Girl (footage of atomic explosions, carpet bombing, burning cities). The southern voiceover, as in the first film drawls a deadpan narration: "Our big, blonde super hero, built like a Sherman tank with a V8 pussy...."

When she hears Trailita's tale of woe, White Trash Girl springs into action and vows vengeance, with the words "Any day is a good day to kick some ass!". Thus ensues the demolition of Trailita's greasy, greedy, heartless boss and the destruction of his office.

White Trash Girl leaps on this desk and sexually assaults the terrified sleazeball. To the strains of the punk song "Fuck You All" the two women exact their perverted revenge on all abusive and exploitative men. It's a cathartic scene and reminiscent of the mood and spirit of Stanley's **Our Us We Bone One So Naked Known** in its uncompromising assumption, by the gals, of male power, through parodic acts of sexual desire.

SECTION TWO: BUFFALO GIRLS

INTRODUCTION

Gus Van Sant's queer feature **Even Cow Girls Get The Blues** (1993), though having very little to do with the 'western' does serve to make explicit the connection between lesbian fantasy and the wild west. Even the incredibly anodyne version of **Calamity Jane** (1953) with Doris Day ("Once I had a secret love!") mainlines straight into the lesbian imaginary, not least because real life legends like Calamity serve in the contemporary construction of a female mythology[7] – the iconic power of Doris Day notwithstanding. This female interest represents an important aspect of the revival of the 'western' as a genre in recent years and ensures that its renaissance (with central characters who are not necessarily white men) has effectively turned the value system of the genre on its head – since the values that it fundamentally espoused were personified by confident white man, emblematically represented by John Wayne.[8] For the first half of the century of cinema the western was popular with (white male) audiences, into the second half it was popular with (white male) theorists who in the late '60s and early '70s spilt much ink extolling the virtues of the western's classically compelling thematic and structural oppositions.[9]

At this time, feminist film theory and its foregrounding of sexual difference in film analysis had not yet surfaced and in the lull before the storm, male critics had a field day exploring the western as a generic site of American myth and individual heroism (prowess and plunder). Even after the Women's Movement had usher(ett)ed in other genres for the critical canon, particularly the 'melodrama' which, with its characteristics of emotionality and excess, was a favourite of newly emerging women critics,[10] the western persisted on film syllabuses even though it was blown out of the water in terms of its popular appeal for American audiences – not least because of the national demoralisation experienced as a result of the war in Vietnam.

In addition to international events affecting the genre, there was a significant cinematic development, namely the emergence from Europe of a bastard brother to America's legitimate son – known as the 'Spaghetti Western' by virtue of the finance and production being Italian – notably Sergio Leone's cycle **Fistful Of Dollars** (1964), **For A Few Dollars More** (1965) and **The Good, The Bad And The Ugly** (1966). Such films are distinguished by a level of violence and amorality totally at odds with the American prototype. Taking its cue from the commercial success of the Spaghettis and the marketability of their new star Clint Eastwood, Hollywood retaliated with films like **Coogan's Bluff** (1968) and **The Wild Bunch** (1969). In terms of the requirements of the genre, these films represented bad faith, presenting and celebrating, as they did, characters who were seriously morally flawed in putting personal gain above human life.

As the war in Vietnam progressed, faith in liberty, justice and the All-American way became a sick joke. Pilloried from the margins in the gay and camp classics **Lonesome Cowboys** (Warhol 1968) and **Blazing Saddles** (Mel Brooks 1974), the western, like the nation it mythologised, started tearing itself apart. A number of commercial films were clear indictments of the western 'legend' as a lie and delivered bodyblows to the genre – **Little Big Man** (1970), **Soldier Blue** (1970) and **Heaven's Gate** (1980).

The western, however, was not dead, only sleeping – even though it had gone to ground throughout the '70s, the call of the wild, the pull of the west, could never be completely suppressed. The western was, after all, a fine example of the 'master narrative' of '80s postmodern theory. Throughout the century it had done sterling work in serving to popularise a colonising and paternalistic discourse that left women and people of colour, if not out of the frame, most definitely in the margins where they belonged! Native Americans were by and large represented as primitive, that is, savage and bad, while African-Americans were pretty much invisible and women were either good (goddesses) or bad (whores).

But the repressed always returns, so that when the genre resurfaced, those denied a place or a voice within it in the past were suddenly its heroes. For example, **Silverado** (Kasdan, 1985) featured a black star, Danny Glover; and **The Dark Wind** (Morris, 1991) and **Thunder Heart** (Apted, 1992) both had a native American as the central hero, whereas the surviving white men were frequently depicted as out of place or out of time (e.g. Clint Eastwood in **Pale Rider**, 1985, and **Unforgiven**, 1992). Additionally, in many new westerns there was a commitment to authenticity. The old impulse, when confronted with a conflict between truth and legend, was 'to print the legend'.[11] This was no longer the case. On the contrary there was a desire to expose the old order for what it was, grim, muddy and merciless. The technicolour ranches of '50s westerns were long gone, with their wonderful royal blue day for night glow. Even if they weren't, a lot of the contemporary films felt black and white, straight out of the archive so to speak.

FEMALE WESTERNS

The double bind for women in the classic western was that whether she was a goddess or whether she was a whore, she represented a threat to the man and had therefore to be ejected from their narrative. If the woman was a loyal wife and nurturing mother, servicing the man and safeguarding the family, she was cast in opposition to the genre's project of freewheeling, untrammelled masculinity with its drive towards autonomy, action and adventure. If, on the other hand, she was a single saloon girl, servicing the men and serving them their beer, she was construed as a loose cannon, unnatural and a threat to social and moral codes – patriarchal law and heterosexual order. What could a poor girl do? In **The Ballad Of Little Jo** (Maggie Greenwald, 1993) she passes as a man.

This film, directed and written by a woman, was one of the first of the female westerns that characterises Hollywood film production in the '90s. Just as the '80s saw the demise of the fit white *cowboy* who had served as the 'desirable' role model to young boys for generations and a shift of emphasis to racial others, so the '90s saw women take up the male role. **The Ballad Of Little Jo**, inspired by the real life legend of Jo Monaghan who lived her life as a man, is in many ways the classic tale of a rugged American individualist pursuing freedom and adventure in the west – except that this individual is a woman. The central female character, in order to escape from brutal sexist exploitation, cross dresses, so forcing the audience to interrogate notions of gender as natural and the nature of masculine roles. In assuming the trappings of power – dress, guns, body language – Jo is able to survive without being completely violated which is the fate of many of her single sisters in the film.

The Ballad Of Little Jo is also concerned with authenticity and capturing the texture of the period. Its visual elements are based on photographs of the time. In narrative terms its focus is with those most marginalised in the classic western, namely immigrants (Chinese, Russians), women (wives, prostitutes) and the poor. The grinding poverty and unremitting brutality of the time is carefully depicted and there is an emphasis in particular on sexual abuse and female friendships. Jo is only able to find an equal sexual relationship with a man who is himself marginalised – a Chinese man. In bed together they make a fascinating couple, he with his long, sleek ponytail shaken loose and Jo with her short crop – the ultimate role reversal.

"BUFFALO GIRLS"

Another film made initially as a mini-series for TV that deals with role reversal and some degree of historical authenticity is **Buffalo Girls** (Rod Hardy, 1995). **Buffalo Girls** is also something of a female buddy film which focuses centrally on the friendship between Calamity Jane (Anjelica Houston) and Dora DuFran (Melanie Griffiths). Like Little Jo, Calamity Jane is based on a true life character and, again like Little Jo, Calamity Jane cross dresses but does not pass as a man, although most of the time she acts like one, carousing and shooting up saloons. Anjelica Houston certainly looks the part[12] and much of the film's somewhat meandering narrative (the overindulgence of the mini-series) is based in fact, such as Calamity's relationship with Wild Bill Hickok and her touring with Buffalo Bill's Wild West Show. The minor characters have also been carefully researched and the film includes some fine sequences featuring sharpshooting Annie Oakley and some nice moments between her and Calamity. But by far the most powerful aspect of the film is the central relationship between the two women, depicted with the intensity of a melodrama, which renders the central men somewhat secondary. This relationship is something we will return to in the discussion of Anie Stanley's **Hours Of The Idolite** below.

"BAD GIRLS"

This fantasy role-reversal film, produced commercially, boasts a strong female input: co-scene writer Yolande Finch, editor Jane Carson and executive producer Lynda Obst. It is a definite female gang western which depicts collective female power when a group of young women escape from prostitution to become outlaws. The film opens with the women in servitude in the local whorehouse situated above the saloon where there's a confrontation between one of the women and a town dignitary who's trying to rape another of the prostitutes. After she shoots him dead, the town gets ready for a lynching but the girls get away, and so begins their life as wanted women.

The film does not go for an authentic look, being much closer in style to the bright look of '50s classic westerns. The four female outlaws are more pin-ups than regular buckskins lasses; they are all attractive, use cosmetics and there's not a hair out of place. That said, they stick together, help each other and fight, shoot and party with panache. The gang of four are carefully individualised, representing a sort of Spice Girls range of young female characters. There's Cody (Madeleine Stowe), the tough competent one, a survivor who, after the death of her boyfriend, gets involved with a bandit gang; Lilley (Drew Barrymore), another tough cookie, a blonde tomboy with American apple-pie good looks; Eileen (Andie McDowell), a brunette farm girl passing as a New Orleans lady; and Anita (Mary Stuart Masterson), a redhead and most conventional of the gang, a widow who is naïve and vulnerable. There are some good individual men in the film but it's clear that the world the women inhabit is for the most part hostile and sexist. Anita finds to her cost that the deeds to the land she co-owned with her husband became invalid when he died and they have all survived abuse and brutal treatment at the hands of men.

The gang, as individuals and collectively, is active, attractive and powerful. They handle guns and horses with casual style and although from time to time they rely on the help of men, generally they are an autonomous group. At the end of the film, with the exception of Eileen who decides her destiny is with a small dirt farmer, they ride off into the sunset to continue their life as outlaws.

A LESBIAN WESTERN

Anie Stanley's Super-8 film **Hours Of The Idolite** (1995) is dedicated to "all the forgotten women of the Wild West". Like her film **Our Us We Bone One So Naked Known**, discussed above, it is a raunchy home-made affair focusing on an angry and highly sexualized gang of outlaw women. It exploits the authentic western style by producing black and white grainy images which recall old photographs and by utilising the *mise-en-scène* of a rough frontier town with a battered saloon and a whorehouse.

The all-female cast also features a strutting sheriff, and there's a series of faces behind bars that dissolve into posters of wanted women. To highlight the contrast, the poster images of bad girls are intercut with porn photos –

HOURS OF THE IDOLITE

the male perception of fluffy cowgirls – displaying buttock and cleavage with Stetsons and Colt 45s as peek-a-boo props and simpering smiles for the camera. The wanted women in Stanley's film who, like cameos from the silent movies or portraits from middle distance, snarling into camera, are unladylike, anti-social and undesirable. With names like Trixie Delight, Hilda Matilda, Dolores Tiara and Scarlet Harlot, these gals are wanted dead or alive for whoredom, adultery, armed robbery, nudity and non-heterosexual behaviour. With each successive portrait the list grows to include sodomy, piracy, gambling, spitting, grave-robbing, bar brawls and obscene activities.

As the portraits come to life, the ladies in question preen and posture to camera. Trixie Delight licks the barrel of her revolver, others suck at cheroots and blow the smoke into the camera lens, play with guns, point knives and shuffle cards in a menacing fashion. All this overlaid with the sound of ricocheting bullets and galloping hooves. The law, like the outlaws, is entirely female with Sheriff Slit Pickens and Deputy Dee Dee, two fearsome bulldykes who make Wyatt Earp look like a pussy cat.

But the highlight of the film is the 'Clammy Jane' episode where footage from **Buffalo Girls** with Melanie Griffith and Anjelica Houston is cut in for ironic effect. This raiding and reworking of the mainstream version begins with the sequence where Calamity Jane (Anjelica Houston) shoots down a chandelier in the saloon. On the soundtrack we hear snatches of the jaunty number "Buttons And Bows" from **Oklahoma**. The central set piece involves the sequence where Calamity is lying in the bath in her girlfriend's hotel room. Stanley's scurrilous editing draws out the buried lesbian sub-text making them a butch-femme couple. As Melanie lights Anjelica's cheroot (footage from **Buffalo Girls**) we hear snatches of the song "Don't Fence Me In" followed by images of the women smoking a joint, snogging and finally making out in the bath using the barrel of a pistol as a sex toy. In a series of carefully matched edits, the female buddies have become lovers. Then a cut to a silhouette of Calamity Jane on her horse and with her dog riding off into the sunset (footage from **Buffalo Girls**) is followed by an intertitle "The hand is quicker than the eye" and a cut back to more passion in the tub to the strains of "Down Mexico Way".

The reworking of 'found footage' is a common strategy in the Underground and Anie Stanley uses it to perfection. At a stroke she has unleashed the deviant desire that Hollywood is forever at pains to repress. And, as Calamity Jane rides downstream, we see an eagle wheeling overhead and realise that at last she is free. There's a final cut to a shoot-out in the sun, Stanley-style, and a few bars of "Smoke Gets In Your Eyes" and then sadly this wonderful film comes to an end. Maybe, though, it's just the beginning....

SECTION THREE: FEMALE BONDS

INTRODUCTION

Notions of liberation are also the theme of the films in this section and all the films discussed share an approach to filmmaking that challenges simplistic notions of realism. Social realism which underpins Hollywood illusionism professes to hold a mirror up to nature – the film being its uncomplicated reflection. In spite of the fact that each of the films has a very distinctive and different style to the others, they all do, to some extent, challenge straightforward notions of the difference between drama and documentary, distinctions between acting and being yourself and the separation of narrative from experimental forms. In challenging these traditional oppositions and incorporating them into their film, these women filmmakers provide examples of work in progress in the search for radical alternatives to mainstream male meaning systems.

It's no coincidence either that in every case the films represent groups of women from minority or marginalised groups within the context of mainstream white society. **Liberty's Booty** focuses on prostitutes in New York City; in **Mi Vida Loca**, a Chicana home girl gang living near Echo Park in Los Angeles is the central subject; a diverse range of old women are the topic of **The Company Of Strangers** which is set in Canada and, finally, a community of Gullahs, the descendants of slave settlers living in the islands off the South Carolina coast, provides the narrative interest in **Daughters Of The Dust**.

In every film, the filmmaker and/or their female characters express their identities both in terms of their gender and the racial or social group to which they belong. As African-American women or as Latinas, as old women or as prostitutes, the experience is of a double oppression. The films, which were all made in North America, come out of the margins and depict a world that is completely at variance with the standard Hollywood image.

"LIBERTY'S BOOTY"

While **Mi Vida Loca** is a drama that looks like a documentary and **The Company Of Strangers** is a documentary that is structured as a drama, **Liberty's Booty** could be described as a (somewhat unusual) documentary. Its ambiguity is perhaps best summed up be J Hoberman in the following words: "(Vivienne Dick) purposefully blurs the distinction between spectacle and document, licence and exploitation, prostitution and daily life. Although filled with digressions and apparent non sequiturs, the crux of the film is its frank subversion of male-stereotyped sex roles."[13]
Vivienne Dick is a filmmaker who has been identified with the New Wave of the '70s, a Super-8 New York-based film movement that addressed street sub-cultures and revived the flagging Underground from its increasingly empty formalism. Working on a very low budget using music and voiceover and the minimum of sync sound, Vivienne Dick's loose hand-held visual style invokes the spirit of the '60s filmmakers like Jack Smith, Andy Warhol and Ken Jacobs. Her opus overall betrays an interest in individual transgression, urban street life, kitsch and popular culture but is framed from a female point of view with an overriding interest in sexual politics and women characters. Like many of the films of Vivienne Dick, there is a fascination in this one with debris (accumulated over decades), the artefacts of fashion and style. The *mise-en-scène* in **Liberty's Booty** is a clutter of dolls, ornaments, toys, televisions and fairy lights in the interior shots and the effects of urban decay – graffiti, rotting doorways, broken windows and derelict buildings on the outside.
Watching **Liberty's Booty** is to share the fascinated, yet non-judgmental gaze of the filmmaker herself, as if you were seeing the world anew. The camera circles textures and light, pausing as it meanders along on characters and objects that take its fancy. The film's prologue gives the flavour. There's a hermaphrodite doll in a black bin bag and a woman in a room surrounded by Christmas chintz who acts as a midwife as the doll gives birth. We cut to a shot to a woman riding in the sidecar of a motorbike down a street. She arrives at a doorway and gets out. There follows a title sequence which consists of an animation of the Statue of Liberty transforming from statuesque woman to striptease artiste to gun-toting militant; from goddess to whore to activist in three moves!
In the following sequences we see women talking together or to camera about their life as prostitutes, their reasons and their aspirations. Dick uses an undefined mixture of verité, reconstruction and talking heads without ever clarifying which of the women are prostitutes and which are not. The blurring of boundaries is deliberate since, as the filmmaker suggests, all women prostitute themselves in some way, to some degree; who's to say where we should draw a line and why. The challenge to conventional attitudes also characterises the filmmaking styles – the mixture of documentary and underground codes. Jump edits, shaky hand-held camera and long takes, strange gels and black leader between reels, intermittent

LIBERTY'S BOOTY

sound, digressions and weird characters are all recognisable as features of underground filmmaking. Interspersed with these features there is the talking head of the traditional documentary and decor to die for; much more typical, in fact, of the excesses of Douglas Sirk's Hollywood melodramas[14] with clocks, decanters, cheap trays, album covers, pictures of kittens – the paraphernalia of people's bedrooms – or are they brothels? – all filmed in wild colour. Sometimes, like a fly on the wall, the camera skirts around a room while a group of women chat about their johns. Then, like a TV docudrama, there's an argument between a woman and her client which seems to be authentic (real) except that the man is, in fact, an actor. The 'direct cinema' technique – where Dick films a woman with a leopardskin print scarf talking direct to camera, who acts as a kind of tragic chorus punctuating the acts of the film and who is endearing, incoherent, paranoid and out of her head by turns, recalls the Maysles Brothers' film **Grey Gardens** (1975).

In **Liberty's Booty** the voiceover carries many of the views and opinions of the women in question and the visuals often provide texture as much as context. The debates include the economic and gender oppression that forces women into prostitution and there's also a sense in the film of connecting oppressions when, in a sequence where a group of women sit in McDonalds, we hear an Irish male voiceover discussing a strike in a McDonalds in Dublin about low wages. This is followed on the soundtrack by a female Latin voice talking about oppression in the Third World set against images of militant graffiti in front of which stands a black woman. This multi-layered approach gives the film a richness and unpredictability. We digress to a

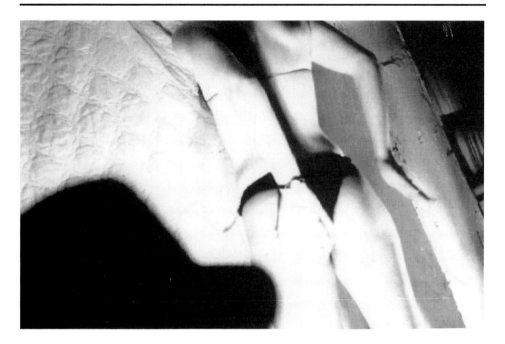

LIBERTY'S BOOTY

discussion of the Pope's visit to New York. First a TV report, then a voice talking about the economic oppression of religion over an image of scruffy kids sucking lollies in a doorway. Suddenly a cut, completely unexpected, to the countryside. In complete contrast to the city footage this is lyrical, with a group of women walking together on the hills smiling and laughing, their hair blowing in the wind while the mellow strains of "She's Not There" plays on soundtrack. Then, halfway through the song, an abrupt, almost brutal cut back to the brothel with the endless TV, the interminable phonecalls, the inevitable discussions of johns, schedules, bedrooms; the chaotic stream of consciousness through which the women describe their lives. (See Appendix for interview with Vivienne Dick.)

"MI VIDA LOCA" ("MY CRAZY LIFE")

Although perhaps not as experimental as **Liberty's Booty**, this film – made in 1993 – is a fresh, original and almost unique representation of the life of young Latin women living in the USA that has achieved commercial distribution and a measure of critical acclaim for director Allison Anders. Her films to date include **Gas, Food And Lodging** (1991) and **Grace Of My Heart** (1996) and are positioned around female characters whose point of view provides the identification of the films. Although basically a fictionalised version of the real life girl gang phenomenon in Los Angeles, **Mi Vida Loca** goes for a strong social realist, almost documentary, feel using a cast composed of some actors and some real gang members, under whose protection the film was made, and employing a number of voiceovers to

MI VIDA LOCA

narrate the story as well as intertitles, both more typical of a documentary than a drama. This strategy, the technique of using the codes associated with non-narrative films for a narrative is a way of unsettling the complacency of the spectator and challenging conventional modes of meaning in cinema. Errol Morris' film **The Thin Blue Line** (1988) achieves the same effect in the converse way – by making a documentary in the style of a film *noir* thriller. For example, Morris' film uses a musical score, almost unheard of for a documentary, written by Michael Nyman, to construct mood and suspense. Conversely, Anders' film, which is not a documentary, is almost without extra diagetic sound since most of the music, both classic and US salsa, comes from within the world of the film – radios, hi-fis, clubs, etc.

Along with Darnell Martin's vibrant feature film **I Like It Like That** (1994) set within the Latin community of Spanish Harlem, **Mi Vida Loca** begins to redress the lack of authentic Hispanic representations coming out of Hollywood. Furthermore, the film is centrally concerned with the lives and hopes of young women, a gang of homegirls from Echo Park. Its focus is the continuing friendship of Sad Girl and Mousie, two old school friends, and the rift created between them when they realise that Ernesto, a small time local drug dealer, is not only two-timing with them but also the father of their respective babies.

The homegirls' spirit in the face of poverty, discrimination, violence and police harassment is impressive. Their options are few and the choice available is crime or (single) motherhood or both. Their dreams and aspirations are never matched by the realities of their limited existence. While their men (also gangsters) fuck around, steal cars, deal drugs and shoot one another, the young women are shown attempting to build a serious support group. This impulse is in part motivated by Giggles, an older home girl, who, after serving time in prison, realises that her only hope for any kind of future is by going straight and getting a job. At the same time she realises solidarity rather than petty feuds is crucial for the women if they are to survive.

Others in the gang include Whisper, a teenage drug dealer, Baby Doll, Dimples and a number of real gang members playing themselves. One of the film's subplots involves La Blue Eyes, Sad Girl's sister, who cuts herself off by not joining the gang and pins her hopes for a life on finding love. She tries to contact the man of her dreams through a penfriends network but this project, like so many in the young people's lives in this community, is inevitably doomed. In spite or this, the fresh and basically optimistic attitude of the girls is inspiring. Without sentimentalising them in the least, Anders depicts the gang as a source of strength and joy. The central friendship between the two main young women is repaired and they bounce back with humour and fortitude. The film also captures their style, the rhythm of their daily routine, the hot music and the colourful clothes, their wit and their fiery repartee. Anders, while showing their flair, at the same time reveals the systematic waste of their potential.

This is not to suggest that the film is ultimately a message movie. In many ways, like **Liberty's Booty**, it mixes its styles and so unsettles a simple description. At times it is poetic, almost dreamlike, achieved through slow motion filming and contrapuntal editing. At other times it's fast-moving with a mixture of montage and music to accelerate the pace. Mostly, though, it's the tableau scenes where the women just sit around (at home, on the porch, in jail) and talk together that provides the crucial fascination of the film. For so long has this group been hidden by Hollywood that the sight and sound of the homegirls is mesmerising.

"THE COMPANY OF STRANGERS"

This small feature made in 1990 with money from the Canadian Film Board was written, produced and directed by women and uses the true life stories of its female cast to construct the narrative. Cynthia Scott directed this, her first feature film (she was a documentary filmmaker) when she was in her mid '50s. She cast the movie before she wrote the script and held auditions for women over 65 years old for a four month period. Then she loosely scripted the film around the seven women she had chosen. It revolves around a group of senior citizens thrown together for a coach trip. When their coach breaks down they are forced to get to know one another and work as a team so that they can survive in the wild open country. The women are all over 70 with the exception of the coach driver who is a younger African-American woman. The women have an assortment of cultures and backgrounds which include a native American, a cockney, an out lesbian, a nun and a smart middle-class widow; their real life histories are woven into the story when they are forced to open up to one another in the face of the immediate crisis. As they struggle with hunger, thirst, the need for shelter, repairing personal injuries and fixing the coach, their individual experiences, attitudes and memories come pouring out. Discussions around aging, racism, herbal remedies, celibacy, pleasure, men and marriage are conducted in large and small group situations.

In a case of life imitating art, the cast, who worked on location in a remote part of Quebec in temperatures which were often over the 100°F mark, were bussed from a nearby hotel on a daily basis. On one occasion their coach came off a bump in the road and landed in a ditch. The old women endured exhaustion, heat and swarms of mosquitoes and blackflies but they never complained. Their spirit was wonderful and it shines in the movie.

Unlikely alliances are formed and the women having established a base in a deserted shack, where they spend the night huddled up against the elements, drift off in ones, twos and small groups the next day to explore, go bird watching, mend the coach, go fishing or just hang out in the sunshine. What ensues are small vignettes of unscripted dialogue between the various characters. The cockney and the lesbian chat about their lives and their sexuality over a spot of birdwatching – sharing binoculars and having a laugh. The real life reminiscences are illustrated by photographs from the past of the woman in question and function to break up the narrative.

This feel-good film evokes the themes and debates of the Women's Movement in the '70s. As the women pull together, finding strength and pleasure in solidarity, the film not only provides a rich and varied document of older women's lives but also offers strong role models using characters who are rarely seen, let alone heard, in mainstream cinema. Though made in the '90s, this film is closer in spirit to the feminist documentaries of the '70s and early '80s; films like **Union Maids** (Jim Klein, Julia Reichert and Miles Mogulescu, USA, 1976) in which a number of older women talk about their experiences in terms of their race and gender and as organisers in the Trades Union Movement during the Depression. Such films, and **The Company Of Strangers** too, work to challenge stereotypes, raise consciousness and highlight women's issues. By placing these elements within a loose narrative structure, the film manages to avoid didacticism and political worthiness while allowing the patterns that shape the women's lives to emerge in exciting and unexpected ways.

"DAUGHTERS OF THE DUST"

Whereas **Liberty's Booty** and **Mi Vida Loca** focus on young women and **The Company Of Strangers** focuses on old women, Julie Dash's film covers the spectrum from not yet born girlchild to great-grandmother. Dealing exclusively with African-American characters, the film is basically a costume drama set in 1902 which explores among other things the experiences of women within the extended family of the Gullah community, descendants of slaves living on the islands off the South Carolina coast. As such, it is a reconstruction of a history; the African-American reality and culture effaced by dominant white society, and as such it uses a structure and form that is totally unlike the traditional linear narrative of conventional costume drama or historical epic.

The film provides the basic details, date and place through sub-titles and is concerned with events on the day when most of the family members are leaving the island to find their future on the mainland. It is, however, in terms of its narrative development and dramatic exchanges, almost experimental, using rhythm and ritual to merge notions of temporality – past, present and future – and developing its plot and characterisation through filmic techniques that are more poetic than discursive. Female encounters serve as the touchstone for developing action and drama and through the women's voices across four generations a rich pattern is woven. In a sense Julie Dash is laying the cornerstone for a national African-American cinema based in history and research as well as imaginative reconstruction – and her central focus is female.

The matriarch Nana Peazant is the link from the past to the present. Her words, her wisdom and her visions serve as the fount of knowledge and the unifying element for the whole community. She refuses to leave the island and by the end of the film she is joined by her great-great granddaughter. Meanwhile the women in the family have different attitudes and varying social expectations. Aunt Hagar believes in progress and wants to leave, whereas her cousin Yellow Mary, a lesbian who as returned from Cuba where she made her living as a prostitute, has different ideas. Throughout the film the women in particular talk together and share their hopes and fears and these group encounters take the place of the action or drama of mainstream cinema.

In the course of the day we see the family engage in a number of shared activities and community rituals. These include preparing food, dyeing garments, making bricks, harvesting and the set piece family picnic during which a number of characters make speeches. The diversity of female positions within the extended family – wife, mother, child, cousin, auntie – and the relationships between them is something that the film celebrates and the images of women in groups against the sea or the river are hauntingly beautiful. The film's visual power, particularly in expressing natural beauty – the light, the colour, the rural scenes of harvesting, the young girls dancing in white dresses on windswept beaches – constructs a kind of dreamlike quality which is matched by the traditional music with its drumbeat like a pulse.

The formal aspects of the film are quite unique. The use of fluid elements, dissolves and tracking shots predominate. The film also uses the fade, both to black and to white, to punctuate the rhythm. There are very few middle distance shots and we cut from longshot to very big close-up on a number of occasions or the moving camera takes us in and out of close ups in very long takes. There's also use of slow motion, fast speed, pixillation and changing camera speeds to express the sense of time itself being relative to a particular character or situation. For example, as the bottle tree is being smashed by Eli when he discovers his wife Eula is pregnant and thinks the child is not his, time slows right down. The bottle tree is an important motif for the family and the film highlights the almost ritualistic power of particular objects, focusing on drapes, boxes, sea shells and other ornaments. The elements are also central in the film's development, the sea, the rivers, the sky, mist, clouds, smoke and fire, and time itself is lengthened, contracted, punctured through a range of techniques including jump cuts, inserts, cross cutting and cut aways. When the matriarch tries to guide her grandson from his folly and anger, the sequence seems almost endless; we cut away to so many different groups and encounters. Again, when a group of women are shown talking together sitting on a tree trunk plaiting each others' hair, there's a kind of theme and variation effect. We return to the basic sequence on a number of occasions, meanwhile it's intercut with the men getting their photographs taken on the beach and on another part of the island a young girl finding a broken parasol in the sand. The rhythm of these repetitions produces a trance-like effect, a mystical or magical quality, epitomised perhaps by the slow motion shot of a little girl running along the sea's edge, an insert initially that we return to at the end of the film and understand that it was a flashforward – a vision of the little girl not yet born whose voice we have heard on the soundtrack, guiding us through the intricacies of family and narrative. It is her birth at the end of the film that guarantees continuity – the women it is who carry the cultural legacy of their African origins and for Nana Peazant the birth of her great-great granddaughter will preserve family and culture and ensure that legacy.

SECTION FOUR: UP AGAINST THE STATE

INTRODUCTION

"Black women, be ready.
White women, get ready.
Red women, stay ready."
—Born In Flames

The films discussed in this section are a mixture of feminism, fantasy and realism in varying degrees. All of them feature female characters engaging in active resistance to the state by taking direct and militant action. **A Question Of Silence** and **Born In Flames** are radical feminist features from the early '80s. **Set It Off** is a recent commercial film which is influenced both by the Black Power movement and blaxploitation films of the '70s.

"A QUESTION OF SILENCE"

Dutch director Marleen Gorris' first feature is the ultimate male punishment movie, tapping into the 'wild zone', the no-mans-land of female experience discussed in Chapter One. The premise of the film is that conceptually, emotionally and linguistically men and women inhabit different universes and it shows that men don't have the faintest clue about where women are coming from; whereas women know exactly where men are situated and find it pathetic, laughable and directly in opposition to their (women's) needs.

As much a female conspiracy film as a girl gang movie, **A Question Of Silence** is based around a central incident in which three women, Christine, a mute housewife, Annie, a talkative, greasy-spoon waitress and Andrea, a cool secretary, join together in battering to death a male boutique assistant. Even though the women do not know one another and throughout the film never directly communicate with one another, they share a secret bond which brings them together for this one event, a murder of solidarity. Witnesses to the murder, an older white woman, a middle-aged black woman and two young women who are always arm in arm seem to share this bond and leave the shop in a conspiratorial huddle and afterwards go their separate ways. They have all met in the wild zone – a place where men cannot enter.

In order to make sense of the collective murder, a female psychiatrist, Dr Janine van der Bos is employed by the state prosecution to interview the defendants and assess their sanity. It is around the transformation of Janine that the film's narrative revolves. At the beginning of the film, she is sleeping with the enemy – her husband who is a lawyer. Because of her class position and her marital and social status, Janine is initially unable to make sense of the murder. But during her separate interview sessions with the three women, she begins to challenge her learnt assumptions about gender, class, sanity, madness and the family.

In the final denouement in court, Janine sides with the defendants (and the silent witnesses to the murder who are sitting in the spectators' gallery) and joins in the female laughter when the male prosecutor demands to know whether the women are sane. The court session ends with manic laughter and the witnesses are led out still laughing while representatives of the law, the judge and the lawyers look on bewildered. The film ends with Janine walking away from her furious husband towards the female witnesses who are standing watching outside the court. In the end, Janine casts aside her masquerade and enters the wild zone. Needless to say, **A Question Of Silence** was hugely popular with female audiences – and panned by male critics.

"BORN IN FLAMES"

Lizzie Borden's low-budget feature is a similarly female-empowering film. It is energetic, anarchic and analytical by turns, based around the contemporary issues that were being raised by the Women's' Movement. Set in a hypothetical future where the Revolutionary Regime of Social Democracy is celebrating the tenth anniversary of the War of Liberation, **Born In Flames** is actually about sexual inequality in the New York of its time.

Filming on a shoestring budget with help from her friends, Borden weaves a loose and freewheeling narrative that incorporates home-shot footage of actual demonstrations and pickets that were happening at the time and uses a mixture of real people and actors as well as documentary and reconstructed sequences to give a flavour of the city. The film raids and reworks TV news items and uses tape-slide, voiceover and New Wave music to knit the narrative together. This gives the film its raw and authentic feel and provides the background for its focus which is the diversity of female political positions. In the film these are represented by two radio stations, a direct action group called The Women's Army and a group of middle class white intellectuals.

The sense of street culture is provided by the female music stations. Phoenix Radio plays black music and is run by a deejay called Honey who

BORN IN FLAMES

plays laid-back reggae dedicated to "the liberation of women and the freedom of life that is found in music". By contrast, Radio Regazza is fronted by a white, wired anarchist called Isabelle. She plays rebel music from Hendrix to punk and spouts a manic mix of violence and voodoo.

Liberation of a more directly political nature is provided by The Women's Army, a radical, non-hierarchical, separatist, vigilante group composed of a range of women from different racial and class backgrounds and of all ages. This group responds to injustices against women at street level – intervening when they see rape or harassment in progress. Central to this group and to the film's plot is Adelaide Norris, a black lesbian, feminist and Trades Union activist. Her mentor is Zella Wylie, an older black activist who comments, "We have a right to violence. All oppressed people have a right to violence."

When Adelaide dies in police custody after a solidarity visit to the Western Sahara Liberation Front, the women from all the organisations join together to demand an inquiry into her death which they suspect to be murder. After a mass leafleting campaign and a group break-in to a television station where the women force the technicians at gunpoint to broadcast a revolutionary message from Zella Wylie in which she denounces government, surveillance and censorship, the women's radio stations become galvanised. Together they form Phoenix and Regazza Radio and broadcast from a stolen truck as they drive around the city and Isabelle announces: "It's time to fight, sisters!". Even the white, middle class socialist feminists come on side and we hear a clipped voice reading their statement condemning the government over images of the street women breaking into a haulage firm and hot-wiring the truck which will carry the merged radio station, now dedicated to the liberation of women. Again, as a manifesto from the Women's Army goes out over the airwaves we hear black funky music and cut to a group of women making a bomb which they will use to blow up the World Trade Centre.

Apart from its radical message, what's notable about **Born In Flames** is the central role given to black women in the struggle. Not only does this serve to redress the invisibility of black women in cinema but also to acknowledge the vanguard role that black people in general and black women in particular, play in revolutionary struggle.

"SET IT OFF"

Black women taking up arms is also the subject of **Set It Off**, a film in which Magdalen Carol succinctly observes: "Four friends who grew up and went to school together in the 'Hood decide that they have had enough of lying down to the system, pick up a few guns and rob a bank ...."[15] With three of the women we are given detailed accounts as to why they would want or need to turn to crime. Stony watches her innocent kid brother gunned down by white cops, Frankie is unfairly dismissed from her uptown bank job and Tisean is a single mother struggling to keep herself and her child together. Cleo, the fourth and informal gang leader, has no such reason – she's a dyke with attitude and that speaks for itself!

This big-budget movie has a divided agenda, caught between the social realist depiction of life and conditions in the projects and the pull of the swaggering heroines in the fantasy world of blaxploitation cinema. Cleo, the larger than life character played by larger than life Queen Latifah, falls into the latter category – she's big, boisterous and deviant – the Ms Bombastic of the 'Hood – who takes no shit and is fearless, witty and sexy. She's a direct descendant of **Cleopatra Jones**, **Foxy Brown** and **Coffy**[16] – as her name suggests.

Cleo, who is connected with and respected by male gangstas, galvinises the girls into action and generates most of the energy and action in the film. As a consummate car thief, Cleo always checks the CDs when she breaks into a new car and throws them out the window in disgust. She then drives away with her own music blaring. Cleo is definitely the kind of character who requires a funky by-line (as in "Coffy – she'll cream you!"). She's so outrageous – French-kissing her bleached blonde girlfriend in the street and leading the sisters into ever more daring escapades in bigger and bigger banks!

The excesses of Cleo's life are matched by her death. Heroically, she leads the cops away from the rest of the gang after they're trapped in a police ambush. Cleo's last stand is magnificent; a mixture of speed, skill and style. Finally surrounded by squad cars, she's caught in what seems like an endless hail of bullets and dies like Bonnie and Clyde, a legendary death. **Set It Off** is one of the best and freshest commercial features made around women for many years. It deserves much wider recognition and distribution than it has had so far and Queen Latifah should have been nominated for an

CLEOPATRA JONES

FOXY BROWN

COFFY

Oscar for her performance. Hopefully it will become the cult classic of the decade.

Set It Off combines black political and cinematic movements with feminist influences and comes up with that rarest of representations, the powerful black woman. Rarer still is the sight of four young black women acting in solidarity, armed, active and dangerous, occupying centre frame. It also taps into the politics of the Black Power Movement of the late '60s and '70s as well as the Women's Movement with its commitment to female autonomy and sisterhood. Cinematically, as we have seen, it references blaxploitation cinema as well as the more recent **Boyz 'N' The Hood** (John Singleton, 1991) social message picture, and the fantasy female buddy film **Thelma And Louise**.

The film may have been directed by a man but it is directed at women, particularly a young, black audience. En Vogue's hit single "Don't Let Go (Love)" comes from **Set It Off** and the film is obviously commercial, but the central characters (the girl gang itself) remain tough and cool throughout, resisting the over-commodified flakiness of the Spice Girls, say, and providing much needed funky contemporary role models.

feminist solidarity to sisters, to home girls, but rather to give a sense of what is available.

The growth of the 'girl gang' film directed by women has been a notable development of the '90s. In the context of the British film industry, Gurinder Chadha's **Bhaji On The Beach** (1993) represents a landmark. The first feature to be directed by an Asian woman in Britain, it presents a sense of cross-cultural fertilisation in its Blackpool-meets-Bombay setting.

When a group of Asian women of various ages and attitudes go on a day trip to Blackpool (a gaudy English seaside town) they find themselves, after a catalogue of crises, thrown into unexpected solidarity. They also find strong links between Asian and British culture, a connection that is marked visually by the famous Blackpool illuminations which transform the place into a magical Bollywood film set.

Gurinder Chanda's wonderful, serious, funny, political, poignant film has a strong feminist message mixed up with the absurd humour of the **Carry On** British comedy films. The representations of Asian women range from two young sex-mad teenagers to an aging traditional matriarch and everything in between. At the end of the film there's a real sense of their collective power when all the women finally forget their differences and gang up to support Ginder, a young mother, against Ranjit, her bullying husband who's trying to abduct their son.

In short film terms, in the British context, the feminism of so many '80s 'girl gang' action films, is referenced in Ann Frankel's low budget video **Snatched** (1995) in which a group of vigilante women kidnap a judge. The four angry young women hold the judge for questioning and challenge him on his notorious leniency to rapists. And, on a more comic note, Carol Morley's film **The Day Elvis Died** (1997) features a gang of tough primary school girls who terrorise nerdy ten-year-old Karen. Karen finds solace in her pet rabbit, Elvis, and eventually hits back in a quirky and unexpected way. A stylish short, the film features a cameo appearance of Tony Blackburn, the radio DJ who's an emblem of '70s Britain. Apart from the sheer originality of **The Day Elvis Died** it is also remarkable in that the film was financed by individual contributions, fund-raising events, benefit screenings and auctions, initiated by the production company TriAngel Films. As such it is an object lesson in what can be achieved with perseverance and dedication and is an inspiration to film makers living on the margins.

POSTSCRIPT: Since the publication of the first edition of *Renegade Sisters: Girl Gangs On Film* there have been a number of new low & no-budget short films made by women on the theme of girl gangs. Below is a list of some of the titles to watch out for: **Yo Yo Gang** (GB Jones, USA 1996); **Junky Punky Girlz** (Nisha Ganatra, USA 1996); **She's Real Worse Than Queer** (Lucy Thane, USA 1997); **Marijuana Moment** (Zalcock/Chambers, UK 1999); **Girl Gang 2000** (Katrina Del Mar, USA 1999); **Shari Shapiro's Slumber Party** (Samara Halpern, USA 1999); **Women In Black** (Amanda Raine, UK 1999); **Chicks With Guns** (Jennifer Arnold, USA 2000).

NOTES

1. See *Queercore: Lesbich/Schwule In Den USA* by Inka Petersen. Hamburg/San Francisco, Summer 1994.

2. See the single "Rule Britannia"/"Jerusalem" by Suzi Pinns, from the outrageous soundtrack album *Jubilee 1978*.

3. Published by Black & Red, Detroit: 1970.

4. See Mulvey's article "You Don't Know What Is Happening, Do You Mr Jones?" in *Framing Feminism: Art And The Women's Movement 1970–85*, ed Rozsika Parker and Griselda Pollock. Pandora Press, London and New York: 1987.

5. We recall Poly Styrene's screech "Oh Bondage! Up Yours!" in X-Ray Spex' song of the same name (Virgin Records, 1977).

6. From a poem by Nancy Labonte, *Nous Jous/We Play*.

7. See *Cow Girls* by Candace Savage (Bloomsbury, 1996).

8. See *Guide For The Film Fanatic* by Danny Peary (Simon and Schuster Inc, New York: 1986) for references to films starring John Wayne.

9. For examples of such work see Jim Kitses' *Horizons West*, Secker and Warburg, London: 1970; and Peter Wollen's *Signs And Meaning In The Cinema*, Chapter 2: the discussion of Howard Hawks and John Ford (Secker and Warburg and BFI, London: 1969).

10. See *Home Is Where The Heart Is: Studies In Melodrama And The Women's Film*, ed Christine Gledhill; BFI, London: 1987.

11. The reference comes from **The Man Who Shot Liberty Valance** (John Ford, 1962).

12. See *Pictorial History Of The Wild West* by James D Horan and Paul Sann, The Hamlyn Publishing Group Ltd, London/New York/Sydney/Toronto: 1961.

13. From MIT Press for the Institute of Architecture and Urban Studies.

14. See for example Sirk's **Written On The Wind** (1956) or **Imitation Of Life** (1959).

15. Film review in *Black Film Bulletin*, London, 31st March 1997.

16. **Cleopatra Jones** (1973) and its sequel, **Cleopatra Jones And The Casino Of Gold** (1975) star Tamara Dobson. **Coffy** (1973) and **Foxy Brown** (1974) star Pam Grier. These films are female versions of black action fantasy (blaxploitation) films like **Shaft** (1971) and **Superfly** (1972), which surfaced in the early to mid-'70s.

CHAPTER SIX

TWO GIRL GANG CLASSICS

ONE: "SWITCHBLADE SISTERS"

AFTER the decline of the female biker movie in the early '70s, the all-female gang on film grew increasingly violent but – sadly – abandoned its wheels. Three titles are worth mentioning as they keep the girl gangs visible. Ted V Mikels' **The Doll Squad** (1974) and **Ten Violent Women** (1982) continue the tradition of the deadly female[1] as well as referencing its camp reworking in more mainstream films like **Goldfinger** (1964) which featured Pussy Galore and her Flying Circus. Mikels himself maintains that **The Doll Squad** provided the prototype for the subsequent TV series *Charlie's Angels*. Made four years earlier, **The Doll Squad** features a highly trained group of female agents who work for the CIA, six of whom blow away an entire army garrison and three hundred troops. Mikels continues his rampaging females in **Ten Violent Women** in which a group of women miners, bored and frustrated with their

THE DOLL SQUAD

jobs, turn to a life of crime, successfully robbing a jewellery store. The third significant title of this period, **Switchblade Sisters** (1976), is a return to the girl exploitation movies of the '50s – but typically with a lot more sex and violence (if only the gang had sported motorbikes as well as flick knives!).

Switchblade Sisters is one of the most interesting girl gang movies to come out of the exploitation fold. It's a heady cocktail of JD film, WIP movie, High School drama and Revolutionary Action picture. It was directed by Jack Hill, who began his filmmaking career in the '60s, doing much of his work for Roger Corman, and who became in the '70s one of the foremost directors of the exploitation cinema. His credits include such classic titles as: **Spider Baby** (1964); the previously-mentioned **Big Doll House, Big Bird Cage, Coffy,** and **Foxy Brown; The Swinging Cheerleaders** (1974); and **Hollywood Boulevard** (1974).[2]

In **Switchblade Sisters**, the teenage delinquent hard girl hybrid develops into what could almost be described as a female rites of passage movie which charts the coming of age of a group of juvenile girls, "The Dagger Debs". By the end of the film the female characters have become women who are realising their full potential and their autonomy from men. They call themselves "The Jezebels".

The monikers are instructive. Jezebel was a seductive and immoral woman who lured men to their death and in street slang a 'dagger' describes a butch lesbian. The women in the film are strongly sexualized and, while the focus is resolutely heterosexual, there is the suggestion of an erotic bond between Lace, the female gang leader, and Patch, her best friend and sidekick. There is, anyway, always a suggestion in exploitation films that groups of wild and violent women are somehow 'deviant' and this is frequently plugged into a repressed lesbian sub-text. On the surface though, each of the girls has a male counterpart, boyfriend or date, in the male gang 'The Silver Daggers'. Lace, the leader of the girls, is going out with Dom, the leader of the boys and her status is secure for as long as this lasts. The girls are thus structured as subservient to the men and dependent upon them. Additionally, in the beginning of the film, the male gang is represented as more powerful and much harder-edged. They control the rackets – drugs, prostitution and protection – at their school, with the covert approval of the headmaster. They use and abuse their women with indifference or casual violence and, initially at least, the girls, like the film itself, appear to support the status quo.

All Jack Hill's films manage to combine a tacky low-budget feel with a genuine visual flair. In the title sequence of **Switchblade Sisters** we are introduced to the characters and the neighbourhood via a series of black and while stills. The gals look tough and their stalking ground looks seedy; high rise projects against a flat land of urban dereliction. The action opens with Lace getting ready to go out, posing in front of her mirror against a pumping soundtrack, the refrain from "Big Hearted Woman" accompanying Lace as she puts on her leather cap and jacket. She enters the living room to find her mother and small siblings being bullied by a fat slob repo-man. As he leaves with the last of her mother's money, Lace follows him into the elevator, cutting her eyes at him seductively as they begin the descent. At every stop

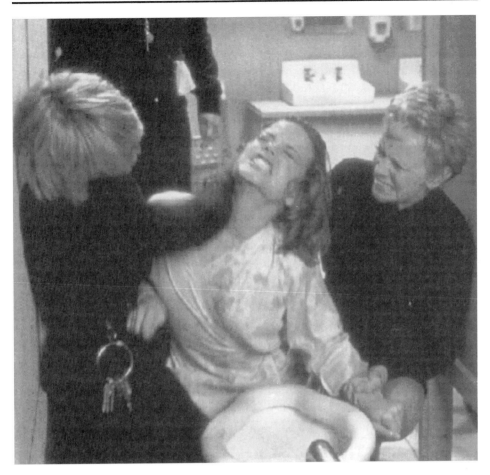

SWITCHBLADE SISTERS

a new tough-looking girl gets in until the sleazy rent collector is surrounded by leather clad, gum-chewing gals. With a flourish they take out their switchblades and he is left at the end of the ride with his clothes cut to shreds. The Dagger Debs have made a killing and move off laughing. They hook up with their men at a local burger joint and start giving customers a hard time. The customers all slink off scared, except for Maggie, the new girl on the block, who refuses to be hustled out. She fights her corner and a ruck ensues.

Maggie is arrested along with the Debs, including Lace, Patch and the fat girl known as Donut (played by Lenny Bruce's daughter, Kitty Bruce). At the Juvenile Detention Centre they face matron and her guards in a scene straight out of a WIP film. Matron is a frustrated bull dyke with a penchant for 'hot little chippies'. Maggie refuses her advances and is bundled out of the dorm for a spot of strip searching. Matron has her rubber gloves at the ready and the scene is played for laughs. Lace and the girls rise to defend Maggie and in the mayhem that ensues beat up Matron and her sadistic entourage. Lace respects Maggie's spirit and they bond. Patch is jealous of this new friendship. The plot thickens.

Next Maggie, in hot pants and high boots, tangles with Dom. She is delivering a love missive to Dom from Lace. The boys hoot and jeer as Dom reads out the letter. Dom is not only weak but nasty. He breaks into Maggie's home later that evening, rapes her and assaults her mother. At this point, Dom's misogyny goes unchallenged by the film. He tells Maggie, "You asked for it didn't you," and she appears to concur. It seems she really fancies him. But the film takes a turn for the better and demonstrates that you can't keep a good woman down. Maggie, not Lace, becomes the figure the girls start to respect and the focus of the identification shifts. Two jealous triangles form between Dom, Maggie and Lace, and Lace, Maggie and Patch, in which Maggie occupies the apex as the object of desire. This takes care of the human interest aspect of the film and provides the motor for the continuing action.

The violent set pieces that follow are splendid. The first is a gang war shoot-out at a roller rink which leaves Dom wasted and Lace hospitalised. Maggie begins to take over the leadership. She encourages the women to throw the worthless men off their turf. They're fed up with being bullied and prostituted by the slobs, so they act swiftly. Who needs them anyway! The girls change their name, they are no longer The Dagger Debs, the possessions of men, they are the Jezebels – powerful and seductive in their own right.

With their new found power and Maggie at the helm, the girls branch out. The Jezebels meet a group of black revolutionary separatist sisters who occupy an abandoned precinct uptown and they agree to pool resources for a daring operation. The plan is to attack a criminal group who are pushing drugs among little kids in the neighbourhood and to seize their huge arsenal of weapons for the revolutionary struggle. The black sisters, who mean serious business, are prepared to work with the Jezebels because they know and trust Maggie. They're pleased that the gang have ditched their men: "The only thing a man's got below his belt is... clayfeet," and welcome their support in the struggle against racist violence and injustice. Quoting Mao they assert: "Political power grows out of the barrel of a gun."

By now the action is really hotting up and the Jezebels, under the tutelage of the black women, work out and learn how to handle guns. In the street battle that follows the women unleash a frenzy of firepower to the rallying cry "Come on girls, for the revolution!" as they blow away the enemy.

For the final scene, Lace returns to the gang and tries to win back her leadership. She badmouths Maggie but her duplicity becomes apparent to the women and with the exception of Patch they line up behind Maggie. There's a bloody fight between Lace and Maggie and, as Maggie plunges the knife into her rival, the police arrive. Filmed in silhouette, each woman pledges her loyalty to the Jezebels and the film ends on a note of solidarity and resistance: "You can beat us, chain us, lock us up. But we'll be back. We're the Jezebels!".

Jack Hill's films are strong on female revenge and often feature some kind of revolutionary struggle. **Switchblade Sisters** doesn't disappoint and is arguably Hill's best – though unfortunately last – film as credited director. In typical exploitation style, it was shot in eighteen days for $250,000 and was originally released under the title of **The Jezebels**. Despite its current cult status – with Hill's blaxploitation pictures touted as a major influence on Tarantino's **Jackie Brown** – the film never did well at the box office and Hill observes: "It was my only real loser".

TWO: "A GUN FOR JENNIFER"; A GIRL GANG FILM FOR THE MILLENNIUM

A Gun For Jennifer is about a group of female vigilantes who work out of a seedy New York Go-Go bar as a front for their undercover activities. The five women who are survivors of abuse, poverty and imprisonment share a collective mission: to blow away the worst exploiters of women, those who rape and torture and make money from it. While they target fat cat sex-industry bosses and small time street gang operators, no man is immune from their vengeance.

While this rings a bell with old time radical feminism, **Born In Flames** it is not! This movie, with its by-line "Dead men don't rape", takes the female revenge drama and the exploitation films of the '70s to extremes. Its graphic violence and pumping action makes Tarantino look tame. These gals are *heavy* and take *no* prisoners.

Jesse, the leader, is a borderline psychotic and directs operations with a murderous zeal that is terrifying. Punishment meted out on offending men is swift and bloody, castration and death is the agenda. The women inhabit a nocturnal city that is shot through with psychological and physical violence. New York provides the backdrop for a descent into hell where men prey on women as a matter of course.

Into this maelstrom comes Allison who is seeking anonymity and escaping a violent husband. No sooner does she arrive than she is ambushed by two hoodlums who are in the process of raping her when the vigilante girls show up. They dispatch the scum without missing a beat and persuade Allison (who tells them her name is Jennifer) to join them. She is reluctant but has no choice and embarks on shooting practice and combat training with them.

At this point we, and Jennifer, become acquainted with the women as individuals and we hear their stories. All have suffered at the hands of men and of the state. Jesse and Trish are sisters, Priscilla is a Latina and Becky is black. Becky has done time for taking part in revolutionary activity. They sit around a campfire toasting marshmallows and talking about their lives. They work out; playing basketball and doing martial arts. They hone themselves into revenge machines; they are superb specimens. These are the quiet moments! The film has comic moments too, as in the Go-Go bar when the group turn the tables on two sexist customers and, at gunpoint, force them to dance and strip – giving them a taste of their own casual objectification of women – a taste of humiliation and terror.

Mostly though, the film is choc-full of adrenalin-laden action and the plot revolves around an NYPD investigation into the dead, mutilated men who are beginning to litter the city. The police hunt is spearheaded by a black woman cop, Detective Billie Perez, who is determined to solve the mystery of

A GUN FOR JENNIFER

the murdered men. Much more insightful than her sexist colleagues, Perez has an inkling of female revenge. She understands the motivation precisely because she is a woman and, unlike the male cops who cannot credit that women could be organised and violent, she has a strong instinct for what is going on. She finally tracks them down alone (her partner, the one sympathetic man in the film, has been mown down by the gang earlier) in a denouement of unremitting violence, involving a graphic torture scene followed by the vigilante's raid and bloody shoot-out.

The two surviving group members, Jennifer and Priscilla, persuade Billie Perez to let them walk away and the film ends up with Perez getting promotion while Jennifer and Priscilla sit in a diner getting hassled by more neanderthals. For them, nothing has changed.

A Gun For Jennifer, made on the slimmest of budgets, is an extraordinary *tour-de-force*. Exhilarating and disturbing by turns, it offers no easy answers but provides a powerful image of a civilisation moving into the new dark ages.

Deborah Twiss, the producer, co-writer and star of **A Gun For Jennifer** was in London for the premiere of her film at the ICA. I spoke to her about the powerful impact of the movie and her unorthodox methods for raising the cash to make it.

A GUN FOR JENNIFER

AN INTERVIEW WITH DEBORAH TWISS

BZ: Your representation of the female vigilantes is quite complex. The film never idealises them.

DT: If you have a group of women friends there's always little conflicts and little ego plays and all kinds of subtle little things that go on between them. Even if you're all into the same thing; if you all have the same purpose, the same drive, the same focus, there's still things that go on within relationships and I think it's really important to show that.

BZ: It seems important that the gang is racially mixed.

DT: I definitely wanted a spectrum of women 'cos the film wasn't about white women or black women. It's about women. And I really didn't want anybody to look at it and say "this race isn't represented". And this story takes place in New York and New York is very mixed and so everyone had to be represented in this film.

BZ: The black female cop and the older woman were very interesting.

DT: The older woman actor does a lot of theatre and often couldn't make our shooting schedules which was unfortunate because she's a very, very good lady. She is a lesbian and a feminist activist.

BZ: Yes, and I felt she had a lot to contribute in terms of an analysis of the gang's position.

DT: I know that's one thing that still disappoints me with the 90 minutes... you know, the campfire scene. That was complete improvisation. We were into about four weeks of shooting and I was having a lot of problems with

A GUN FOR JENNIFER

the feeling that it wasn't getting to grips with my ideas. I come from a theatre background, so when I wrote the script everyone had monologues, everything was explained and you can't do that in film, it would have dragged. So when Todd (Todd Morris, director, editor and co-writer) took what I did and made it into a screenplay, a lot of the motivation went to the side and the little things about the characters had to come through in the acting. And about four weeks into the shoot I was getting really frustrated, so I got everyone together and I said "Look, I want to do something here and I'm going to tell Todd. And what I need us to do is for each of us to work on a core. You have to decide why you're with this group, why you believe in what they're doing and justify working out of the Go-Go bar. 'Cos these are issues that are not addressed in the script and they have to come out and this is your chance as an actor to develop the character and show everything." So I sent them away for a week to do that while we were shooting other things. And then we went up to Hunter Mountain and the campfire scene happened at 2 o'clock in the morning. We did 40 minutes of footage and everyone was talking and debating and it ended up working our really well.

BZ: It is important to understand the gang member's individual motivations.

DT: Yes, and you get a sense of their backgrounds also with the basketball game. Todd did a wonderful editing job there. He's a great editor. A brilliant editor I think. He did about 90 per cent of the edit on the film and we brought in a female editor at the end to help restructure certain scenes and bring in the female perspective for the final edit, but overall Todd did a really fabulous job.

A GUN FOR JENNIFER

BZ: The film never explores the sexuality of the gang members.
DT: That was deliberate. We left their sexuality open-ended. We didn't show any sexual relationships involving the women or between them. We felt that would be exploitative. In fact, there's no sex in the film at all. The film focuses on violence and abuse.
BZ: Who is the character the audience should most identify with? Is it Jennifer?
DT: She's with the audience. She has an outside perspective on the group. Even at the end she's toying with the idea of leaving.
BZ: Is she the focal point? You are Jennifer in the film. Are we supposed to identify with her?
DT: There are three women: Jennifer, Billie the black cop and Jesse the gang leader. It's almost as if they're the same person; three different parts of the personality of the same person – or the same person at different stages of development.
BZ: What do you feel about Billie, a black woman working in a sexist police department?
DT: Ultimately she does what she believes is right as a woman. And manipulates things the way a man would. Puts a spin on the press and moves up. She gets promoted. So she ends up being the cream on top. You remember the one woman who's in the gang hideout, the one who the vigilante gang execute and Jesse says: "She chose her friends poorly, kill her". If you sleep with rapists and murderers you should die as such.
BZ: I found that very harsh.

A GUN FOR JENNIFER

DT: If that was a group of male terrorists, would they hesitate for a second? Jesse's nuts and this is something the group feel very strongly about. This gang are selling crack and raping children. They're monsters and the woman wants to have a relationship with them. If you collude you're also guilty.

BZ: It's a very hard-edged film.

DT: I know, I know but there were so many things I wanted to expose and this was in my mind for a long time. I was in New York for about four years before this started happening in my mind.

BZ: Your message is strongly about male violence and its effect on women. In many ways it's reminiscent of radical feminism of the '70s that 'all men are rapists' and it begins with the female vigilante group castrating a pornographer who rapes and tortures women. Most of the men in the film are represented very negatively. How have male audiences reacted to **A Gun For Jennifer**?

DT: It's so funny because men are some of our biggest fans. It's so weird to me because I did not make this film for men, I made it for women, definitely. It's exciting that men have embraced it so much. I think it shows ultimately that the message in the film is not about men or women, its about right or wrong and how strongly some people feel about things that have gone wrong and to show that you can't fight violence with violence. It's a constant thing that people are wondering about; there's so much injustice and what's the answer? It taps into something that is an issue to many people and it goes beyond gender even.

BZ: You have said that the film is anti the violence although it shows such extreme violence. In the end the two surviving members of the female gang walk into a diner and are subjected to sexual harassment.

DT: All that they've done, they still have not achieved what they set out to do. All they did was lose many of their friends and become even more hardened and sad.

BZ: What, then, is the message of the film?

DT: I wanted to set off writing the film, my dream... I was writing this film while I was still dancing (in a topless bar). I was working at a place where I was dancing half an hour on stage and then half an hour off and in my half an hour off I would run into the bathroom and write. And the whole time I was doing this I was fantasising that what I would have at the end was a film that people would watch. They'd all go out to see it together and afterward they'd have to go to a bar or café and talk about it for hours and debate and say 'what's the answer'? And the answer that I want people to come up with – is if you remember in the film, all the women come from very abusive, hostile backgrounds. It goes back to the family. And that is the ultimate answer. You can't fight violence with violence. You know the death penalty, jail, all of that, you know, that's just a product of the violence. But, if you go back into the family and you have children educated properly by their parents... don't give the responsibility away to the government or to teachers or anyone else. It goes back to the family. The good core family with no abuse.

BZ: But it is still an indictment of men. It's very anti-men.

DT: All the men are bad except for Grady and it's so sad when he dies. And that's the beginning of when everything starts to fall apart.

BZ: For me the film is an image of a descent into hell, leading to the final shoot-out where Jesse is being flayed alive in a frenzied torture scene.

DT: The place where the final party was, it's called 'The Vault'. It's an S/M club and it's actually a basement.

BZ: I know the film has a tongue-in-cheek, exploitation quality but it's also very scary.

DT: That character, Carl Varna, is based on a real criminal. All the crimes that are in the film are things that are in the news in the US over the past ten to fifteen years. Everything. At the end we had to do something symbolic of what women have endured throughout the centuries at the hands of men; graphic image of torture. People are living in terror of violent and abusive crime, eg, children disappear on a regular basis in the US and are used in pornography.

BZ: The film highlights what the media and society denies – particularly violent crimes against women.

DT: Yes, it's not recognised. It's open to interpretation.

BZ: The women in your film, because they had been abused were putting themselves into situations where they would be abused. Almost that the damage was being reinforced by being in those kind of occupations (ie the sex industry).

DT: I have this theory (because I still dance to pay for my films) that most of the girls I dance with do come from weird backgrounds. I think I have one of the most stable backgrounds at that job. I'm doing the job simply to pay my

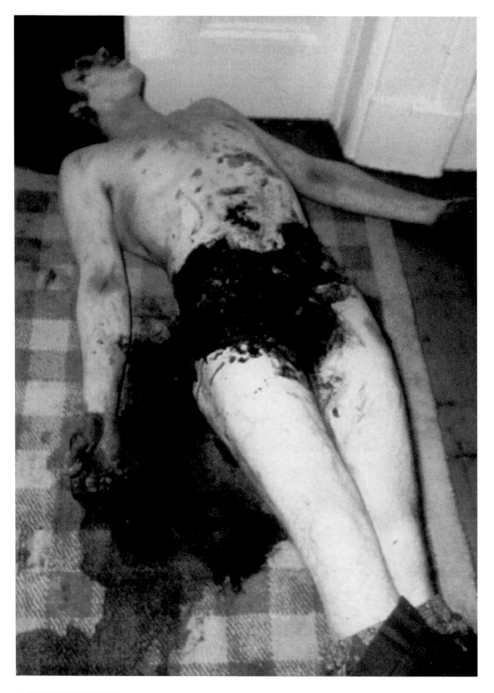

A GUN FOR JENNIFER

debts but I'm also getting a lot from it, character-wise. I'm learning about people. But what happens is that whenever there's been some kind of abuse in the background, people keep trying to relive it – try to sort it out, work it out. So they keep getting drawn into situations that logically are bad for them. But emotionally and mentally they have to work it out. So many times a woman will come from an abusive home and then hook up with a guy that hits her. It's one of the things I wanted to show in the film. There are patterns that have to be broken. You have to stop them and ultimately you have to make the decision to change your own behaviour. And that's how you change the world. The choice of the individual, you know.

BZ: Could you talk a bit about your collaboration with Todd Morris.

DT: It was 50/50. We work very well together. Everything that I'm weak in, he's strong in and the other way around. It's a perfect working relationship. He's not a typical American man. [Laughs]

BZ: How much did the film cost and how did it get financed?

DT: It cost $400,000. It's a low-budget movie but it's very slick and Todd is very, very picky and detail oriented. So it was all about focusing and hard work because we didn't have the money. So I had been dancing. And we had written the screenplay and we were going to shoot it on credit cards originally. And that was just not working out because we realised we needed more cash. So I promised Todd in the summer I was going to work so hard that I would bring in ten grand cash. But then I was working and it was hard and I was only making about two hundred a day. I was working five times a week and I thought, no way am I ever going to do this. So I started telling every customer that I was trying to make this film. And very quickly I found out who were the assholes and who wasn't – 'cos the ones that were assholes were "God, a film like that!!" But then ultimately it came down to three different guys who were very interested in doing it; they felt very strongly about it. They were not your typical guys who come in to a topless bar in Manhattan. Within eight weeks I wanted to start shooting so I told each of them that the other was going to give me a cheque for ten grand that following Monday. Until finally the one said "No, you tell those other two to go away. I'll give it to you on Friday". And that Friday he came in and gave me the money. I thought "Oh my God, this can't be real". I held on to the cheque for a week before trying to cash it. I was convinced he was going to call me and say "Oh I was just kidding," you know! "Rip it up." But he kept calling me and saying "Did you deposit it yet?"

BZ: Did he get a credit on the film?

DT: No, he's in jail now! There's a lot more to this story.... So then we started the account and the money kept rolling in. Ultimately it turned out to be $315,000 that he gave us. And the principal photography was over. Now it was New Year of 1994. And we were all excited because Christmas was over and we'd be going into post-production and get this thing done fast. And he called me and said "I have something bad to tell you. You'll be having a private detective coming to your house because all the money I gave you was embezzled. I'm not a loan officer for a Japanese corporation, I'm an accountant." Next day a private detective comes to our house and a couple of days later the Japanese corporation freezes all our bank accounts and tries to seize the film. For six months we were in a huge law suit. I had to go testify at the District Attorney's office in New York City. Show all our receipts. Prove everything was for the film. I mean, we got nothing for ourselves; I didn't even pay myself – every penny went into the film. And so finally they believed us. Everything was fine and we got a new contract with the Japanese corporation but they weren't going to give us another penny and we still had all this footage and no way to finish it. So we go back to the credit card idea. We had $100,000 worth of credit among twenty different credit cards. We'll finish the film on the credit cards and I'll go back to dancing and just dance really hard so we can make a minimum payment. Do the pick up shots that we need to do and we'll finish it that way. So we did it and it was really, really hard but it got finished. We finished it in 1996 on March 1st. We did the New York Underground Film Festival. Then we started getting into all these other festivals all over the world, including Cannes. We've done seventeen festivals so far. I've been dancing constantly because the credit card payments are so obscene and I come to Europe a lot – at least once a month. The film came out in France in January 1998 and it's doing very well. Our distributors have already made their money back and other countries are now interested. I'm trying to raise money for the new film, to shoot this summer. It's been really tough and I'm so angry that I still have to dance.

BZ: What kind of reaction has the film had?

DT: Audiences really love the film. Even if they don't love it they are intrigued and they want to debate and I love that. That's all I wanted. I wanted people talking.

BZ: That's what makes it political rather than just a piece of entertainment.

DT: Exactly. Every film that I want to do for the rest of my life as a producer, actress or writer has to be something that gets people talking. I really believe with cinema that you have the power to change the world. It's such an amazing medium. You can reach hundreds of thousands of people and it's so difficult to reach them any other way.

BZ: What about the press?

DT: We've had a favourable review in *Variety*. All the reviews have been good. *Le Monde* and about fifteen different publications in France alone have carried reviews and raved about the film. Reviews in papers throughout the US, in Montreal and all over Germany have been positive.

BZ: Could you talk a bit about your own background?

DT: I come from theatre. Theatre though is unfortunately a dying art form – it's so difficult, it's so expensive in New York. If you're going to charge ten dollars for an off-off-Broadway theatre ticket, people aren't going to see that. People are going to go to Sony or Loew's, pay eight dollars and see **Titanic**. Also film is a much more personal medium. You don't have to be big and grand; it's not about performing. It's about truth. And theatre is more musical theatre and it's not in my heart. I believe in subtle things between people. Contacting people with their eyes and their hearts and their minds, you know. I've always been very fascinated with film. I was three years old when I told my mother I was going to be on the TV someday. [Laughs] It's always been there. I moved to New York when I was seventeen to study at NYU. I was studying drama and started doing a lot of off-off-Broadway plays and community theatre, independent films, independent commercials – all non-union stuff. Then I started getting involved in producing plays that I was in. Around that time I met Todd and the idea for a film grew. I thought "Why don't I try to raise the money for a film where people have the possibility of maybe making their money back and then I can do what I want". The whole reason I wanted to start producing was that I didn't have to wait any more for somebody to cast me or to hire me – you know to be playing bimbos in stupid movies. You create your own medium, you know. If I want to do a film I'll make it. Ultimately, now that things are starting to happen, there's a film that I'm going to be acting in – nothing to do with the production of it – in April 1998 in Chicago. I want to be able to produce one film a year of my own and then act in as many films as I can. Especially in European films; I really want to do European films.

BZ: What films have touched or moved you or influenced you?

DT: Mildred Pierce, All About Eve and **Thelma And Louise. Gloria** with Gena Rowlands, she's one of the goddesses of cinema to me.

BZ: How did you cast the film?

DT: We put an ad in *Backstage*, a trade paper in New York and we received about 2,000 head shots. We got to 200 people. We auditioned 100 men on Saturday and 100 women on Sunday. I thrive on a heavy workload. We quickly broke it down into who would be right in the roles.

BZ: How did you decide on the locations, which are very powerful in the film?

DT: Me and Todd drove around for days sometimes. I would get home from work and we'd get in the car at two o'clock in the morning and we'd drive around Manhattan for like three or four hours, looking at places, taking down notes, taking polaroids. We were very particular about what we wanted to show, how we wanted Manhattan to look. The extremism of the film is about the extremism of America and the emotional violence of New York which is partly expressed in the settings.

BZ: You really worked hard to get this film made.

DT: Yes, it is about commitment and there can be no doubt. When I raised the money for this film, no one believed that I'd get the money. But I knew, somehow, I just knew that it would happen.

BZ: You are a woman with a mission.

DT: Yes, and every film that I produce or write or that I'm in has to be about strong women. That's my message. Women have to write and really get things happening. Cinema has to become much more strong between women and, no matter what, we have get our messages out.

NOTES

1. Note also Mikels' penchant for female gangs in sci-fi horror, including **Astro Zombies** with Tura Satana (1967) and **Blood Orgy Of The She-Devils** (1973).

2. Hill also directed a quartet of wild, ultra-trashy horror movies in Mexico, shot back-to-back in 1968 and all starring Boris Karloff: **La Muerte Viviente (Cult Of The Dead** *aka* **The Snake People); Macabre Serenade (Dance Of Death** *aka* **House Of Evil); La Camera Del Terror (The Torture Zone** *aka* **Chamber Of Fear);** and **Invasion Siniestra (Alien Terror** *aka* **Sinister Invasion).**

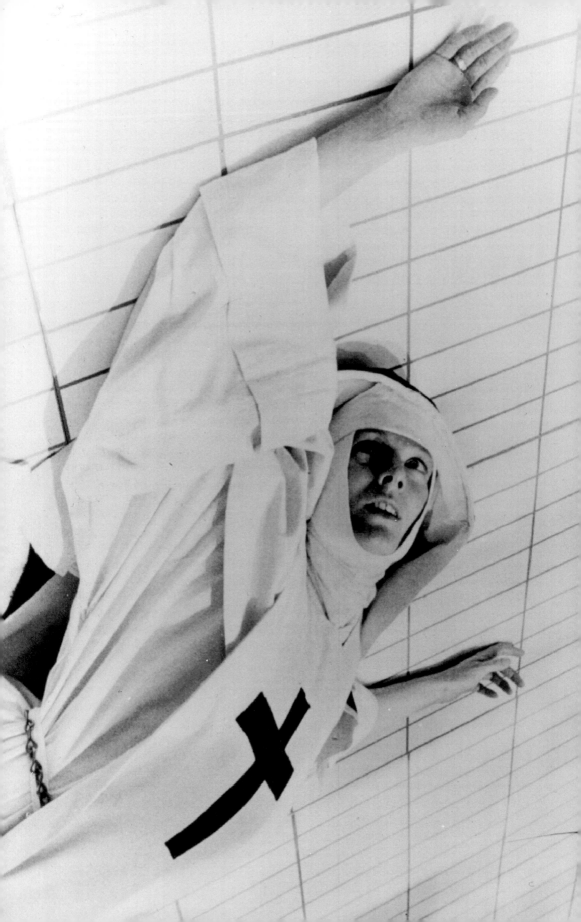

CHAPTER SEVEN

THE SISTERHOOD

INTRODUCTION

The image of the nun has been historically a powerful one, in literature and cinema alike, and many of the most celebrated movies featuring female religious orders are based on literary works. In fact, representations of the cloistered sisterhood have been a part of popular Western culture for centuries; Chaucer's "The Nun's Tale" being an early example from classic English literature. In cinema, from the silent period to the present day, stories about nuns have excited a combination of critical and prurient interest.

British cinema was among a number of national cinemas to tap into the inherently erotic appeal of the image of the celibate, nubile nun. Hammer's **To The Devil – A Daughter** (Peter Sykes, 1976), based on a novel about Satanism by Dennis Wheatley, is an obvious example. The film features a sultry sixteen-year-old Nastassia Kinski as a young novice in a delinquent religious cult, whose innocence is corrupted by devil-worshippers. Nastassia rips off her habit more than once, to full frontal effect, and is shown *in flagrante* with Christopher Lee, Satan's high priest!

More serious depictions of nuns behaving badly include Ken Russell's **The Devils** (1971, based on Aldous Huxley's *The Devils Of Loudon* and a play by John Whiting). The story of Urbain Grandier, priest of Loudon, was first committed to film by Jerzy Kawalerowicz in **Mother Jeanne Of The Angels** (1961). But the subject matter of such movies, and their often graphic (sac)religious iconography of flagellation, scarring and other sado-masochistic activities, inevitably invites some sort of cross-over from the serious to the scurrilous. There's always a *frisson* of the forbidden in nuns' stories, so that while every film discussed in this chapter is not an exploitation movie, there's always a strong erotic (i.e. renegade) sub-text in such narratives.

GET THEE TO A NUNNERY

Like cinematic desire in general, the structuring gaze of sisterhood movies is underpinned by the fearful nature of female sexuality and the need to avert the castration threat. The nun as an archetypal symbol of innocence – and thus also of corruptibility – evokes the concept of first temptation/sin and the loss of Eden in Judaeo-Christian cultures. The seemingly innocent (biblical) temptresses like Eve, Jezebel, Delilah and Salome, are antecedents of the nun who falls from grace – the corrupt, treacherous and castrating female,

TO THE DEVIL – A DAUGHTER

MOTHER JEANNE OF THE ANGELS

seducing men from behind the veil. Father Grandier, the liberal priest in **The Devils**, comments on the suppressed sexuality dormant in the sisterhood: "They give themselves to God, but something cries out that must be given to man." Grandier then traces the chain of this desire from punishment, to pain, to physical arousal, love, repression, and ultimately hatred.

In Western culture, the way the image of the nun is perceived is as contradiction. She is in fact the personification of duplicity; for the patriarchal gaze she is both the virgin and the whore, representing at one and the same time meditation and madness, restraint and excess, purity and profanity. The continuing connotive possibilities of this image can be measured by the range of references for which the nun, as signifier, is used on moral, political and personal levels. The scope of films about nuns is wide, their appeal elementary. Classics of European cinema such as **Les Anges Du Péché** (Robert Bresson, 1942/3: France), **Black Narcissus** (Powell and Pressburger, 1947: Britain), and **Viridiana** (Luis Bunuel, 1961: Spain) exemplify the serious theological, philosophical and political concerns associated with nun narratives. But even the most outwardly serious of these narratives can carry a high sexual charge. **Black Narcissus** is a case in point.

"BLACK NARCISSUS"

This British film classic is based on a novel by Rumer Godden and is concerned with a female religious order situated in India. A select group of nuns, headed by Sister Clodagh (Deborah Kerr), is instructed to set up an annexe high in the Himalayas. The film's setting is a visual *tour-de-force* constructed out of stage lighting and painted backdrops. The nuns in **Black Narcissus** are not a closed order, and their mission is to serve the people through medicine and education.

The group sent to the mountains is composed of Sister Briony, a strong and reliable medical nun; Sister Philippa, a vegetable gardener; Sister Blanche, loved by all and known as Sister Honey; and Sister Ruth, a troubled and increasingly demented nun, who is set on a collision course with her superior, Sister Clodagh. Reverend Mother's deadpan comment about Sister Ruth before the group's departure – "Sister Ruth is ill, she's a problem!" – turns out to be something of an understatement in the end. Ruth is a jealous hysteric, who undermines Sister Clodagh and the project at every turn.

To add to Clodagh's problems, the local British agent is a cynical and initially unwelcoming man. He seems bent on discouraging the nuns from staying and comments drily that the site of the building and its original function – built to house a prince's harem – make it "no place for a nunnery". Indeed the intense atmosphere of the place, exacerbated by the rarefied altitude and the constant wind, begins to take its toll on the vulnerable sisters. They begin to have strange reactions and start behaving oddly out of character. Sister Philippa plants forget-me-nots when she should be cultivating cabbages; Sister Honey behaves irresponsibly and her actions leads to the nuns being blamed; Sister Clodagh starts getting flashbacks of her past – the doomed love affair in Ireland which led to her taking the veil – and Sister Ruth just gets madder.

It is as though the constraints that their vows have imposed have become loosened, so that each woman reverts to some extent to the person she was before she became a nun. Their personal discipline and sense of collective order simultaneously start to disintegrate, and we see the sisters, white habits flapping in the wind, vainly trying to restore an equilibrium while increasingly losing control. Sister Ruth becomes insanely jealous of the growing friendship between Clodagh and the agent, Dean, and in a powerful climax they face each other off across a table in the candlelight.

This scene, the most sexually charged of the film, is memorable for its composition. The confrontation between the two women, symbolising the struggle between good and evil, is visualised in terms of a mirror image in which Clodagh, in her starched white habit, piously reads the bible while Ruth, in civvies and with hair flying, wantonly puts on lipstick. She is a scarlet woman; and as Clodagh snoozes Ruth absconds to the village, where she tries to seduce Dean. Enraged by his rejection of her advances, she returns to the convent next morning in murderous mood and tries to push Sister Clodagh off the mountain as she sounds the bell for the Angelus. Clodagh keeps the faith, but Ruth is a fallen woman, bitter and twisted, and she plunges to her death as the bell tolls.

The simmering passions and frustrations which test each of the women are powerfully conveyed in **Black Narcissus**. The notion of a seductive and exotic otherness, which the film's setting and title suggest, throws into relief the cold and limited vision of missionary zeal which the religious sisterhood represents.

The struggle between repression and desire which **Black Narcissus** explores was reworked in a short experimental film by the American filmmaker Su Friedrich, **Damned If You Don't** (1987), in which a young lesbian spectator inspired by images from the Powell and Pressburger original, fantasises about her erotic pursuit of a solitary nun.

"LA RELIGIEUSE"

Jacques Rivette's **La Religieuse** (1966: France) uses a nun's story to focus on the plight of women in a patriarchal society. Based on the celebrated novel *The Enlightenment*, by Denis Diderot, the film illustrates the collusion of Church and State in 18th century France to perpetuate injustice against the vulnerable, particularly women. Outrageous in its time, **La Religieuse** was subjected to strict State censorship, being banned by the Gaullist government.

The film's protagonist, Suzanne, is confined to a convent against her will. Because she was conceived adulterously her formal father, a rigid bourgeois lawyer, refuses to maintain her financially – having spent a fortune marrying off his other two daughters. Thus, at sixteen and a half, she is persuaded to enter a nunnery by her mother, whom Suzanne loves. Having agreed to take the vows as a way of atoning for her mother's adultery, Suzanne rescinds at the eleventh hour, knowing she is not suited to a cloistered life. Again she is coerced by her father and pressured by her mother, and finally takes her vows in a feverish reverie.

The film catalogues Suzanne's suffering behind the convent walls. She

LA RELIGIEUSE

is a sensitive soul who loves God, but also loves her freedom. When the benign old Reverend Mother dies, a new and much more draconian regime commences. The new Superior, Sister Sainte-Christine, is a punishing sadist, who institutes regular whippings and cell searches. In fact, she runs the place much like a high-security prison. Suzanne's formal request to renounce her vows makes her particularly unpopular with this monster, who seeks to break her – but doesn't quite succeed.

The other sisters collude with the sadism because they are scared of the personal consequences of dissent. Eventually, Suzanne is examined by a priest to ascertain whether or not she is possessed, as the demented Mother

Superior now claims. Suzanne is exonerated, and the mad Mother is warned against her unreasonable and sadistic behaviour. She cannot be punished, because her family are particularly influential, so Suzanne is transferred to another convent – her request to leave the sisterhood having been denied.

The new convent is the complete antithesis of the one Suzanne has left. It is a lesbian arcadia, hedonistic, sensual and virtually pagan. The Mother Superior is a deranged lesbian, always dressed for a party, and with a strong penchant for her young charges. Suzanne, who is pure in body and soul, is tormented in this new environment. She rejects the Reverend Mother's persistent advances and is distraught at the prospect of being seduced against her will. Her father-confessor, a priest as regretful of his vows as she is of hers, arranges for the two of them to escape under cover of night. Yet, no sooner is Suzanne free of the convent walls, than the priest tries to force himself on her sexually. Still an innocent, she goes on the run alone. But she is unable to find the freedom she desires; she is now a wanted woman finds it difficult to get work without revealing her identity. Finally reduced to prostitution, she hurls herself off a balcony to her death.

Having spent her entire adult life behind closed doors, Suzanne is fatally institutionalised and unable to function in either the nightmarish convent confines or in the society which first spurned her. **La Religieuse** is a desperate indictment of a social system that condemns its unwanted daughters to a life of misery.

SISTERS ARE DOING IT

The expression and repression of desire present in **Black Narcissus,** would later provide the thrust of a graphic sub-genre of exploitation cinema known as "nunsploitation", in which the more deviant and excessive strands of renegade sisterhood are explored[1]. Heavy manners and bad habits: sado-masochism, lesbianism, even Satanism are constant features of European nunsploitation films. Like the WIP genre to which it is closely related, nunsploitation boasts stock characters in endlessly reworked scenarios. Nun narratives usually feature an innocent, a novice, who has arrived at the convent under duress, having been forced to take the veil by her family (or, in particular, her father). As such, the convent represents a prison, and its strict regime a form of prolonged torture. All the publicity for Eritando Visconti's **The Nun Of Monza** (1968: Italy) accordingly centred on the torments and mortifications (clothing in barbed wire, lashing by cat o'nine tails, thumb screws etc) suffered by the young novice of the title.

In **Flavia, The Heretic** (Gianfranco Mingozzi, 1974: Italy), the young girl of the title is so brutalised by life both within and outside the nunnery, that the narrative ends up as a 15th century rape/revenge drama, with Flavia on a murder spree. The film's graphic scenes of sex and violence include a woman raped in a pig sty, naked nun orgies, and sadistic tortures culminating with Flavia herself being skinned alive.

The sexually frustrated and thus demented Mother Superior is another nunsploitation stereotype. This stock character is first cousin to the predatory matron of the WIP film, stalking the corridors for her prey. It's no surprise

FLAVIA, THE HERETIC

that convents in nunsploitation are something of a sinister cross between a female detention centre and a girls' boarding school.

Walerian Borowczyk's **Behind Convent Walls** (1977: Italy) again portrays the convent as similar to a prison, ruled by an old Mother Superior whom the nuns secretly refer to as the "Anti-Christ". Typically, Borowczyk

BEHIND CONVENT WALLS

concentrates mainly on the sisters' sexual activities, with voyeuristic episodes of lesbian sex, nuns masturbating with wooden dildoes, and general lascivious titillation.[2]

In **Story Of A Cloistered Nun** (Domenico Paolella, 1973: Italy), Suzy Kendall stars as a sex-mad Superior, while Guilio Berruti's **Killer Nun** (1978: Italy) stars Anita Ekberg as Sister Gertrude, morphine-addicted Reverend Mother at a sanatorium/asylum. Sister Gertrude's transgressions include drug abuse, anonymous sex with men, and a lesbian affair with a younger nun; she raves about inquisitional tortures and is prone to homicidal hallucinations which may or may not happen in reality. Once again, the image of the nun is dragged through the mud in this bizarre, claustrophobic movie.

Exploitation directors, as we have already seen, easily move from one sub-genre to another; for example Jack Hill or Jess Franco, who between them have worked in sexploitation, horror, WIP, SS torture, JD and blaxploitation. Bruno Mattei, director of **The Other Hell** (1981: Italy), had also produced several gems of WIP and SS torture, so nunsploitation was a natural progression for him. **The Other Hell** is a truly extreme attack on religion, in which a secluded convent is stricken by a series of sudden deaths. An investigation by male priests reveals the whole convent to be possessed by Satan. The strange images here include genital mutilation of both sexes, bleeding from the mouth and body, an attic full of hanging mannequins, rooms piled with bones and skulls, and the devil's red eyes burning from the darkness. An insane film.

Another Italian director adept in all genres of exploitation, Lucio Fulci, produced his own addition to the nunsploitation canon in 1990. **Demonia** (1990: Italy) begins in style, with the crucifixion of five nuns by an angry mob.

THE OTHER HELL

The action progresses to a sequestered Sicilian convent, where the five dead nuns (who were devil-worshippers) take their revenge via a series of bloody murders. Punctuated by flashbacks to mediaeval atrocities, **Demonia** is the nun (non)narrative you would expect from Fulci.

Dark Waters (Mario Baino, 1993) brings the Italian fascination with nuns up to date. The film's heroine is sent to investigate a convent which her late father has been supporting financially. Needless to say, she soon discovers that the nuns here – headed by an ancient, blind Mother Superior – worship a sinister cult of their own. With Lovecraftian plot elements and sumptuous photography, **Dark Waters** is one of the more intelligent and well-crafted entries into the "evil nun" sub-genre.

The audience for exploitation movies remains, essentially, the same; only the stock roles, settings and scenarios vary in different sub-genres. There are, however, subtle differences in terms of the erotic impulses which each narrative seeks to exploit. With WIP movies, for example, the accent is on rampaging females; whereas by contrast, the captive female in nunsploitation is more passive, more likely to suffer in silence than her WIP sister. In this sense, nunsploitation constructs a more sadistic and controlling gaze for its audience, as thus offers more overtly depraved pleasure.

The forbidden fruit of religious thinking constructs taboos which are obviously pleasurable to break. Additionally, the graphic sado-masochistic imagery at the heart of Christianity – the stations of the cross, and the lives of the saints, for example – provides rich pickings for exploitation studios.

DARK WATERS

Blasphemy is a particular feature of nunsploitation (and, to some extent, of all cinematic representations of the nun). The fundamental instability of the virgin/whore duality and the ambiguity of what lies behind the veil, imbues the habit with a notion of guise/disguise. Sin, masquerading as goodness – a typically patriarchal anxiety – finds in the image of the nun a powerful suggestion that things are not what they seem; see, for example, **Vertigo** (Alfred Hitchcock, 1957), **Ms.45** (Abel Ferrara, 1984), or **Dark Habits** (Pedro Almodovar, 1995). The destructive power of female sexuality is at the heart of the fear that the image of the nun evokes in these films[3]. This destructive potential is most powerfully unleashed in **The Devils**.

"THE DEVILS"

Maligned by some, but generally regarded as Ken Russell's best film, **The Devils** provides the perfect outlet for the director's trademark of excessive over-the-top imagery, which is here perfectly appropriate and expressive of a world in chaos. The film takes as its central subject the diabolical possession of a closed order of nuns. The setting is France in the 16th century, a country riven by religious bigotry and decimated by plague. Louis XIV is a feckless monarch, his chief minister Richelieu an ambitious politician and cardinal. The visual representation of something rotten at the core of the State is superbly realised by Russell and his art director, Derek Jarman. The film's set-pieces seem framed in black like an *in memoriam* card, and the clothing, habits, priests' vestments, royal standards and ribbons are also black, signifying pessimism and death. The nunnery, like the town itself, is depicted as a prison – all brick walls and barred windows. The convent walls have a white-tile

THE DEVILS

sheen, reminiscent of a public toilet, and much in keeping with the scatological images of waste and corruption which prevail.

Like the settings, the objects and instruments of religion (exorcism and torture) are suggestive of brutality, cruelty and ignorance (for example, the leeches and insects used by the quack doctor to "cure" a plague victim. In fact hot oil, leeches and suction cups conspire to kill rather than cure the patient). Corpses rotting on wheels, huge enemas, thumb-screws, whips and deathsheads suggest a chamber of horrors or a descent into hell. The city is a charnel house, the State is a sewer.

Within the monastery resides the Holy Order of St Ursula, headed by its crippled (inside and out) Mother Superior, Sister Jeanne of the Angels (Vanessa Redgrave) – a hunchback. The motifs of torture and suffering continue within the convent walls, with the stations of the cross and self-flagellation part of the daily regime[4]. Repressed sexuality is represented by Sister Jeanne in a series of masturbatory, blasphemous fantasies involving Father Urbain Grandier (Oliver Reed), priest of the parish and notorious womaniser, as Jesus Christ. In a highly aroused state, the deformed nun imagines Grandier/Christ getting down from the cross and making sexual advances toward her. The implications of these visions are soon made clear, when the nuns are used by Richelieu's agents to accuse the priest (who in fact has never seen them, and who they have only glimpsed through the barred convent windows) of witchcraft and collusion with the Devil.

The context here is important for a number of reasons. Loudon, during the time of the alleged possession, is one of the four remaining walled towns in France. It is a relatively self-governing citadel, which is opposed to

THE DEVILS

the persecution of the Huguenots and is led by the liberal priest, Grandier. Richelieu, an arch political manoeuvrer, has designs on Loudon and must, therefore, dispose of Father Grandier. The rumours and gossip about the nuns' diabolical possession, and Grandier's recent secret marriage, provide Richelieu with the means to destroy Loudon. His agents, the witchfinder and the inquisitor[5], conspire to whip the nuns up into a frenzy, so that they will publicly denounce the priest.

The social realities, especially as they relate to the position of women in 16th century France, are also important in **The Devils**. The women who take the vows are frequently those deemed too ugly to marry, or those who have been rejected by their families as illegitimate, barren, or too much of a financial burden. The nunnery, in the 16th century, is only one rung up from the madhouse. Many of the women are there against their will, or have been excluded from a society that has no use for them. These sisters are in most instances bitter and frustrated, victims of coercion rather than vocation, locked away from life and love (and sex). It is not hard to imagine what effect the *frisson* of sexual scandal, within their midst, would have.

Once the sisters abandon themselves to falsehood/fantasy and impure thoughts, the lid blows off and they plunge into an escalating orgy of mental and physical frenzy. The sexual debauchery, including lesbianism and masturbation, provides entertainment for the King and his nobles, who enjoy the spectacle of naked shaven-headed nuns cavorting wantonly around the convent. The idea of diabolic possession has quickly grown into mass hysteria, and Russell's visions here reach an apotheosis of excess.

THE DEVILS

Russell's film depicts the nuns as horrifying, but also vulnerable – victims of political manipulation. Father Grandier is more ready to condemn Richelìeu's servants, from both Church and State, than the sisterhood that has condemned him. As he says to the witchfinder: "You have seduced the people in order to destroy them."

Sated with their excesses, the nuns eventually calm down and begin to relent, but they are threatened by Richelieu's men not to retract their accusations. Sister Jeanne, the main accusor and ring-leader, finally acknowledges: "I have wronged an innocent man." But when faced with Grandier's measured reproach, she falls back into a frenzy of hatred, repeatedly accusing the priest of being a devil. Unhinged by frustrated desire and self-loathing, Sister Jeanne has been the instrument for converting the nunnery into a travesty: the wimpled, walled-in women are exposed as dangerous, raving mad, as tortured as the characters in a Bosch painting. She finally hangs herself, as Grandier is burnt at the stake.

While the image of the sisterhood in **The Devils** is not a positive one, neither is it totally negative. The film illustrates the consequences of denying basic human needs like freedom, love and sexual desire, and shows how easily repression can be turned into abuse and self-loathing. When the cloistered sisters are manipulated for political ends, they flaunt themselves in much the same way performing animals do for a ringmaster. It is an image of abject exploitation and, in the final analysis, the women are more to be pitied than blamed – more sinned against than sinning.

CONCLUSION

The enduring fascination of the nun in popular culture is today as strong as it ever was. The holy sisterhood is rarely depicted in cinema as a threatening girl gang, but nuns are often depicted as objects of pity and terror. As the bearers of a simmering, sometimes delinquent sexuality, these sisters are constantly on the precipice of revolt. And while ostensibly the image of the nun serves as a measure of morality, her plight historically is also a measure of the misogyny underpinning patriarchal society.

NOTES

1. Nonetheless, exposing the corrupt power of the Church, the political machinations of religious leaders, and the hypocrisy hiding behind holy orders, is in many ways as much an objective of pure nunsploitation movies as it is of a more serious film like **The Devils**. Ken Russell's arthouse production, which also features a famously mad Reverend Mother, often comes close to its exploitation correlative in its vision of convent hysteria.

2. An independent British short, James Havoc's **Crimes Against Pussycat** (1989, about the heretic Gilles de Rais), samples images of naked girls from Borowczyk's **Immoral Tales** and re-shoots them through a triptych of inverted crosses to invoke a *demi-monde* of sexually depraved nuns.

3. William Friedkin's **The Exorcist** (1973) deserves a mention in this context; in terms of blasphemy, its image of an eleven-year-old girl masturbating with a bloody crucifix is near-impossible to beat, while the girl's demonic possession may be read as a grotesque allegory on the effects of puberty, the advent of female sexuality which brings with it physical distortion and torrential, unchannelled power (see also Brian de Palma's **Carrie** [1975]). (Incidentally, the girl's voice – often multi-tracked – at times sounds like the cacophony of a gang of girl demons; the main vocal was provided by Mercedes McCambridge, a B-movie character actress previously noted for playing a leather-clad, female gang leader in Orson Welles' **Touch Of Evil** [1958].)

4. The self-flagellation of nuns tempted by Satan can be seen as far back as Benjamin Christensen's **Witchcraft Through The Ages** (1921), a film awash with grotesque religious/ anti-religious imagery.

5. The introduction of these two characters, and their sadistic methods – which include the insertion of grotesque instruments into nuns' vaginas – links **The Devils** to another strain of religious persecution cinema, namely the "witchfinder" sub-genre as exemplified by Michael Reeves' **Witchfinder General** (1968) and Michael Armstrong's **Mark Of The Devil** (1969). Adrian Hoven's **Mark Of The Devil 2** (1973) features scenes of a convent's Mother Superior viciously whipping a young novice across her exposed breasts.

CHAPTER EIGHT

TWO INTERVIEWS

INTRODUCTION

COMING from two very different traditions of cinema, the films of Vivienne Dick and Julie Jenkins illustrate the range and richness that is available to anyone interested in representations of groups of women or girl gangs. With their very individual styles and approaches to filmmaking, they offer images that are original and witty. Their respective influences could not be more different. Vivienne cites the N. American Underground of the '60s as an important influence, whereas Julie talks about the impact – from childhood – of British film comedy.

ONE: VIVIENNE DICK REASSESSES HER EARLY FILMS

I talked with Irish-born filmmaker Vivienne Dick in her 18th floor council flat in North West London where she lives with her son and her cat. The focus of the discussion was the films from the late '70s made in New York which gained critical recognition in the context of the 'New Wave' or 'punk' film, a movement with which Vivienne Dick is crucially identified.

Made on Super-8 using friends and neighbours as subjects, the experimental narratives of this period revived the flagging underground filmmaking culture and were shown in the bars and rock clubs of downtown Manhattan. An unsteady camera, abrupt transitions, jump cuts and changes of mood were the hallmark of Vivienne's inimitable style. In terms of content her films are preoccupied with female sexuality, relationships and 'transgressive behaviour'. Women in ones, twos or in groups are the subject matter of a number of films including **Guérillère Talks** (1978), **She Had Her Gun All Ready** (1978), **Beauty Becomes The Beast** (1979) and **Liberty's Booty** (1980).

Bev Zalcock: Could you talk about your influences?
Vivienne Dick: New York was a big influence. Seeing women there who were creative and experimenting. There was a lot of encouragement to experiment. The first films I saw at Anthology Archives were basically American Underground cinema. I saw Maya Deren, Ron Rice, Ken Jacobs, Jack Smith and Warhol there. This was my first time to see work that wasn't Hollywood film

and seemed to be made by one or a few people, home movies really. I'm interested by films that are made by women because it's unusual, still. I remember some time in the '70s seeing Margarethe von Trotta's work **The Two Sisters**, and later Pat Murphy's films.[1]

BZ: What is your view on representations of women taking up arms?

VD: I'm interested in how women can have power in the world as they have so little power. I'm interested in incorporating political ideas into a narrative in an oblique way or with humour. I'm not cut out to do straight narrative though. I bring these issues to do with women and power in terms of psychoanalysis and in terms of their place in the world. Or issues to do with a mother for example, which is something I've been thinking about a great deal this past year and work out how to represent that somehow in a film.

BZ: How do you work 'issues' into your films?

VD: Liberty's Booty and **Beauty Becomes The Beast** particularly come out of this incredible anger that I was feeling. A sort of rage. I see it as more complex now. I saw women being oppressed in the world and a difference between how men and women are brought up. Seeing the church as an oppressive institution, in having been brought up with a heavy dose of Catholicism – reacting against that, you know. There are little scenes that come up in **Liberty's Booty** like the one in McDonald's, connecting capitalism and low wages. It's not *about* capitalism but the issues are there. Like the graffiti on the wall by Samo (Jean Michel Basquiat): "TELEVISION=CHURCH=STATE= MCDONALD'S=OPPRESSION" (or was it "McDonald's=Church=State=Television= Oppression"?). The voiceover is somebody recounting the story of McDonald's in Dublin where there was a strike against low wages which lasted over a year.

BZ: There's a sense of random connections in **Liberty's Booty**. Could you comment on this?

VD: Instead of focusing on a narrative structure in the conventional way, the film links things in a more open-ended way. I'm showing another kind of link that's there anyway. It's a looser kind of link. Things that crop up all the time whether they're on the radio or something on the wall, that you see in the street or whatever, which connect in unexpected ways. I'm aware of all that when I place them in the film – they're not altogether by chance. But at the same time they're captured in a chance way. You're walking round the street and you see something and you say – I want to film that and I know it will fit into the film somewhere.

BZ: Could you talk a bit about your approach to editing?

VD: I learnt to edit as I went along. I had plenty of time to mess about because I was working at home and still usually do. There's a kind of abruptness in the Super-8 work which is there partly because it's inherent in Super-8 single system and live sound. There is a hole in the soundtrack when the camera stops and starts. I like abrupt switches – like channel hopping.

BZ: What about the music?

VD: Sometimes the music comes later. It's something I find that seems to be appropriate and sometimes it's music that's happening at the time I'm filming; it's literally on the radio or someone's playing it or I say "put that record on again, I want that in the shot, playing while I'm shooting". That's how I shot

LIBERTY'S BOOTY

then, very crudely. Now I want to work with people who play with sound – composers.

BZ: Can you talk about the influence of popular culture on your work, as there seems to be a lot of references to it?

VD: It wasn't a conscious thing. We're influenced so much by everything around us and everything we hear. It infiltrates our brains, our consciousness. You know, old programmes coming up on TV. People dressing (we're talking about the late '70s) in the clothes of the '60s. You know, this sense of other times which, of course, we are so aware of now. At that time it was fairly unusual to have someone dressing up in their apartment in completely '60s paraphernalia. Someone who was only a tiny girl in the '60s, playing that music and just fantasising. It is a result of growing up on TV culture and looking at old movies on TV and being influenced by different looks of women, different images of women that allows us to see these representations as constructs. As images of femininity, as possibilities only. In those dance scenes in **Beauty Becomes The Beast** I'm playing with an image of '60s femininity, obviously with irony. The 'male' dancing partner is a woman in drag. At the beginning of **Liberty's Booty** there is a scene with the woman with a large doll or mannequin. It is a woman ostensibly but it was really a man who had a sex change. And it's a male-female doll.[2] I wasn't thinking about gender in a theoretical way. I just found it fascinating so I had to film it.

BEAUTY BECOMES THE BEAST

BZ: Another aspect of your films, particularly with **Liberty's Booty,** is the extraordinary décor, a sense of accumulation of objects. Did you set it up?

VD: The clutter in the rooms was there. It's like seeing a place and saying "I want to film this". It's full of things which spill out of the frame – it's going on, it's continuing. It's to do with the way some of the people I was hanging out with in New York were living – a lot of kitsch and trash. Stuff they collected in their apartments. A bohemian type of lifestyle, full of people who didn't quite fit into society or have jobs or anything. A lot of fantasy in the world, in their world. Eccentric. Probably a lot to do with being in your twenties or early thirties! Like in **Liberty's Booty** when Trixi opens the fridge in her apartment and she has a broken doll with bloodstains inside the freezer. She didn't put that there for the film. That was there! What the hell does that mean? You know! [Laughs]

BZ: How do you get your characters to perform? Are they acting or are they for real?

VD: Usually it's something I've seen them do many times and think I'd like to film, like the dance scene in **Beauty Becomes The Beast.** There is a collaboration there because people would often produce their own costumes and props. There was a great playfulness there. I did not have to explain myself. A fantastic atmosphere, full of possibilities; because I think I grew up in a very critical and judgmental culture. **Guérillère Talks** was the first film I made. It consists of six cartridges of Super-8 strung together, each running for

BEAUTY BECOMES THE BEAST

three and a half minutes. The women in each could say and do as they wished. It must have been influenced by Warhol's work I'd seen. I certainly didn't direct them. I remember feeling so thrilled just filming looking at them.
BZ: And what about your work with Lydia Lunch? She's in a number of your films.
VD: In **Beauty Becomes The Beast**, Lydia Lunch plays a young girl who has been abused or who could have been abused. She said it freaked her out because it wasn't something she could talk about at the time. She told me that she had been abused years later when she asked to see the film again. I had picked it up somehow – but it was never discussed, never talked about. So on the one hand the 'characters' are one-dimensional – we don't 'know' them in the usual narrative sense, but on the other hand there is a documentary element there. So we are seeing 'real' people, with 'real' apartments, gestures, clothes and views. That boundary is deliberately made unclear. In **Liberty's Booty** it is difficult to tell who is a prostitute or who isn't. Maybe it is a kind of evasion?
BZ: How far do you think your films are about relationships between women?
VD: In **She Had Her Gun All Ready** I've always sort of thought that could as easily have been a man and a woman, as two women, in terms of their relationship. Pat [Place] – the blonde-haired one – the more passive one, people who saw that film thought she was a boy. The film is about a relationship. It's about someone feeling overwhelmed by the other person.

SHE HAD HER GUN ALL READY

That mirror in there seems to be such a big feature of the film. Pat's looking at herself and suddenly the image turns into the image of Lydia [Lunch]. There is this identification which turns into a huge hostility, you know, a need to kill – get rid of the other person. This may be is more of a feature between mothers and daughters, or amongst women, as it's easier for men to break away on account of being another gender; they can move away from that very close bond with the mother. Perhaps. In the film, Lydia tells a story and Pat is sitting there pulling at her hair, full of anxiety. The voiceover is about Ed Gein, the serial killer, who loved his mother to death. He identified with her to the extent that he put on her body suit – disembowelled her and had her skin hanging up in the cupboard. The most extreme end of loving someone to death. Psychoanalysis is a valid way of looking at the film it seems. At the time I seemed to be very preoccupied with relationships being something overpowering; being something where one party can be really overwhelmed by the other. It's still an area we haven't worked through, especially in heterosexual relationships. There is often not enough reciprocity. It seems to me now that this notion of reciprocity is related to respect for the other or another point of view, where we get away from the polarised 'right' and 'wrong' or 'good' and 'bad' which is entirely caught up with Cartesian patriarchal culture. Take relationships within the family set up. It's breaking down now. Women are beginning to demand a more equal place when it comes to children and the value of what they do. Women have really been

SHE HAD HER GUN ALL READY

taken advantage of where children are concerned. Now that families are breaking up, people are forced to realise the value of what it costs to raise a child, for example, when it comes to maintenance. We still live in a society where raising children and doing housework is not considered part of the GNP. It's not considered to have value which is an extraordinary thing. That is the new Pandora's Box! Open that one and the whole of society as we know it will collapse.

BZ: What was your attitude to feminism in the late '70s?

VD: I was interested up to a point because I was quite intimidated by the academic thing. But at the same time I had my ears open; I was listening. I'd feel intimidated by material I didn't understand because there was this kind of slightly academic snobbery about this new stuff that was coming from France. I hadn't read that much. It was very dense and undigested.

BZ: At the time did The Women's Movement take up your films?

VD: Betty Gordon had this screening over in her loft and invited Yvonne Rainer and other women. And I was invited as well and I felt very shy. Nobody spoke to me. They saw **She Had Her Gun All Ready** but they didn't talk to me about it so I felt estranged. Betty was the person I knew the most in that group and her friend Karen Kay wrote about the film in one of the magazines connected to 'The Collective' which was a downtown alternative cinema at the time. Amy Taubin also wrote about the work. I think the film really upset Yvonne Rainer. And the same thing happened when I went to Edinburgh and showed the films there – I don't think Ulrike Ottinger liked the work, though her editor did. It was difficult for me to talk about the work. I felt incredibly vulnerable – unsure – although I wasn't that unsure as I made the damn thing! Right. And I was always there when they were being shown. But I felt like I was really exposing myself in some way. But it was very gratifying in another way. There was always a very strong response. It was not your usual film audience at all, as the early screenings took place in music venues. It was interesting that people didn't find the films too confusing. It all happened outside of the academic thing, outside of all the feminist thing.

BZ: Did you feel you were making films for women in particular?

VD: All my life I've been looking at films which foreground men. I wanted to make films where men are peripheral. In the background – the way women usually are. I also feel that I could relate to women easier. I spent five years in a boarding school. [Laughs]. I used to show the films then and there would be discussions afterwards. You know. People were interested in these strange 'punk' films that were coming out of New York. Women certainly responded to them.

BZ: Does it bother you that recently your films are being shown in a more rarefied atmosphere, in art galleries for example?

VD: In the past year the work has been shown in The Museum of Modern Art [New York City], and the Tate Gallery [London]. I think it is good that galleries and museums are taking an interest in lo-tech work. They might start buying tapes! But it is usually more satisfying to screen in smaller places. The Whitney showed a programme of mainly Super-8 work from the late '70s/early '80s in conjunction with Nan Goldin's photography retrospective. She took some stills for the early films and one was shot in her loft.

BZ: I know that in your New York films you worked autonomously, at least where the technical side of the filmmaking is concerned. How do you find working with a crew?

VD: It was hard for me working with a crew in **London Suite** [1989] which was shot on 16mm. I found it very hard letting go of the camera – having someone else shoot it. It is hard to explain intuitive movement verbally; to explain what it is I want to frame or how I want to frame it is quite a challenge. If you can do that then I would adore to make a film with somebody else shooting part of it. And I would shoot part of it. I can use the little camera, someone else can use the bigger camera. I would love to work with a crew. You know, I've always worked with musicians – worked with music and of course the people in the films have always been collaborators. It's not all directed by any means. They give so much of themselves and of their own ideas, and so on.

BZ: But if you work more formally with a crew isn't there a danger that your films will lose some of the spontaneity, the meandering style that people associate with your work?

VD: Oh yeah, I'm aware of the dangers of that because I experienced it working on **London Suite**. I have a tendency sometimes to become stiff or petrified. It's something in my personality and it's something that could occur consciously with a crew – feeling overwhelmed. It is something I am more aware of now; not that it doesn't ever happen. It would be interesting to incorporate this in some way in a film. Basically I am looking forward to collaborating more and working on a larger scale.

BZ: But isn't the small scale nature of your films part of their particular aesthetic appeal? And wouldn't getting a large amount of funding change what it is about your films that makes them special and original?

VD: Well, for a start, it costs money to make any kind of film; you can spend all your life going for small amounts of money but it would be nice to do something more ambitious too and it would be interesting to work something out on paper. A structure is worked out and it *can* change. Funders need the assurance that you know what you're doing. That you've got a plan. What you're saying is the results of what comes out of very low-budget filming is something you'd never be able to get in a more formal funded situation. I know, yeah, it's true. But maybe a film can be made that has elements of both, where there's a space somehow in the script for bits of filming that would operate off chance or off something more instinctual. It's difficult to get funding bodies to allow you to do that, but I am about to try!

BZ: How *did* you finance your earlier films?

VD: I was working as a waitress and bartending as well. The ratio was about 2:1 or something crazy and we shot over time. That's what you have to do; when people are available, when people are free.... So it was shot little bits here and little bits there. And people giving me their time and help and everything, you know, and not getting paid.

BZ: Looking at your work overall, two things especially interest me: your approach to narrative and your representations of women. Could you comment on these?

VD: I see narrative as basically the male story. If you look at the history of narrative films, for the most part it's from the male point of view. There are other stories. Women make narrative films too but from another perspective. I'm extremely interested in making films which play with narrative – stretch it – let it flow in other directions. Films which are fragmented, playful, which have another kind of coherence. It happens with music, dance, theatre. Why is it so hard for films like this to get made I wonder? Is it to do with its power as a medium? On the subject of representing women and images of the female body, take the mother, right. The mother is never sexualized. She's not allowed to be a sexual being. There is a scene in **Beauty Becomes The Beast** where the woman who plays the mother is ironing. And then she's putting on makeup and looking very strong; and she's wearing '50s corsetry and there's that really aggressive music on the soundtrack. She's represented as powerful and sexual in that image. It's the same with the sewing. The things that women do have been demeaned by our culture. I think I am trying to show that. Then take women as a commodity in our culture. **Liberty's Booty** is about prostitution. It's about the split between sexuality and emotions. But its also about the complexity of sexuality in that we see ourselves as feminist and can still get off on fantasies of being dominated. It's there in popular culture – in the music. In that song "96 Tears" for example, where it's about one person controlling another person. Experiencing 'in love' as something where you're overwhelmed by someone and losing your own power, you know. And the situation being reversed. Men still distance or control women by placing them in this body place. By sexualizing them because they're afraid of reciprocity. I believe there is a connection between this kind of relationship between men and women and capitalism. Where relationship is like one culture dominating another culture. Freud uses the term 'the dark continent' when speaking of femininity (female sexuality). We're still somewhat stuck there in that place and it hasn't moved beyond that too much. I think playing with gender is an empowering thing. It's about changing identities, as well. Playing at different roles. I was aware of women in our culture being placed in a particular place and there being an attempt to keep that fixed. The images of what women can be are changing. For example, Sigourney Weaver has a powerful role in the **Alien** series.

BZ: Finally, could you say a bit about how your Irish identity informs your work and also the effects of being a mother on your filmmaking?

VD: It's always been a struggle for me to combine the mothering job and anything else that I do. A battle almost, you know. Now, finally, this year, I've deliberately and willingly put my child first and I'm finding that, to my amazement, it's turning right round and feeding my work. And maybe finally, after all these years, become at peace with this conflict. In terms of being Irish, in a way, the film **London Suite** deals with Irish people living in the margins. I have made two films in Irish; one was **Pobal, The Artist**, produced by Bob Quinn for RTE; the other was an Arts Council funded film, a landscape film called **Rothach**. I've always felt a kind of an outsider in Ireland anyway. I feel that everywhere I am. And I've decided that's just how it is. Now I've accepted it, you know. It may be to do with me being part of a large family. [Laughs] I identify with being Irish because I grew up there and have an understanding. But I think no matter where I go – it seems that I'll always feel somewhat of an outsider, 'cos it's just sort of the way it is. And maybe it's not a bad thing either because it detaches you a little from stuff. Maybe that's why I'm making films even. Always trying to figure things out. And making films is like trying to make sense of something – trying to understand something. If everything was all easy and I slotted in to somewhere, I'd just be doing that wouldn't I!

TWO: AN INTERVIEW WITH JULIE JENKINS

I talked with Welsh-born Julie Jenkins in her 'short life' flat in South East London. Julie has, to date, directed two films – released on video by 'Dangerous To Know', a British Lesbian and Gay Video distribution company – **The Housewife And The Plumber** (1993) and **MUFF Match** (1996), which she describes as 'sex romps'. Prior to that, in the late '80s, she worked on a lesbian and gay video magazine called *Pout*. I began by asking her to explain her involvement.

Julie Jenkins: *Pout* was an idea basically before all this interactive TV came in. We wanted to make something that was interactive for gay people and so the idea was to set up a video magazine, we called it, and the idea was to have people sending us videos and we would edit them all together and make this sort of magazine type thing and I was asked completely out of the blue by Darren Brady who set it up. I think originally I was the only lesbian that they knew, so that's how I got drawn into it and there were three of us and we set up a whole group which then grew so big that it became impossible to make decisions so we ended up being the people that would look at what was sent and we'd be the ones that would end up at the BBC and put it all together. We did three issues all together and, by the time of the third one, we were making absolutely everything ourselves 'cos we kept getting birthday videos sent in and stuff like that and it was like 'this is access TV gone mad' you know, and we just thought "Na!". Basically we'll try and get people to make issue based stuff – make fun stuff whatever, so it actually changed during the course of bringing it out – from 'send us anything you want' to 'if you would like to make something for us', you know, and we would have an overall idea of the kind of things that we wanted to do in it. So the involvement was to write stuff – I wrote a few of my own pieces and had a couple of ideas about what I wanted to see, and making it, filming it ourselves and then editing it and then putting it out – so we did basically everything.
Bev Zalcock: What kind of response did you get from women?
JJ: Lesbian content was 70:30 gay men to women. Out of all that time we got one woman offering us stuff – it was predominantly men that would send stuff in. The first thing I did was about women's sexual fantasies – and I remember one of the comments I got from that was "Oh, you're the people from *Pout* that film people really close-up and make them look really ugly!". A lot of gay men commented on it, much more than the women. A lot of women were actually shocked by it.
BZ: Was there much criticism?
JJ: The main complaint throughout the whole thing was the quality of the video work, the quality of picture and the quality of sound – the first one was terrible – the second one we kind of sorted it out. We had to change the concept and put more work in and try to be a bit more professional about it which meant the cost of it went up. But when you're buying something for £15 you really don't want to watch it and wipe it. The novelty value of it was the most important thing and having access stuff for gay people was great.

BZ: Can you talk about your first credited film **The Housewife And The Plumber**?

JJ: It was originally part of *Pout*. I had this thing that (at the time) you didn't read much about lesbians and their sexuality – and how they feel about sex and their fantasies and all of that – having read Nancy Friday and all that kind of thing I just wanted to indulge in it. Which is why the very first thing I did was to get women in a room, put the camera right up against their faces and say "What do you fantasise about?" and some of the stuff that came out of that was great. **The Housewife And The Plumber** I thought of as a natural progression. It was one of my fantasies – based on a straight porn film I saw years ago when I was working as a waitress. We used to watch porn films at the end of the day. And it was exactly the set-up that I had. It was a corny old housewife. It is a really John Waters-type housewife in the kitchen and the plumbing goes wrong and the plumber comes in and services her. And I just thought I really want to see two women doing that. You know, I really love that reversal thing just by putting two women into a set-up that's already been established as a straight set-up/porn thing. I thought 'that's nice'. I just wanted to see it. It's part of that. And then I had to do another version which was put on with the lesbian shorts thing (**Lesbian Leather Shorts**[3]) and that version was different. With *Pout* we just broke every single rule – we just thought 'sue us, we haven't got any money – might as well!'. So we had things like, you know, footage of Valerie Singleton and Princess Anne in Africa with **Love Story** music over it – we just thought 'we could get in real trouble for this' and then using *Blue Peter*[4] footage and a bottle of washing-up liquid that became a dildo and stuff like that. Then Tom Abel, who was putting money into *Pout* and distributing it for us wanted to use **The Housewife And The Plumber** on something else. I had to rework it a bit and put different music. I couldn't use the music from **Deliverance** I'd used, which kind of washed it out a bit. I wanted it to be all stuff taken from mainstream culture like a straight porn set-up with two women with music from a rape scene in another film. I just wanted it all to be that because I just wanted that contrast. It's a shame that to put it out on another collection it had to be changed. 'Cos it kind of takes that difference out and that contrast of taking really, really mainstream things and turning them into gay stuff.

BZ: What are your influences?

JJ: John Waters seems to have the same obsession that I do with housewives, 'cos that was another thing. I wanted to get a 'Tupperware Party' video but I... when I was a kid I used to watch loads and loads of British sex romps. I just laughed at them and loved them – all the **Carry On** stuff, Benny Hill and Morcambe and Wise. And then I went through teenage-hood and became political. I would sit there and refuse to laugh at it, hated it with a vengeance, particularly Benny Hill. And then as I got older I just thought you don't have to lose the politics. You can just ease up a bit on yourself and enjoy. All the **Carry On** stuff is so bad you laugh at it. I wanted to use that kind of stuff. You know, the way the British are so embarrassed about sex. That's why they can make sex comedies so well. A lot of women when they come out had to desex themselves because you weren't meant to objectify women and so you sort of take it all out and then you start being a bit embarrassed about it. That kind of thing tied in with the sex romp thing. So I wanted to make something that was just having a real laugh and being slightly embarrassed about sex and I wanted to make it for lesbians, basically because I didn't want lesbians to be really earnest about sex in films. So that really connected up with the **Carry Ons**, Benny Hill, etc. And also it's just about where you come from. John Waters is a total mid-west American with an upbringing that sees those big women in nightgowns. Mine, I just saw that in *On The Buses* and in the **Carry On** films. They were from when I was a kid, still part of my sense of humour. **Carry On, St Trinian's**, Benny Hill. Also American stuff. When I saw a Russ Meyer film I absolutely loved it. The first one was **Faster, Pussycat** and then I saw **Beneath The Valley Of The Ultra Vixens** and I can take in so much – but I would never go and see him talking about it at the ICA; Meyer discussing the politics of his films, I just think that's just taking it too seriously. The absurdity of the characters, the campness of it all is what I enjoy. The bit I don't like is that nasty edge when it goes further into violence. But those stupid sex scenes where the music is going over and all the sound effects and everything is great! To me that's like coming from the same kind of place as the **Carry On** stuff. You know 'cos it's a bit 'let's laugh at it 'cos its easier to laugh at sex', it just takes all the pressure off you.

BZ: Can you talk a bit about your views on female sexuality and how it's represented in your films?

JJ: With women it's more politicised than with men because politics has always been attached to women's sexuality and women's bodies, you can't just freely make something that's connected with sex. You can't just think – what kind of things do I want to see? What kind of fantasies do I want to put here? I think that's what men can do really easily because none of their stuff has been connected with politics. When I did the lesbian fantasy on *Pout* a lot of the women were talking about rape fantasies and I knew if I included that there'd be so much response. And even talking about it, the women would never say the word. They would always say "a very restricted fantasy". So women's sexuality can't just be thought of as erotic. In terms of fantasy and imagination there's always been that connection with politics. I think that's really shown by what women put out in the media, write about, sing about, put on film. I think they always have to connect it. Even if they're not aware of it. I think it always is connected to politics. So the kind of stuff that turns me on is bizarre anyway. I knew Dangerous To Know wanted a woman to make a very heavy porn film but (and this was a problem from day one) we should have decided then what it was going to be. 'Cos all the way through **MUFF Match** we had a problem. I wanted to make **St Trinian's**-cum-**Carry On**. I wanted to use that stupid sense of humour, that naïve sense of humour with lesbians. Again, people make a lot of assumptions when they think about lesbians and sex. It's either going to be black and white or women dancing in a forest, or it's going to be some cheesy S/M scene where they're really, really trying to look like they're really hard. The big word to me was earnestness. I didn't want them to look terribly earnest about sex. I wanted them to lighten up! So I wanted to put in a structure that was just a bit silly and embarrassed about it all, which is what ties in with the **Carry On/St**

Trinian's thing. So that's how it got started – they wanted lesbian porn – they didn't get it – they asked the wrong person. The idea came from – I wanted to make a housewife Tupperware Party. We were working with another woman Lotte, and she said the word 'hockey' 'cos we were trying to think of what women we know fantasise about – and of course school girls and hockey came up. I was never a hockey girl – I was netball. So I didn't get any of that stout-legged fantasy. I still wanted to do women in nylon negligées having Tupperware parties! I wanted to have this big teacher (oh, dear it does go back to John Waters slightly doesn't it) who was in charge of it all. I wanted the Charles Hawtrey character in there. I wanted Sid James which was Harriet the main girl and I wanted all those **Carry On**-type things. Another thing that was really important was that I wanted a Joan Sims, because she was a *total* fantasy for me and I absolutely love big-hipped housewifely, womanly type characters. Then I also wanted to get that hideous thing – I went to a comprehensive school and did netball and sometimes we used to go to girls' schools; Monmouth Girls' School. We thought we were hard. We thought Betwys Comprehensive was quite a hard school. We thought we were really hard. When we played those girls they were absolutely terrifying! They were all-girls boarding school and they were so hard, these women. So when I thought of hockey I just thought 'yeah that's what those women are like, that's what those girls are like!'. You know, you think that the slaggy (compy) comprehensive type girls are really hard. But no, it's the bruiser-type boarding school girls that are really hard. So this is where immediately that gang thing came in. I wanted the tarty comp girls and then I wanted the Mother Ulysses Female Fellowship School – the MUFFs – to visit them, to show who really are the scariest. That's where the idea came from. Memories of playing really hard boarding school girls. So that was the structure of it. And then I very dutifully wrote the whole story. Did storyboards for it all. Had everything planned out. Got on location. So little time to do anything that it ended up being... do the scene once, shoot it from this way. Do it again, shoot it from that way. The storyboard went out the window on the first day. But at least I had in my head what I wanted basically. The funding was £6,000 and that all came from DTK. Because of this it had to go out at £15 and we had one camerawoman, one sound and that was it – the basic crew – no lighting or anything! Only the camerawoman was experienced. The rest of us had never done anything like it before. I've had experience of directing stuff for TV. I had an idea of how a crew should work and what my role as director was. From all the actors, only two of the women were used to performing and could switch it on straight away. And that was fabulous 'cos then you've got a lynchpin – something to pull everyone into line. And we had Amy Lamé as the big Joan Sims character and we had Cathy Piece, and both of them do cabaret and perform a lot. So that was great. But every other person was a friend. So they were sitting around chatting, laughing and having coffee and the whole thing really, really slowed down of course. And it should have been about twenty minutes long really. That's the limit. It's one joke. But because of the way it was financed for video sales it had to go to fifty minutes. So it kind of lost the point really. You lost the joke. I had to keep adding and adding on to it.
BZ: How did you and the crew handle the sex scenes?

MUFF MATCH

JJ: Particularly around sex everyone has very precious ideas about it. I didn't want in my auditions to say 'take your clothes off, let me see what your body's like' which I've heard people have done. That was the whole fucking point. Amy Lamé said it really well. "If you're a lesbian and you say you don't objectify women, you're lying but the difference is a woman's gaze is different" and I just though 'Yeah' that is perfect, that is so accurate. But at the some time what was more important to me (as I didn't see that I was making a porn film but making something funny that had sex in it) I wanted to show that women could be light about sex and their sexuality and what they do in bed. So in the auditions I would just say to women 'This is going to be very **Carry On**. Do you like that sort of thing? Do you have a sense of humour about your body? Do you have a sense of humour about sex?'. That was more important to me than the size of their tits of whether they had any stretch marks on their body. That doesn't bother me at all. The one element of control that I wanted but I couldn't get was that we had a shower scene in it but none of the big women would go in. Which is fair enough. I would never want to push them. Since you've had it from ten years old that you have to occupy less space than you do. So I wasn't going to say 'Get your kit off! You're fat, get your kit off!'. 'Cos people just don't want to do it. Which is understandable unless you are like Amy. With Amy that's part of her personality – she's huge. So. There were other women who were involved with it who had very different ideas about how they wanted to show lesbians as having sex. I wanted it to be very Russ Meyer. I wanted it to be bang, bang, bang – I'll put sound effects on. Stupid sound effects and all that. So I'll show women fuck really hard. But I'll show that funny, you know. Like Russ

Meyer does – with funny sound effects that take the edge off it. Anyway there were points in it where the camera would hold seductively on a nipple being licked and all of those kind of things and I should have been stronger and said 'that's not the kind of thing that I want'. So that infiltrated it and that's not **Carry On**. That's not girl gangs coming to visit and having a bonk! That's trying to make it look really, really sexy and soft and seductive. Sure, somebody can make that but it was in the wrong place. I let control of that go a bit. I could have edited it out but I couldn't 'cos I needed everything – the full fifty minutes. That did detract slightly. We got away with it because we had the girl gang outside on the hockey pitch 'rumpy pumpy' out there and then meanwhile back in the office, meanwhile back in the first aid room. But they are very different genres, you know. We had funny little scenes of the women linking arms and doing the Monkees-type walk towards the women and terrifying them. Meanwhile you've got a nipple being seductively licked. You know that's wrong! So then it fell into funny little scenes outside on the hockey pitch and so called pseudo-sexy scenes inside that weren't sexy because it wasn't lit to be sexy. It was cold light of day. It was this is what flesh looks like with all the lights on. You know, wrong place! So that's a problem with it to me. I didn't like that. I wasn't happy about that. At the time I wasn't strong enough to get that tight control on it. I would love to cut it down so that it's basically a hockey pitch and bonky bonky – in the first aid room and that's it. As soon as you put women and sex together you get loads of issues there. That's why I'm talking too much about sex! [Laughs]

BZ: Could you talk about humour?

JJ: I wanted to put humour in it. I really love the British sense of humour. The stupid things – it's all part of British culture. It comes from embarrassment and stiff upper lip and hide it all behind and do really stupid embarrassing things. I wanted to do that because of my own sense of humour and my own personality. It was politicised. I wanted lesbians to laugh at themselves having sex. Using a fantasy, a gang of girls coming to play a hockey match was such a good vehicle. If you do get funding, it's so rare, that you feel you have to make a huge statement. This is the one. And it's going to speak to people – so you can't lighten up about that either. All the politics of having big bodies, small bodies, black bodies, white bodies, Asian bodies. All of that comes into it. You never see a gay male porn thing with people writing in about the fact that there are no fat bodies, as we did it. In male porn the main thing is the size of their dick and the fantasies they're having. It's completely different with women. Completely different and that's another reason for getting humour in there. 'Cos also you can get away with things in terms of certification if it's funny.

BZ: Were you happy with the cast?

JJ: The women that were in it I thought were fabulous, particularly the woman who played Nursie. She'd been used to doing loads of heavy sex scenes and I was like, if you fall off the table just do it. If the dildo drops off, go for it, just do it. That's what happens and its really funny and if you don't mind other people laughing at your inadequacies, then I'll just leave it in. So she was fabulous and she just camped it up. She was so melodramatic. And when things went wrong she just emphasised it even more and that was great

– that was just what I wanted. And then there's the women continually snogging all the way through –I think they turned into a joke. And I like that – that is teenage fantasy stuff – snogging some butch thing in the changing rooms. And because it goes on for so long it's quite funny as well. And snogging is such a British thing as well, isn't it? We'll show people snogging a lot! [Laughs]

BZ: What kind of response did the film get?

JJ: The straight porn press reviewed it and they hated it for all the best reasons. They thought the women were unattractive [laughs]. And I thought 'course you would'. Beth Jordache wasn't there for them. That's what they wanted, that's what lesbians are to them now. They're not scary any more – it's like straight girls – except you can watch them playing with another girl. With women – when we had the first screening, it was absolutely fabulous and the best comment I've had was "thank god, at last a film with women having sex that doesn't make you go ooh nooo, how embarrassing!" [laughs]. And it was because they weren't earnest about it. They didn't take any of it seriously. When it showed in USA I thought 'this audience hasn't had **St Trinian's**. They haven't had that whole culture, their thing is very different'. So I did a little speech at the beginning saying these are the influences, this is very British, to kind of prepare them for it. And it was really bizarre – they laughed in exactly the opposite places that the British audiences did. In San Francisco at the festival, it came at the end of a programme of really earnest, really painful, really tiring films. It got a really sort of *hmmm!* response. They didn't quite get it. It wasn't just the cultural thing though, it was more to do with, like I said, the fact that some of the shots shouldn't be there. Partly that reason, and it being overlong. One woman came up to me and said. "Oh God, at last some energy" and that's great.

BZ: Overall, are you happy with the film?

JJ: There's two things I've really been complimented on, which is so good because it's exactly what I wanted to achieve: women seeing sex differently (sex portrayed differently) and energy and no big huge painful angst about any of it. I wanted it to feel light and breezy and fluffy and I think it's achieved that – apart from the shots that I've talked about. I would love to cut it down. Because it does want to be more that girl gang type of thing. It does want to be a lot of women getting together, rough and tumble on the pitch and then rough and tumble in the changing rooms. That's all it's meant to be. The hockey pitch and that stupid slapstick comedy.

NOTES

1. For example **Maeve** (1981) and **Anne Devlin** (1984).

2. The maker of the doll, who died recently, was Greer Lankton (star of Nick Zedd's **The Bogus Man**).

3. A compilation released by Dangerous To Know.

4. BBC Television children's programme.

CHAPTER NINE

DELINQUENT NURSES

PART 1: THE BRITISH VERSION

An enduring female fantasy-figure in cinema, as in life, is the nurse. This is not surprising, given that nurses are traditionally young, female and in uniform. As well as being nubile and naïve (in the popular imagination at least) they also administer to their patients when they – the patients – are lying helplessly in bed. All in all there's plenty of scope for risqué scenarios. Interestingly, it is British comic cinema that is most successful in realising the potential of the hospital drama and of its key player – the nurse. Because of the number of nurses allocated to a ward, and in spite of the hospital hierarchy, it seems only fair to award them the status of a girl gang.

As with the St. Trinian's film cycle discussed in Chapter 2, whose subject was an anarchic girls' school, British post-war comedy also dealt extremely successfully with madness and mayhem on the hospital ward. Most well known of the hospital films was the cycle that began in the early '50s and ran for almost two decades. These were the "Doctor" comedies that spiced up the basic medical melodrama with plenty of dashing doctors and naughty nurses. **Doctor In The House** ('54), **Doctor At Sea** ('55), **Doctor At Large** ('57), **Doctor In Love** ('60), **Doctor In Distress** ('63), **Doctor In Clover** ('66) and **Doctor In Trouble** ('70), while never popular with the critics, did well at the box office, having as they did a recognisable house style based in working class humour, formulaic plot development and a perennial team of comic actors who tended to play the same role from film to film. *Films & Filming* dismissed the final film in the cycle as "...the cinematic equivalent of an end-of-the-pier summer show".

THE "CARRY ON" FILMS

Beginning later in the '50s than the "Doctor" films, the "Carry On" comedy cycle was to continue production for much longer, running from 1958–1992 and boasting thirty titles. In fact, if "exploitation" cinema is about the endless reworking of a successful formula to purely economic ends, then the "Carry On" cycle of film must take all the accolades. Generally loathed by the critics and loved by the public, these comedies were a combination of farce, slapstick and verbal innuendo. Even in the relatively repressed Britain of the '50s, there was early evidence that "tits & bums" jokes would be a staple. The films are crude and camp in equal measure and the series, taken as a whole provides a fascinating insight into both the class and sexuality of the nation. From the point of view of nurses, there are four titles which feature hospital humour as the central focus. These are **Carry On Nurse** ('59), **Carry On Doctor** ('68), **Carry On Again Doctor** ('69) and **Carry On Matron** ('72).

The partnership responsible for all of the "Carry On" films consisted of Gerald Thomas (director) and Peter Gilbert (producer). Gerald's brother Ralph had worked on **Doctor In The House** and was enthusiastic about the box office potential of the hospital drama/comedy. Both Thomas and Gilbert decided to exploit this potential, with only their second "Carry On" title, **Carry On Nurse**. This was not only a smash hit in Britain but became a cult film across the Atlantic, having been promoted by an independent film distributor by the name of David Emmanuel. Predating the waving of wire hangers at the **Mommie Dearest** screenings and the throwing of rice at **The Rocky Horror Picture Show**, Emmanuel provided plastic daffodils for audiences to wave at the end of **Carry On Nurse**, at the moment when the nurses get their revenge on a particularly difficult and demanding male patient. During this denouement, the nurses insert a daffodil, instead of a thermometer, into a rather embarrassing orifice, much to their amusement and matron's consternation. It was really rather rude and the film *did* have problem with the British censors, notably when matron instructed a nurse to "pick up his balls" after the weights supporting a patient's broken leg had crashed to the ground! Quite raunchy for the time – but the series got much more outrageous as it went on.

LARGE LADIES AND SMALL MEN

The characteristic "balls & buttocks" lavatorial humour of the "Carry On" films tapped into a strong strand of British working class humour, which comes out of the music hall tradition and is most graphically exemplified by the seaside postcard, in which big-busted dominant women smother weedy and hen-pecked men. In fact Andy Medhurst writing about **Carry On Nurse** for *Sight And Sound* describes the film as "...a seaside postcard come to life, a shameless procession of vulgarities... utterly irresistible".

As with the "Doctor" series, the films present stock and stereotyped characters, often with the same actors repeating their roles across a number of titles. The female roles range from the overweight and oversensitive dominatrix (Hattie Jacques) to the well-endowed, blonde, mischievous cockney (Barbara Windsor). The men, on the other hand tend to be tiny, timid and camp (Kenneth Williams and Charles Hawtrey almost always played such roles) or small time villains, spivs and wideboys (Sid James played this type to perfection). Improbable plots, farcical situations – men in drag and women losing their bras – and verbal innuendoes are the hallmarks of the "Carry On" series, and like most other exploitation films they were critically mauled while doing great business. *Variety*'s assessment of **Carry On Doctor** is typical – "The usual unabashed mixture of double meanings, down to earth vulgarity and blue jokes".

Carry On Nurse was the second film in the long-running "Carry On" series. It took six weeks to shoot at Pinewood Studio, and was the top grossing film in Britain in 1959. Although much of the comedy is based in fairly basic slapstick and verbal suggestiveness, the film is much more restrained than some of its later incarnations. In fact, in terms of the film's finely observed characters and its tendency to melodrama, it's closer to the spirit of the "Doctor" films. This is not surprising considering the connections between the two production companies. Not only was there a link between the Thomas brothers, but as well as this fraternal connection, Peter Rogers, the producer of all the "Carry On" films was married to Betty Box, who was the producer of the "Doctor" films. Adrian Rigelsford in his tribute to the "Carry On" films, makes the following observation:

*"For the eagle-eyed viewer there's evidence of an in-joke between Peter Rogers and his wife to be spotted. It can be found in every scene where the doors of the hospital lifts are on show. While Rogers had been ploughing through countless 'Carry On' films, his wife, Betty Box was still producing the 'Doctor' films, with Ralph Thomas (brother of Gerald Thomas director of the 'Carry Ons') directing. Rogers had already cleared the fact that his team were using the word 'Doctor' in their rival series with his wife, by giving her a percentage of the royalties made on **Carry On Doctor**, and as an affectionate nod of appreciation, one of the artists at Pinewood was commissioned to produce an oil painting of James Robertson-Justice. Robertson-Justice had played Sir Lancelot Spratt, the head of the hospital in all of Box's 'Doctor' films, and so in **Carry On Doctor** a bizarre link was formed by having his picture hung in their hospital by the lift doors."* [1]

As has been noted, the final gag of **Carry On Nurse** represents the revenge of the long-suffering nurses on a snobbish, self-centred and endlessly demanding character known as "The Colonel", played by Wilfrid Hyde-White. Their very original use of a daffodil on their tormentor, gives them – and us – the last laugh, and not only provides an image of young women working together to challenge the arrogance of the male establishment, but also represents a class victory. Matron's horrified face when she sees a daffodil sticking out of the Colonel's bare bottom is greeted by his typically patronising response:

Colonel: Come come Matron. Surely you've seen a temperature taken like this before!
Matron: Yes Colonel, many times before – but never with a daffodil!!!

In **Carry On Nurse**, actress Hattie Jacques created the prototype for the Matron that was to be a crucial feature of all the hospital based "Carry Ons". Jacques unique presence – a large lady, but extremely attractive, and her inimitable acting style; her comic timing and her outraged-of-middle-England expression, make her one of the most memorable nurses ever. Because of her ample girth and the strictness of her regime on the wards, Hattie Jacques' Matron has resonances with the stereotypical dominatrices of the "Women In Prison" movies. In films like **Caged** and **Reform School Girls** the matrons terrorise and abuse the young female inmates in their charge, and in the "Carry On" films Matron strikes terror into the heart of the doctors, the

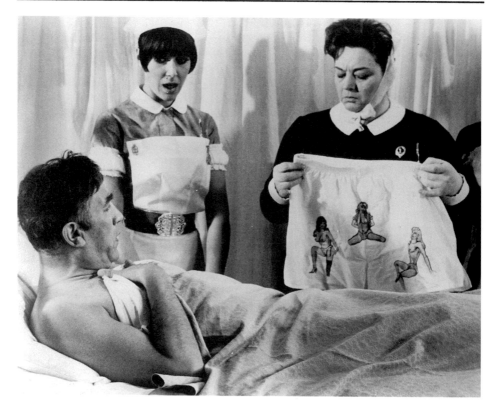

CARRY ON DOCTOR

nurses and, most of all, the patients on the male wards. The men in the hospital beds are for the most part an inadequate bunch, who wilt under Matron's domineering rule. The nurses are an over-worked lot, from the ward sister to the student nurses, who tend to support each other when dealing both with Matron's demands and recalcitrant male patients.

QUEENS OF THE WARD

It's interesting to note that **Carry On Nurse**, which is an early "Carry On" title, is restrained in comparison to the later films, and freely mixes social realism and melodrama with its slapstick comedy and double entendre. At this stage of the cycle's development its much more "Doctor In The House" than "Carry On Up The Ward"! There are, however, hints of what's to come, with Kenneth Williams and Charles Hawtrey vying to be the production's most convincing queen. At one point in the film, when the patients get drunk and rebel against Matron's rule, Hawtrey cross-dresses as the night nurse, while the real nurse is dispatched unceremoniously, tied up on the bed in her underwear. Drag in British comedy is almost routine, but there is something deliciously subversive about Hawtrey's performance. Speaking of camp, Kenneth Williams was notorious for his outrageous behaviour during the "Carry On" productions, renowned in particular for his practical jokes and acerbic wit, while Hawtrey was not above a quip or two himself. Kenneth Connor recalls an episode during the filming of **Carry On Henry**, where Kenneth Williams is putting Charles Hawtrey on the rack in his torture chamber to get a confession from him. According to Connor:

"Hawtrey is seen getting longer and longer every time Williams cranked the rack. Charles was a quiet man but quite capable of the odd remark that was equal to anything Kenneth Williams could say. When the scene was over he turned to the props man and asked: 'Does this thing really stretch human limbs?'. The technician looked a bit nonplussed and said, 'Well, I suppose it does,' and Charles looked him up and down and said, 'Come into my room afterwards because I have a bit of freelance work for you. And bring your smallest rack.' Kenneth Williams' jaw nearly hit the floor while Charles just looked on as if butter wouldn't have melted in his mouth!"[2]

Given the quintessentially British nature of the proceedings, both on and off the set of the "Carry On" films, it's amazing how well **Carry On Nurse** did in the United States, where it ran for two and a half years. This transatlantic success was never matched by the other productions, but it did ensure that nurses would be firmly on the agenda in the coming years. It was, however, almost a decade later before the team returned to the subject of nurses with the film **Carry On Doctor** ('67). Britain, by the end of the '60s, was a much more permissive society and this coupled with the relaxing of the Hays Code in Hollywood[3] made for much more explicit film-making. In **Carry On Doctor** Hattie Jacques reprises her role as Matron, and most of the film's funniest moments come out of the banter between her character and Dr. Tinkle, played by Kenneth Williams. This formula was to be repeated in the next two nurse-based comedies, **Carry On Again Doctor** ('69) and **Carry On Matron** ('71). The following piece of dialogue between them is typical:

Dr. Tinkle: You may not realise it, but I was once a weak man.
Matron: Well once a week is enough for any man!

The "Carry On" films took formula to an almost absurd length. The plots are so contrived, the jokes so inevitable and the visual gags so simplistic, that they came to be regarded with the affection felt for the very familiar. Add to this a familiar cast who play characters with ridiculous, sub-Jonsonian names, (for example, Frankie Howerd is Francis Bigger, Barbara Windsor is Nurse Sandra May) and the vulgarity of the films is almost perfectly achieved. Talbot Rothwell must be given credit for his script, an unending stream of puns and double entendres:

Dr. Tinkle: It's an enigma. That's what it is, Matron an enigma!
Patient: I'm not having another one of those!

The usual assortment of nurses from the statuesque Matron to the busty Nurse May, are pitted against the inadequate male hospital establishment, including men in pyjamas, men in white coats and men in drag. Effeminate behaviour hinting at barely repressed homosexuality, cross-dressing and exaggeratedly limp-wristed acting was the hallmark of the "Carry On" films.

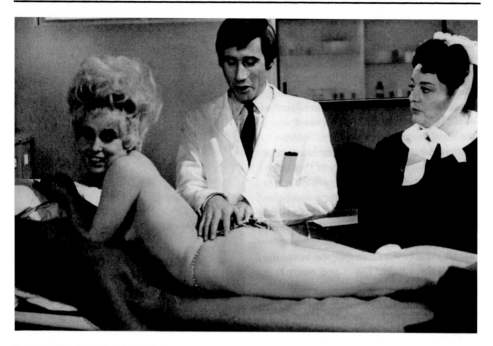

CARRY ON AGAIN DOCTOR

In fact it's no exaggeration to suggest that there was more camping and queening at the Pinewood Studios during this time than at that notorious transatlantic studio, Andy Warhol's factory. Ironically, the "Carry On" films were about as far from avant-garde as it was possible to be, and yet they provided representations of gender play that the entire nation celebrated. Embedded thereafter in the popular imagination is the image of Hattie Jacques as the representation of matriarchal power on the wards, alongside the image of Kenneth Williams as the Chief Surgeon – the camp figure that resides at the heart of the British establishment.

The success of **Carry On Doctor** led to the inevitable sequel, **Carry On Again Doctor** ('69) which featured Matron again, Dr. Carver (Kenneth Williams) and Dr. Stoppidge (Charles Hawtrey), who also appears in drag. Unfortunately there is little else to recommend it. By **Carry On Matron**, the last of the hospital-based films, the formula is wearing thin and the ratings are beginning to wane. However, with Matron, two drag queens and an array of nurses it's still the best "Carry On" film made in the '70s. It's set in a maternity hospital and makes fun of pregnancy, fertility and gender roles. The chief gynaecologist, Sir Bernard Cutting, believes he is undergoing an involuntary sex change and turns to Matron to prove his manhood. Matron meanwhile is more turned on by illicitly watching medical soaps on TV with the hospital psychiatrist, Francis Goode. On the ward, a patient is refusing to have her baby and the student nurses are romping in the nurses' home. Nurse Ball is sharing a room with a new student who turns out to be a man involved in a scam to steal the hospital's supply of contraceptive pills, and they end up wrestling on the bed as Matron arrives. The finale is pure farce, with a safecracker posing as a pregnant woman, concealing his tools in his bulge and a gang of small-time villains being chased around the hospital by a posse of female patients.

Even though the girl gangs in the "Carry On" hospital comedies are an assortment of female stock characters and drag queens, they are nevertheless a powerful post-war image that served to belittle the British male establishment as well as asserting the fundamental fluidity of gender. What is more they were wildly popular and still strike a chord within the British psyche. While drag continues to be at the cutting edge of popular entertainment, its subversive potentially has rarely been so well realised as in the "Carry On" films.

PART 2: THE AMERICAN VERSION

"THE STUDENT NURSES"

In America, a very different kind of nurse-based movie was pioneered by Roger Corman, who always seemed to have his finger on the pulse of the drive-in movie crowd. Following the success of **The Babysitter** (Don Henderson, 1969), dealing as it did with the teenager in distress, Corman felt that a film about a group of trainee nurses would do well. His instinct proved to be correct as usual. To launch his new production and distribution company, New World Pictures, Corman invited Stephanie Rothman to make a film about a group of student nurses. Although not overly impressed with the chosen topic, Rothman agreed to direct. Corman stipulated that the nurses be pretty and naked as often as possible.[4] With this proviso, he left Stephanie Rothman alone, allowing her the freedom to pursue her own ideas.

She worked on the story, with her collaborator, Charles Swartz (who also produced the film) and Frances Doel, the studio's story-editor. It was written in a week and was followed by two months of pre-production and casting, after which the shoot began. Using a small crew and many locations, the film was shot in seventeen days. When Corman saw the rough-cut, he was concerned that Rothman had made the nurses too intelligent and that this would affect their sex appeal. When the film made money he changed his mind.

The success of **The Student Nurses** (1970) inevitably spawned a sexy, Corman-produced nurse exploitation sub-genre, including **Private Duty Nurses** (1971), **Night Call Nurses** (1972), **The Young Nurses** (1973), and **Candy Stripe Nurses** (1974), amongst others. **The Student Nurses** is however a classic of its type, with its Cormanesque subject matter and its trademark Rothman "reversals". This combination makes the film a landmark in exploitation cinema and, thanks to Rothman's influence, one of the most progressive girl-gang films of its time. There were however conditions that had to be met in order to satisfy Corman and the other financiers. In order for the film to do good box-office, as we have seen, it had to appeal to a very voyeuristic, predominantly male audience, and this meant, in typical exploitation style, the inclusion of lots of sex and violence, however arbitrary. Roger Corman, himself, set particular store on the selling power of nudity and as such was a

STUDENT NURSES

strong advocate of naked females in his films. This was clearly not one of Rothman's priorities, but she had little choice but to accede to this basic demand. She observes: "To his credit, Corman did not object to my exploring more interesting or controversial issues as long as homage was paid to that unholy trinity of exploitation values: violence, sex and nudity."[5]

In addition to these requirements, the regional film distributors, who co-financed and distributed the movie, wanted it to have an R rating from the Motion Picture Producers Association of America, which meant that only those aged seventeen and above could view it. It also meant that the film could not show simulated sex from the waist down or full frontal nudity. Rothman describes the prospect of filming the sex scenes with the restrictions of the R-rating as a "gymnastic dilemma". She also discusses her reservations about working in exploitation and how she was able to meet its demands, while at the same time, subtly undermining its values. "Whatever they [exploitation films] were called, there was an aspect of them that was deeply troubling to me: the victimization and sexual objectification of women. Even if I was not acquainted with the word exploitation film, since my university years, I certainly was with the word feminism and I always considered myself a feminist.

"How did I apply my feminist views to the exploitation films I made? The most obvious places where women are objectified in these films are in the areas of sex and nudity. While it was an ironclad requirement that I include scenes of sex and nudity, I tried to make sure men and women were equally nude equally often and the sex was not brutal but sensually evocative for both sexes. When women did experience sexual assaults – which occurs in only two films, **The Student Nurses** and **Terminal Island** – they resist vigorously; in one case the woman frees herself, in the other she is helped to free herself by sympathetic men."[6]

AN UNCONVENTIONAL GIRL GANG

While she was researching for **The Student Nurses**, Rothman remembered a conversation she once had with a doctor, who said that contrary to popular belief, it was the nurses, not the doctors, who had the most powerful role within the hospital. In the collective imagination, nurses provide tender loving care; in reality they keep the hospital running. Although for the purposes of the movie Rothman was saddled with the concept of *student* nurses – by definition even more vulnerable than fully *trained* nurses – who had to be pretty, it occurred to her that she could up-end the expectation that the girls would be vulnerable and submissive. In order to achieve this, she decided to focus on the lives of the student nurses *outside* the hospital, thus dispelling any expectations of innocents in uniform and sex-romps in the wards. Rothman also represents her pretty young nurses as strong-willed and challenging. This is a girl-gang with attitude; a group of four high-spirited young women, who live and grow together; a group who, true to the times, challenge the rules and behave unconventionally.

"It was not my intention to satisfy the fantasies of men at the expense of women, but the reality was that many standard situations in exploitation films did this. My solution was to have women first think and then act unconventionally. For example, each of the four women in **The Student Nurses** consciously violate the rules of the hospital and the profession which they aspire to enter; they choose not to be 'good girls' who are always submissive to men and their elders."[7]

Rothman also decided to use the film as an opportunity to represent the issues of the day. In 1970 the USA was in a state of conflict and change and contemporary events, like the war in Vietnam, were polarising society. Liberation politics and a fledgling youth culture were challenging traditional moral and social structures. The emerging Black Liberation and Women's Liberation movements were making an impact, and the sexual revolution, which had begun in the '60s, was still unfolding; for example the pill was available, but abortion was still not legal. Many of these important social developments are documented in **The Student Nurses**, which, as Rothman describes it, is "a document of its time; a low-budget exploitation film about political turmoil, social change and the sexual adventures of four very pretty nurses who are naked as often as possible".[8]

STUDENT NURSES

A GROOVY GIRL GANG

Of the four young nurses, Pris is definitely the most tuned in. She's a no-bra, mini-skirted wild child, turning on to some free love and hippie action through Jim, her motor-cycling, drug-dealing boyfriend. Although she's majoring in psychiatry, Pris seems much more interested in exploring the scene outside the wards and is very keen to free her mind. Jim persuades her to drop acid and she has her first hallucinogenic experience; getting down in the sand dunes as the waves crash around her.

Fred is the most sexually liberated of the quartet and very early on we see her seducing the eligible young doctor, who gives the girls a ride to the hospital in the title sequence. In fact Fred is so keen to get him into bed that she rushes round to his house and dives into the bedroom. In one of the movie's many comic moments, Fred ends up in the dark with the wrong doctor, who is wearing nothing but a stethoscope. In spite of her relaxed approach to sex, she is the most uptight character and strongly opposes Pris' abortion later on in the film.

Sharon is the most soft-hearted of the gang and her training involves caring for a poor little rich boy with terminal cystic-fibrosis. Her patient is a melancholy and self-absorbed romantic, who initially rejects her overtures, but later succumbs to her generous and understanding nature. Indeed, so generous is Sharon that she ends up sleeping with her patient because she realises he has very little time to live and she wants him to die happy.

Lyn, whose specialism is Public Health, is drawn to social medicine in a very practical way and ends up helping the disadvantaged Hispanic population who live in the ghettos of LA. As she becomes increasingly involved in community activism she is ultimately persuaded to embrace the revolutionary struggle, and when her Mexican boyfriend shoots a cop she decides to go on the run with him. Like the others, Lyn learns more about life and her chosen role *outside* the hospital and she is the one who undergoes the most radical transformation.

As we have seen, each one of the female characters is involved in breaking the rules. From the outset of the film the nurses are represented as independent minded and willing to take risks. They also work together and support one another, even though they are strongly individualised from the start. This is a film where sisterhood is powerful. In the final image of the film, the group enter the hospital together to receive their diplomas. There's a strong sense of solidarity, even though their destinies will be very different. Sharon is off to Vietnam to nurse the wounded soldiers, whereas Lyn will join the guerrilla struggle against "amerikan" imperialism.

COMIC REVERSAL

Stephanie Rothman's commitment to unsettling audience expectation is evident in **The Student Nurses** from the very start. During an early scene on the ward, one of our young heroines is assaulted by a deranged patient. In place of the expected (standard) violation sequence, the young woman is shown fighting back, dispatching her attacker with a swift knee to the groin. Expectations are further dashed, when two orderlies arrive with a giant syringe and plunge it into the man's bare buttocks. Ironically, the film's first image of nudity is that of a man's behind; a disappointment, no doubt, to certain sections of the audience, but a bit of a laugh for the rest of us. Another of Rothman's strategies is also in evidence: "I tried to make sure men and women were equally nude equally often and the sex was not brutal but sensually evocative for both sexes."[9]

The scene in which Pris and her boyfriend drop acid and make love on the beach illustrates this principal perfectly. There is an equality of explicitness insofar as framing and point of view are concerned. The scene is also shot to show the love-making as both sensual and consensual, and although Pris later comes to regret the interlude, there is never a sense of her having been violated. She wanted to experiment and she has to deal with the consequences. Her abortion is one of the most radical scenes to come out of exploitation cinema and it is as shocking and controversial today as it was at the time. With the help of her gang and a sympathetic doctor, Pris is shown having an illegal home abortion, because the hospital has refused to authorise it. Watching this scene in the context of today's fundamentalist backlash against a woman's right to choose is a salutary experience and a reminder that the women's struggle far from over.

A CULT CLASSIC

As well as the radical representations within the film, **The Student Nurses** is also distinguished by its filmic flair. For example, the style of the film changes to suit each of the protagonists. Pris, who's dating a drop-out drug dealer, and is attracted to a hippy lifestyle, is described by languid long-takes in sun-drenched picturesque locations, against an acoustic guitar soundtrack. Lyn on the other hand is getting involved with activists and is filmed in edgy, urban settings in a newsreel style, with rapid cutting and hand-held camera. The film also uses a variety of styles to enhance expressiveness. In the sequence where Pris discovers she's pregnant she is filmed with a series of jump-cuts moving along a number of different streets, with voice-over, which produces the kind of lyrical realism we associate with the "nouvelle vague". And to create a sense of her paranoia, there are incongruous matches and a weird point of view, which are very surrealistic.

Rothman's celebrated talent for creating a strong sense of place and somehow capturing the texture of the time is very much in evidence in **The Student Nurses**. The crew filmed events as they happened in a number of locations in LA, which are then used as the back-drop for the drama. This is not only very cost-effective, but also accounts for the movie's visceral quality. Footage of the agit-prop street theatre and of the love-in in the park, which happened to be going on during the production, provides the film with an aesthetic of authenticity. There is a real sense of the moment about the film, as well as a strong feeling for filmic pleasure; the acid trip is wonderful, all slow-mo waves, gels, dissolves and head music; and the abortion scene is truly disturbing, with the unsettling cross-cutting between the love-making on the sand including Pris' point-of-view of the voyeurs watching her (Pris had a bad trip and this is a flashback) with the illegal home operation, taking place in a bedroom where the primary colour is red. In other emotionally charged scenes the use of colour has been crucial. Yellow is used to underpin Pris' paranoia, and in the interior sequence where Fred is warning Pris about the difficulties of being a single mother, the long take, the abstract art and the yellow crockery are strongly reminiscent of the stylistic elements of Jean-Luc Godard's **Pierrot Le Fou** (1965).

Once again the filmic references in **The Student Nurses** seem closer to the "nouvelle vague" than to exploitation cinema. Apart from Rothman's films, very few American films of the early '70s point to the radical developments in film-making that had been going on in France for over a decade. As well as its radical style, as we've seen the film boasts a radical content, particularly in terms of its feminism. At one point in the film, Lyn's boyfriend, Victor Charlie, quotes from a leading Black Panther: "You're either with us or you're against us!" and in a sense this sums up the underlying political message of the film. What seems special about this film apart from its ideology is its political optimism, which is partly a reflection of the time and partly a hallmark of Rothman's unique approach. She humanises, rather

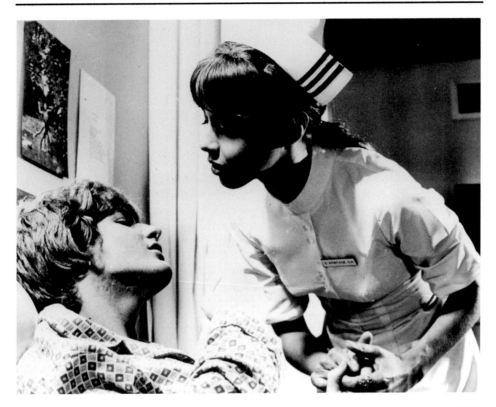

STUDENT NURSES

than fetishises her characters. The women are never victimised and violated to such a degree that they transmute into the castrating bitches so beloved of the revenge fantasy genre. Nor are the men unremitting sleazeballs looking for a chance to abuse women. Gone from Rothman's films are the familiar sexist stereotypes; and yet they did well on the exploitation circuit; it's a tribute to her ingenuity and her sense of humour that they did.

CONCLUSION

Exploring cinematic representations of nurses has uncovered some unexpected variations on the theme of the girl gang. The representation of nurses within the tradition of British comedy has revealed that, while it provides an opportunity to depict plenty of saucy women, the main object of the humour is the insecure man, whose lack of confidence in his masculinity, is the basis for most of the jokes. In a sense the "Carry On" films are not about women at all, but about gender trespass in post-war Britain. As such, the nurses in these films constitute the most unorthodox "girl-gang" to date.

The nurses that feature in the exploitation movie, **The Student Nurses**, are equally unexpected. The representation of the four student nurses who comprise the girl-gang is completely at odds with the usual sexist stereotypes of exploitation cinema. On the contrary, the film provides a strong and original image of sexually liberated young women in '70s America. By personalising the female characters, the film's director, Stephanie Rothman is able to show their struggles both as individuals and as a group to show in other words, how the personal *is* political.

NOTES

1. See *Carry On Laughing: A Celebration*, by Adrian Rigelsford. Virgin Books. London, 1996, p66/7.

2. Ibid., p90.

3. Hollywood's self-regulatory code, which comprised a set of rules that guaranteed the moral respectability of its product. Started in the early '30s in response to religious pressure, the code was relaxed by the end of the '60s.

4. See "Notes About **The Student Nurses**" written and presented by Stephanie Rothman at the Feminale Conference, "Girls Gangs Guns" in Cologne 1999 and published in German translation in *girlsgangsguns: Zwischen Exploitation-Kino und Underground*; Carla Despineux, Verena Mund (Hrsg.) Feminale Edition, Schuren 2000, Germany. With financial support from *Bundesministerium fur Familie, Senioren, Frauen und Jugend gefordert*, Feminale was able to contribute to a restored colour and sound transfer of **The Student Nurses** from 35mm to Beta. One copy of which is in the archive at UCLA.

5. See "Everything You Never Wanted To Know About Exploitation Films", written and presented by Stephanie Rothman at the Feminale Conference, "Girls Gangs Guns" in Cologne 1999 and published in German translation in *girlsgangsguns: Zwischen Exploitation Kino Und Underground*. Op cit. p47.

6. Ibid.

7. Ibid.

8. See "Zu **The Student Nurses**" by Stephanie Rothman in *girlsgangsguns: Zwischen Exploitation-Kino Und Underground*. Op.cit.

9. See "Everything You Never Wanted To Know About Exploitation Films", written by Stephanie Rothman in *girlsgangsguns*. Op cit.

CHAPTER TEN

AN INTERVIEW WITH STEPHANIE ROTHMAN

INTRODUCTION TO THE ROTHMAN INTERVIEW

Stephanie Rothman started making films commercially at AIP studio, by then under the control of Roger Corman. Her first directorial assignment was on **Blood Bath**, released in 1966, a film started by Jack Hill and completed by Rothman. Although they share the director's credit, they never actually worked together. The film itself is notable for being the first vampire movie to be directed by a woman. It's a theme Rothman returns to in her 1971 film, **The Velvet Vampire. Blood Bath** was also released in a TV version known as **Tracks Of The Vampire.**

So began Stephanie Rothman's career as a film-maker, which was to last eight years (1966–74) during which time she directed seven films: **Blood Bath** ('66), **It's A Bikini World** ('66), **The Student Nurses** ('70), **The Velvet Vampire** ('71), **Group Marriage** ('72), **Terminal Island** ('73) and **The Working Girls** ('74).

As a student, Rothman's subject had been sociology, which presumably provided the grounding in political analysis that shows up in her films. Subsequently, Rothman studied "cinema" at the University of Southern California, where she distinguished herself in being the first woman to win a Director's Guild Fellowship. After proving her obvious talent and ability to Roger Corman on two titles, **Blood Bath** and **It's A Bikini World**, Rothman was invited by Corman to make the debut movie for his new studio, New World Pictures. As a result she directed **The Student Nurses** in 1970. Working for New World and latterly for Dimension Pictures, Rothman began to acquire something of a reputation for being able to give low-budget films, destined for the drive-in movie slot, a politically progressive edge.

From **The Student Nurses** onwards, there is a tendency in all Rothman's pictures to explore contemporary themes via a female focus. In his article "Stephanie Rothman: R-Rated Feminist"[1] Danny Peary makes the following observation: "Rothman's pictures are all certainly about interesting contemporary women, exploring new occupations, relationships and living situations and confronting the ever-changing values of the 1970s".

In direct contradiction to most female characters in exploitation cinema, Rothman's young women are neither fetishised nor objectified. They are shown naked (an absolute requirement of the Corman production) but only as often as their male counterparts and they are not subjected to the usual statutory sexual violence and abuse. By challenging the standard stereotyping of female characters in this way, Rothman is able to create much more humanised representations of both men and women (see the discussion of **Terminal Island** in Chapter 1). In place of the mindless violence characteristic of exploitation cinema, Rothman substitutes humour and parody. Rothman's use of comic reversal is a trademark feature and has been well documented. In fact her use of laughter to undermine patriarchal power is generally acknowledged as an important element in the uniqueness of Rothman's films.[2] Another notable feature, as Peary has observed, is Rothman's strong sense of setting, of place and space. Peary describes her depiction of LA as "sunny, sandy, washed-out, wacky, decadent LA".[3]

Stephanie Rothman's remarkable achievement has been her ability to work within the exploitation genre without sacrificing her politics and her humour. In fact she was able to use these qualities to transform what were basically teenage trash films into something that is radical and challenging; to express in fact, her feminist, and ultimately humanist, convictions. As such the films of Stephanie Rothman are an important demonstration of how it is possible to combine the commercial with the progressive, and come out with artistic integrity intact.

I was lucky enough to meet up with Stephanie Rothman at the conference, "Girls Gangs Guns" held in Cologne in November 1999.[4] Her films had been enjoying something of a renaissance in Europe, in the late '90s; particularly in Germany. Screenings in Cologne, Munich, Hamburg and Berlin were ensuring that a new generation of film audiences could sample Rothman's comic and deeply subversive take on "exploitation". The Feminale conference in 1999 was therefore an opportune moment to showcase a number of rarely screened Rothman titles as well as to open up the debate around the progressive potential of exploitation cinema, with particular reference to the films coming out of New World Pictures. Stephanie Rothman as a speaker at the conference, was able to provide a unique insight into the modes of production of low-budget cinema in '70s America. In a witty and fascinating presentation entitled "Everything You Never Wanted To Know About Exploitation Films", Rothman discussed the advantages and strictures of working for Roger Corman.[5]

History shows us that Stephanie Rothman broke the mould of exploitation film. Not only was she a one-off, a woman director in a world of male movies, she also challenged the very assumptions upon which the films were based – the objectification of female characters. In turning the standard sexist stereotypes on their head through "comic reversal", Rothman's films provide a striking counter-point to the most abusive aspects of the genre, as well as offering a unique example of filmic subversion in the interests of feminism. I talked with Stephanie about this, and other aspects of her work, earlier on this year.

THE STEPHANIE ROTHMAN INTERVIEW

Bev Zalcock: What made you decide to go into film-making?

Stephanie Rothman: The catalyst was Ingmar Bergman's film **The Seventh Seal**. It was the first time I saw a film that shared a world view similar to my own.

Q. What other films influenced you when you studied film-making at the University of Southern California?

A. I was mostly interested in the remarkable films coming out of Europe and Japan at the time. In particular, Francois Truffaut's **The Four Hundred Blows**, Jean-Luc Godard's **Breathless**, Michelangelo Antonioni's **L'Avventura**, Federico Fellini's **I Vitelloni**, Ingmar Bergman's **Wild Strawberries**, Akira Kurosawa's **Seven Samurai**, plus every film ever made by Jean Renoir. Of course, I was also influenced by a lifetime of watching American films whose titles are too numerous to list, everything from Vincent Minnelli's **Meet Me In St. Louis** and **The Bad And The Beautiful** to Stanley Donen's **Singin' In The Rain**, to Stanley Kubrick's **Paths Of Glory** and Orson Welles' **Citizen Kane**.

Q. To what extent did the Women's Liberation Movement provide the inspiration for daring to make it in a man's world?

A. I entered film school in 1961, nearly a decade before there was any organized effort to break down barriers to the employment of women, so I cannot say the women's movement inspired me to do it. But I never had any patience with the subservient roles women were expected to play in society.

Q. Feminist themes certainly *do* recur in your films, in a sense it's an "auteurial" feature. How far was the Women's Movement a driving force in your work?

A. In the 1970s, when I made most of my films, the U.S. women's movement was gaining momentum. Women could no longer be silenced and I felt encouraged by it to create female characters who were unconventional, although I think I would have tried to do that anyway.

Q. Before you had your directorial debut working for Roger Corman did you have a strongly defined idea of the kind of films you wanted to make, not only in content, but also in style?

A. Yes. As far as content, I wanted to make art films like the European ones I so admired, in which the characters wrestled with provocative existential choices. As far as style in my films, the subject of a scene has always dictated the particular style I chose to film it in.

Q. How did you get the job with Roger Corman?

A. Roger wanted to hire an assistant. I was sent to meet him by Bernard Kantor, Chairman of the University of Southern California Cinema Department.

Q. You obviously impressed Corman with your work on **Blood Bath** and **It's A Bikini World** because he gave you the project of directing the inaugural film for New World Pictures, **The Student Nurses**. Was there a downside? Did you encounter jealousies, and rivalry in what must have been a very small and highly pressured world?

A. Very little. There was too much real work to be done. The New World office was just that: a few administrative offices with no production facilities. The actual screenwriting, production, and post-production work was done elsewhere. Most of the people who worked on the film tried to do their best work. During filming some of the crew were sceptical about the film's quality,

STUDENT NURSES

but when they saw the final version, they liked it.

Q. When Roger Corman asked you to make the film to launch his new studio New World, you became involved in writing the script as well as directing the film. Could you talk about this aspect of your work in constructing the overall meaning of the movie and also say something about your collaboration with Charles Swartz on **Student Nurses** and subsequent films?

A. Roger wanted us to make a film about student nurses because he thought it would appeal to a young male audience, which then, as now, was the largest group to regularly attend films in the U.S. Aside from requiring scenes that contained some nudity and violence, Roger left Charles Swartz, Frances Doel, his story editor, and me free to construct whatever story we wanted. The three of us agreed the only way to avoid making a tawdry little fantasy about nurses was to have the characters involved in the some of the controversial issues of the day. From the beginning, I liked the idea of constructing different stories for each nurse, because it would enable me to shoot each one in a different visual style. Our entire production schedule was very rushed and we didn't have time to do our pre-production work and also write the screenplay, so we hired a promising young writer named Don Spencer to do it. We worked very closely with him on his drafts to ensure that it contained the tone and perspective that we wanted throughout. My collaboration with Charles Swartz began when we met at USC Cinema, where we were both graduate students and where, ironically, he directed the first student film I worked on. Charles subsequently produced all the films that I directed and co-wrote their screenplays; the only exception was **The Working Girls**, which I wrote alone.

Q. Could you give us some idea about the scope of production on **Student Nurses** e.g. budget, schedule and your personal involvement with areas like casting, editing, music and so forth.

A. The film cost $140,000 and was shot, as best I can recollect, in seventeen days. It was made entirely on location in Los Angeles and its environs. Charles and I did the casting. We hired all the production and post-production workers, including the editors and composer. The rough cut was made by the film's editor, Stephen Judson, while we were still shooting. Roger Corman saw it and, after making some helpful suggestions, left the completion of the film to us. Roger began work on a film of his own and did not see ours again until it was already playing in theatres.

Q. How was the film received and reviewed? How did you feel about it then? How do you feel about it now?

A. I don't know what kind of reviews it received elsewhere, or if it even received many reviews, although it did have lots of playdates and was a commercial success. The reviews it got in the Los Angeles newspapers were unfavourable. But the reviewer for the trade paper *Daily Variety* liked it and described it as "an exploitation film to be sure, yet it has a surprising depth". I was astonished to get even one good review, considering the stigma that exploitation films had. Today, I am even more astonished – and gratified – that a low-budget exploitation film made over thirty years ago, which got so little attention when it first appeared, is still remembered.

Q. Working for New World and hence making films destined for male audiences in drive-ins and late-night double-bills, how much compromising did you have to do? Did you have a bottom line of what you were prepared to do?

A. Yes, my bottom line was that I would not show scenes of rape, and if a film required nudity, there had to be nudity for both sexes. Most films that were made then showed only female nudity and I refused to cooperate in this objectification of women. Also, I decided there would be no violent action without showing its ugly consequences. When violence occurred, it would not

TERMINAL ISLAND

be free of the pain and mess of real violence. Sometimes this made the violence more graphic and upsetting, but that was my intention. For example, there is a scene in **Terminal Island** in which a man's throat is cut. I filmed a close up of this, but the Motion Picture Association of America, which assigns the age ratings for films, made me take it out and show it in long shot in order to get an R rating.

Q. How did you get around the economic constraints of that kind of film production?

A. The films were shot on live locations, which were far less expensive than building sets and renting studio stages. We hired excellent people who normally worked on major studio films to fill the key crew positions and paid them their usual price. Since this was proportionately more than the budget could afford, we compensated by working very fast and having very short shooting schedules.

Q. How did you manage to meet the requirements of the exploitation picture whilst, at the same time, turning in a film that had (despite the odds) flair and integrity?

A. I was given a lot of freedom to develop ideas as I wished, as long as I put in enough nudity and action. Exploitation films were distributed in the U.S.

GROUP MARRIAGE

by regional film distributors, some of whom also financed my films. They were businessmen who wanted to make a profit, and they were willing to book films with provocative or controversial ideas if they thought audiences would pay to see them. Historically, this was the niche that exploitation films had always filled. Since they lacked stars, masses of extras, lavish sets, or other things that major studio films could afford, the films had to show and tell things one couldn't see in the majors' productions.

Q. In her book *From Reverence To Rape*, Molly Haskell talks about the dearth of strong female characters in the films of the '70s, which attributes to a backlash against feminism in popular culture. Why do you think at the time, exploitation was the one area of film-making where women characters were still centre frame? It does seem ironic that the exploitation cinema was able to provide what more responsible movies lacked, namely strong female characters.

A. I think the reason was market driven. Young men were the biggest audience for exploitation films and, at the time, exploitation films showed more female nudity and were more ribald and lively. To give the narrative some interest, the female characters had to be strong and exciting.

Q. Given the recent revision of the contribution of exploitation cinema, do you feel, with hindsight, that it was a productive place to work from?

A. For me it was. I got the opportunity to make films in different genres, using different styles of composition, lighting, and camera movement.

Q. Apart from a theoretical interest in your films from feminists, did your films

SHE'S WAITING TO LOVE YOU...TO DEATH

Climax after climax of terror and desire...

where the living change places with the dead.

IN METROCOLOR

THE VELVET VAMPIRE

Michael Blodgett · Sherry Miles and Celeste Yarnall A NEW WORLD PICTURES RELEASE

get any screenings in the burgeoning women's film festivals of the time? How were they received?

A. The only festival I know of was the 1973 Toronto Women's Film Festival where **Terminal Island** received a polite response.

Q. It's not only your representations of women that are progressive, but also your films provide a range of representations that are humanised and non-stereotypical. In **Group Marriage** there's a gay couple who actually get married! In **The Velvet Vampire** the central character/vampire is a woman; in **Student Nurses** we see Chicano activists (justifiably) shooting policemen. Such images are still so unusual in cinema and in the context of the '70s were almost unprecedented, so how did your audiences react? Were they shocked? Did they protest? Did they applaud?

A. They did all those things. Of course, I can only tell you about the audiences with whom I watched them. I never got the opportunity to see **The Working Girls** with one. But audiences reacted very favourably to **The Student Nurses, Group Marriage,** and **Terminal Island,** laughing in the right places and staying silent in the right ones too. **The Velvet Vampire** was another matter. At every screening I attended, a vocal minority disliked the parts of it that were humorous and lacked the solemnity of a traditional vampire tale. To my surprise, it was a very polarizing film, while the other films, with far more radical content, were not.

Q. Given the recent reassessment of exploitation cinema and its potentially challenging role within popular culture (e.g. the discussions that were had at Feminale) do you feel that, after all, exploitation was a productive site for you to work from, or do you regret not being in the position to make art-house films or even more mainstream commercial films?

A. Yes, to both questions. Making exploitation films gave me the freedom to work in many genres and experiment with different styles of lighting, composition, and camera movement. It was a great training ground. But I deeply regret that I never got a chance to make art-house or mainstream commercial films.

Q. All films to a certain extent are "of their time", but your films convey a really strong sense of the "texture" of the time, a real feel for the revolutionary spirit of the day. How and why do you think this is? Is it simply that you used real locations, or is something else going on?

A. I have always liked the texture that is added to a film by putting the actors on the streets or elsewhere among crowds of real people going about their ordinary business. You can see it in all my films, not only **The Student Nurses, Group Marriage,** and **The Working Girls,** but even **Terminal Island** and **The Velvet Vampire.** I think it contributes to the perception that a film is rooted in its time. But I suppose what makes these films appear timely is that different forms of social change are explored in their narratives. That, I think, is the source of what you describe as giving them a feel for the revolutionary spirit of the day.

NOTES

1. See *Women And The Cinema: A Critical Anthology* edited by Karyn Kay and Gerald Peary. EP Dutton, New York 1977.

2. For further discussion see "Exploitation Films And Feminism" by Pam Cook in *Screen* #2, 1976. p122–127. See also *Script Girls: Women Screenwriters In Hollywood* by Lizzie Francke, British Film Institute, London 1994, p91–97.

3. See "Stephanie Rothman: R-Rated Feminist" by Danny Peary in *Women And The Cinema: A Critical Anthology.* Op cit.

4. The Feminale Conference "Girls Gangs Guns", dedicated to a discussion of female representation on exploitation and underground cinema, was held in Cologne in 1999 and

featured Stephanie Rothman as one of the guest speakers.

5. See *girlsgangsguns: Zwischen Exploitation-Kino Und Underground*, Carla Despineux, Verena Mund (Hrsg.) Schuren, Germany: 2000.

CHAPTER ELEVEN

FANG GANGS: BRIDES OF DRACULA

Looking for girl gangs in the horror genre is a bit like looking for a needle in a haystack. In fact, with one or two exceptions, horror's representations of women are unremittingly negative, based as they are in the misogynist mythology of the female as either virgin or whore.[1] Vampire cinema from the silent period onward is a case in point. In the *Dracula* films, for example, the female characters are traditionally portrayed as either subservient or seductive. The women are good compliant wives and fiancées, who transmute into evil predatory accomplices once they have succumbed to Dracula's unusual charms.

Even though the Count is polymorphously perverse, and is happy to suck the neck of either gender, it is his ability to overwhelm his female prey with sexual power that is increasingly the main point of the films. The sexual suggestiveness of Dracula's oral activities and its potential to win audiences is crystallised by Bela Lugosi in his role as the Count in Universal's acclaimed 1931 movie **Dracula**, in which Lugosi portrays Dracula as a sophisticated and suavely erotic eastern European aristocrat. The character of the Count as a masterly sexual predator is further developed by Christopher Lee in the 1958 Hammer film of the same name. Because of Hammer's notoriously graphic exploitation of the relationship between sex and power in the *Dracula* films, vampire cinema as a whole began to be recognised as the stage on which the psycho-sexual drama between male and female is played out.[2]

Throughout the next two decades, Hammer was able to use the horror genre as the Trojan horse by which soft-core images could be smuggled into mainstream cinemas. The iconography of horror, Hammer style, included images of skimpily clad females and suggestions of sadistic sex and nocturnal perversions. The '70s, in particular, saw the emergence of a rake of Hammer movies featuring female vampires. These films developed the soft-core elements of the genre, while only very loosely referring to the Dracula legend. In films like **The Vampire Lovers** (1970) and **Lust For A Vampire** (1971), soft-core titillation begins to rub shoulders with lesbian sado-masochism. The potential of the female vampire was also being explored in a number of arthouse films in Europe during the same period.[3]

Andrea Weiss, in her book *Vampires And Violets*, argues that the female vampire, especially in a film like **The Vampire Lovers**, provides a not altogether negative image of the female sexual outlaw, by opening up a lesbian sub-text.[4] This is a generous interpretation of Hammer's soft-core cycle, requiring rather a big suspension of disbelief. Women who transgress in the horror (more than any other genre) generally suffer rather unpleasant consequences. In the *Dracula* films, for example, the female vampire is always the first to get a stake through her heart, whereas Dracula usually manages to escape this fate, and even when he *is* dispatched by Van Helsing, he's always resurrected in the next film.

Furthermore, even the coolest, most calculating of the female vampires is unable to compete with Dracula's power. She suffers more, usually because her desire for blood conflicts with her sensitive nature, and this sentimentality inevitably affects her overall performance as a vampire. It's not unusual, therefore, to see representations of the female vampire as either torn, schizophrenic almost – as is the case with the Countess Marya Zaleska in **Dracula's Daughter** (1936) – or alternatively as inadequate and in need of male supervision, as is the case with Carmilla in **The Vampire Lovers**.[5] Even a hardline sadist like the Countess Elizabeth Bathory[6] is ultimately shown to be a figure who needs company, lacking the self-sufficiency of a Dracula. In the film **Daughters Of Darkness** (Harry Kumel, 1971) we see the Countess preying on others more out of emotional neediness than blood lust.[7]

In horror generally, it is the female characters that are the primary victims. They are victims either of hunting and haunting (the woman in peril of the slasher films) or of their own emotional intensity (the raging female monster of the rape/revenge genre). It is, in fact, the lack of detachment that distinguishes the female vampire from her male counterpart. In the *Dracula* films, the Count is completely self-controlled and in charge. He is the master. The extent of Count Dracula's mastery is reflected in his power over the female vampires that he lives with. In the classic *Dracula* films, the female vampire's role is to serve and service her master.

The films that are based on Bram Stoker's gothic novel often feature a trio of female vampires who make an appearance at certain crucial moments. The irony is that while the trio may seem to be a potent girl gang because they appear together and function collectively, suggesting solidarity and power, they are in fact the opposite, existing solely and simply for Dracula's pleasure. They are utterly controlled, and their desires for flesh and blood are thwarted at every turn by their master. They are abjectly subservient and, in this respect, not like a gang at all, but more like a harem. These women are Dracula's brides.

It's worth looking at the literary source of this seductive trio. In chapter 3 of *Dracula*, entitled "Jonathan Harker's Journal (continued)" they make their first appearance. There follows a vivid description of them as sirens:

"They came close to me and looked at me for some time, and then whispered together. Two were dark and had high aquiline noses like the count, and great dark piercing eyes, that seemed to be almost red when contrasted with the pale yellow moon. The other was fair as fair as can be with great wavy masses of golden hair and eyes like pale sapphires... All three had brilliant white teeth, that shone like pearls against the ruby of their voluptuous lips... I felt in my heart a wicked burning desire that they would kiss me with those red lips... They whispered together and then they all three laughed – such a

silvery musical laugh, but as hard as though the sound never could have come through the softness of human lips."

This is followed by a detailed description of their seduction of Jonathan Harker, up to the point where Dracula arrives and forbids them to proceed further. The description of the Count's rage is equally vivid:

"As my eyes opened involuntarily I saw his strong hand grasp the slender neck of the fair woman and with a giant's power draw it back, the blue eyes transformed with fury, the white teeth champing with rage and the fair cheeks blazing red with passion. But the Count! Never did I imagine such wrath and fury, even in the demons of the pit. His eyes were positively blazing. The red light in them was lurid as if the flames of hell-fire blazed behind them... With a fierce sweep of his arm, he hurled the woman from him, and then motioned to the others, as though he were beating them back; it was the same imperious gesture that I had seen used to the wolves."

Although no film version can capture the gothic intensity of the novel, the number of variations on the female vampire theme is fascinating. The three best adaptations of Stoker's original novel – **Dracula** (Tod Browning 1931), **Dracula** (Terence Fisher 1958), and **Bram Stoker's Dracula** (Francis Ford Coppola 1992) – all feature the brides in one form or another. Like the book, the films contrast the feminine wiles of the female vampires with the masculine attributes of the lord and master. In terms of Stoker's narrative all the female characters (both the living and the undead) prove to be unreliable, mainly because they are unable to resist their desire and control their sexual drives. Perfectly respectable women, once they have succumbed to passion, turn into predatory monsters that must be taken in hand for their own safety and the protection of others.

DRACULA 1931

Universal Studio's version of **Dracula** references Bram Stoker's novel only indirectly. The film is in fact based on a stage play by Hamilton Deane and John L Baldeston. This translates into a rather static movie, geared more around the possibilities of the stage than the cinema. For instance the final action, driving a stake through Dracula's heart, is not shown. Yet apart from this anti-climax, the film is a celebrated one, with Lugosi as an unforgettable Dracula who almost seems to float around the stunning sets, which include a great baronial hall with a large sweeping staircase. The first reel, in particular, is notable for its atmosphere; Dracula's castle and the Transylvanian countryside are stunning backdrops, and the gloomy interiors, especially the crypt are eerily memorable.

The female vampires make one brief appearance near the beginning of the film. In this version, Jonathan Harker, recently arrived at Dracula's castle, is drinking wine and becoming drowsy. Enter three wraith-like female vampires who circle Harker and prepare to take him. Just as they are descending towards him, Dracula appears and orders them off with a gesture

and a flash of the eyes. It is obvious that he wants Harker for himself. In spite of its brevity, this scene is faithful in spirit to the book. The film's black and white expressionist imagery gives the scene a dreamlike quality. No word is spoken. The vampires, with ghostly faces and white flowing dresses arrive suddenly and depart just as suddenly, baring their fangs and hissing.

DRACULA 1958

In Hammer's first **Dracula** film the female vampire trio is pared down to one. Whilst taking some other liberties with the story-line, this **Dracula** is much more detailed than Universal's 1931 film. Apart from the impact of Christopher Lee in developing the sexual magnetism of the character, the film is also memorable for its lurid use of colour and its wonderful gothic sets. In this version Jonathan Harker, working for vampire hunter Van Helsing, travels to Transylvania with a view to destroying Dracula. Shortly after his arrival, Harker encounters a beautiful and alluring women in white who pleads with him to rescue her from the castle. Later that night she returns but this time makes a bee-line for his neck. With bared fangs and heaving bodice she is about to take her prey, when Dracula appears with red-eyes and a blood-smeared mouth and goes for Harker himself. Although Harker is bitten, he later manages to drive a stake through the thwarted she-vampire's heart before he himself turns into a vampire. Dracula survives Harker's foray into the crypt, but his "wife" has shrunk to an old crone. He thus sets off to England to replace her with Harker's fiancée, an act motivated by both lust and revenge.

Although **Dracula** has a shortage of female vampires, a number of the Hammer follow-ups amply compensate for this lack. **The Brides Of Dracula** (1960), generally regarded as the best of the many sequels, boasts a bevy of female victims procured from the local girls' school, and fresh nubile prey is also a feature in **Lust For A Vampire** (1971) where we find the vampiress Carmilla installed as a pupil at a Transylvanian finishing school. In **Taste The Blood Of Dracula** (1970), Dracula sets out to destroy the families of three townsmen as an act of revenge, and concentrates on the young women of the families, who are an enthusiastic bunch. As David J. Hogan observes:

DRACULA (1958)

THE SATANIC RITES OF DRACULA

"His [Dracula's] converts are immediately enthralled by him; Alice even sleeps during the day atop Dracula's cold crypt. No pimp ever had such total control of his stable. One vampiress murders her father by driving a stake through his heart, and Alice beats her own father to death with a shovel."[8]

We return to the theme of the out of control female vampire in **The Satanic Rites Of Dracula**. (1973) In an early scene a nobleman strays into a cellar, where a group of hissing and snarling vampiresses are chained to the walls. Showing their fangs and cleavage in a thoroughly wanton way, while begging the man to release them, they illustrate the theory that young women who are sexually active or provocative need to be kept on a tight leash. They represent a threat to all men, and only Dracula is capable of controlling them.

BRAM STOKER'S DRACULA (1992)

Francis Ford Coppola's film **Bram Stoker's Dracula** is, as the title suggests, the most faithful to the novel. It follows the critique of Victorian morality that is present in the Hammer productions, but takes it to its logical conclusion. Blood lust symbolises sexual desire in a repressive society, and female desire,

BRAM STOKER'S DRACULA

in line with the double standards of the day, in this context becomes a pathology – literally, a disease of the blood. Just as in the novel, Jonathan (Keanu Reeves) on the first night at Dracula's castle, is set upon by three rampant female vampires, who use their feminine allures to seduce him, but are repelled at the last minute by Dracula himself. The representation of Dracula's brides in this film is much more elaborately detailed. They appear as wraiths in a swirling mist and set upon Jonathan like three devilish temptresses, their sexuality enhanced by wanton displays of their bare breasts. They never speak, which not only endows them with an animal quality, but also renders them strangely powerless. Their seductive charms can only be resisted by Dracula himself, who controls them and uses them as a tool to his own ends. The relationship is a paternalistic one. When denying them the body of Jonathan, he pacifies them with a freshly caught baby, which they tear apart with relish.

When the Count journeys to England, Jonathan is left in the clutches of the three sirens. They use him for their own diabolical ends and he is unable to resist them. "Dracula has left me with these women... These devils of the pit, they drain my blood to keep me weak... so I cannot escape." In the denouement of the film, Van Helsing defends Jonathan's fiancée from their bloody advances. Thwarted, this time by Van Helsing, who draws a protective circle around himself and Mina to keep the devils at bay, they vent their fury and blood lust on the only living creature in the vicinity, Van Helsing's horse. He finally returns and dispatches them for good, cutting off their heads and tossing them in them in the river.

In spite of the presence of numerous female vampires in the *Dracula* films, the cinematic representation of predatory women is invariably a negative one. Even when they hunt in packs as the three brides do, there is a feeling that rather than being a freewheeling girl gang, they are under the control of a powerful force. Victorian vampire literature reveals a belief in the vulnerability of young girls to the temptations of the flesh, and vampire cinema merely gives this notion a contemporary spin. A young woman, once bitten, will become shamelessly promiscuous, a hussy, a strumpet, and a threat to decent society. Patriarchal control in the form of fathers and husbands can reign in the female's impulse to transgress. But when all else fails, death is the only solution. It seems that even within the society of the undead, the usual rules apply.

NOTES

1. Two women-directed films that reverse the trend are **The Slumber Party Massacre** (Amy Jones, USA 1982 [see Chapter 12]) and **Trial Run** (Melanie Read, NZ 1984).

2. See *Dark Romance: Sex And Death In The Horror Film*, David J Hogan. Equation, Jefferson NC: 1986, p146. "If Lugosi's concept of the character was frankly erotic, Lee's was blatantly sexual. His Dracula bristles with sexual energy and magnetism."

3. See the vampire films of French director Jean Rollin throughout the late '60s and early '70s, including: **The Nude Vampire** (1969); **The Vampire's Thrill** (1970); **Requiem For A Vampire** (1972); and **Lips Of Blood** (1976). Rollin rarely depicted gangs of girl vampires, preferring his predators to operate in pairs, as in Hammer's **Twins Of Evil** (1971).

4. In Chapter 4, *Vampires And Violets: Lesbians In The Cinema*, Andrea Weiss. Jonathan Cape, London: 1992.

5. See discussion of Carmilla in "Female Vampires: Girl Power From The Crypt" by Bev Zalcock in *Necronomicon Book 2*, ed. Andy Black. Creation Books, London: 1998.

6. Elizabeth (Erzsébet) Bathory was the Hungarian Countess who slaughtered hundreds of virgins and bathed in their blood in the belief it would give her eternal youth. Given the nature of these atrocities, she has become a natural figure on which to hang a vampiric legend. Bathory's full story is told in *The Bloody Countess* by Valentine Penrose and Alexander Trocchi (Creation Books, 1995).

7. Ibid. p.178.

8. *Dark Romance: Sex And Death In The Horror Film*, op cit. p.150.

CHAPTER TWELVE

BLOOD SISTERS

INTRODUCTION

In the more radical girl-gang films, sisterhood and female solidarity is a guiding principle. What is less common in such movies is the existence of *real* sisters. In fact films about female siblings are more likely to be concerned with dysfunctionality than solidarity. Contemporary examples of this tendency include films like **Sweetie** (Jane Campion, 1989) and **Sister My Sister** (Nancy Meckler, 1994), both of which deal with disturbing displays of pathological behaviour between sisters. And there are also numerous examples of relationships between sisters leading to no good in the Hollywood classics of the '30s and '40s, in films like **The Dark Mirror** (Robert Siodmak, 1946) and **A Stolen Life** (Curtis Bernhardt, 1946) where rivalry between sisters, often twin sisters, tends to end in tears. The image of twin sisters is also a familiar motif in horror films, such as Brian de Palma's **Sisters** (1972), and especially in the vampire films of cult French director Jean Rollin, and not forgetting Hammer's **Twins Of Evil** (John Hough, 1971).

This chapter will explore two fascinating girl-gang movies, where real sisters feature. One is an exploitation classic from the early '80s, **The Slumber Party Massacre** ('82), and the other, a recent film that already has a cult following, **The Virgin Suicides** (1999). Both films feature a woman director, and both films, in very different ways, explore the dark side of suburbia. **The Slumber Party Massacre**, directed by Amy Jones, was made for New World Pictures to cash in on the success of the suburban horror film, like **Halloween** and **Friday The 13th**. **The Virgin Suicides**, directed by Sofia Coppola, was released the same year as **American Beauty**, and shares its pervasive obsession with suburban repression and sexual perversity. Adolescent angst and suburban suicide was *the* preoccupation of the American indies during the '90s, with director Todd Solondz's **Welcome To The Dollhouse** ('95) and **Happiness** ('99) leading the way. So that while in the '80s it was "slasher" films that spoke of the fear and loathing at the heart of the American dream, by the next decade, the films that depicted something rotten to the core of American apple pie, were more likely to be the independents.

As well as sharing a preoccupation with the dark heart of suburbia, the two films discussed here also have sisterhood in common. Yet they are diametrically opposed in mood. Although **The Slumber Party Massacre** is a gore-fest of a film, it ultimately celebrates the enduring qualities of the girl-gang, where solidarity equals survival. **The Virgin Suicides** is the opposite. Here, the sisterhood cannot sustain itself, but instead is shown to contain the seeds of its own destruction. In **The Virgin Suicides**, the poison of suburbia has not simply invaded the family home, but has seeped into the collective sibling soul. As such **The Slumber Party Massacre** is a celebration, whereas **The Virgin Suicides** is an elegy.

"THE SLUMBER PARTY MASSACRE": A GIRL GANG SLASHER FILM

In 1982 Roger Corman's New World organisation cashed in on the success of the recent slew of the psycho-on-the-loose horror movies with **The Slumber Party Massacre**. Directed by Amy Jones, this film occupies a unique place in film history, for being the only feminist inspired slasher film to be made. But the film is not only of interest for its generic originality, it is also yet another illustration of how Corman's New World provided the opportunity for aspiring women film directors to make low budget exploitation pictures as a way of getting into feature film-making.

Amy Jones wanted to make the switch from editing to directing and approached Corman for advice. He let her shoot the first seven pages of a script he owned, but had never made. It was the script for a horror film written by Rita Mae Brown, writer of *Rubyfruit Jungle* fame. With a crew of four people, Jones shot the opening of the film and delivered it to Corman. When he saw it and realised how little it cost he said: "You have a future in the film business!" So Amy Jones made **The Slumber Party Massacre**. She explains that when she began the project she knew very little about horror: "When I read the script on Roger's shelf, I had stupidly never seen **Halloween** or **Friday The 13th**, so I thought it was so original. In fact it was just a rip-off of **Halloween** and **Friday The 13th** and as soon as he said 'direct it', of course I went and looked at them and discovered the problem. But I think **The Slumber Party Massacre** has a uniquely feminine point of view and it has, oddly enough, its following".[1]

Although working for Corman on low-budget movies had its limitations, Amy Jones like Stephanie Rothman before her, acknowledges the advantages of working for New World: "He [Roger] has hired women directors for years and years. When I first came to Los Angeles I had worked for Scorsese on the crew of **Taxi Driver** in New York, just as his assistant, a gofer. It was my first job; and then I came out to Los Angeles and worked with Joe Dante on **Hollywood Boulevard**, for Roger Corman. And one of the first things I noticed was that almost half the crew were women. Not just the directors, but the crew. He likes working with women."[2]

Amy Jones also discovered, like Stephanie Rothman, how much importance Roger Corman placed on female nudity in his films. As the producer of her second feature, **Love Letters** (1986), Corman required the leading character to be naked as often as possible; "She doesn't have to be in bed Amy, but please make sure she takes her clothes off a lot!" Jones was, however, aware that working in exploitation did not preclude making a film you could be proud of: "Exploitation is not a bad word to me. I mean I came out of there and almost all of the big male directors came out of exploitation films. Martin Scorsese, Jonathan Demme, Francis Ford Coppola, de Palma, all these people made films for Roger Corman. Films you may have seen, or you may not have seen. They were biker movies, Women in Prison movies, they were nurse movies... Jonathon Demme made six of them [laughs]. I'm very happy that I got away with only doing one. I quite like **The Slumber Party Massacre**. I never would have chosen to make **The Slumber Party Massacre**, but I find it a very amusing film and I think it's worth looking at".[3]

It is the unusual reworking of the female-in-peril role that makes **The Slumber Party Massacre** so interesting. By playing with the expectations of the classic horror film, feminist writer, Rita Mae Brown and feminist director, Amy Jones between them are able to construct a female point of view. Furthermore, the comic manipulation of the codes of the slasher movie anticipates the deeply ironic horror films of the '90s which started with **Scream**.

"THE GUY HAD A DRILL BUT I MADE THE GIRLS CUT IT OFF!"

The fact that Jones has confessed to an interest in inverting traditional Hollywood genres by placing women in roles normally associated with male protagonists, is born out in **The Slumber Party Massacre**. She places her girl gang at the centre of the narrative and displaces the boys to the margins. The central group is introduced to the audience as active subjects; we first see them together playing basketball. Trish, Diane, Jackie and Kim are a close-knit group of school friends, although their solidarity is somewhat under threat now that they are beginning to get interested in boys. Diane in fact slips away from the slumber party to meet her boyfriend and this not only disrupts the status quo, but proves to be fatal. The solidarity that the school basketball sequence has promised is never really fulfilled. This is a girl-gang ready to disintegrate.

There is another factor that contributes to the unease of the evening and things not being right between the girls; Trish, who is throwing the party at her absent parents' house, wants to include Valerie her new next door neighbour. Valerie is unpopular with her classmates because she's so attractive. She's also, as we've already noted, rather too good at basketball. The gang members don't want Trish to invite Valerie and even though she does against their wishes, Valerie declines, because she has overheard them talking about her. Valerie is anyway responsible for her younger sister, who she's babysitting for the evening, and even though Courtney is a hormonal adolescent and a bit of a brat, the sisters generally get on well together and ultimately support one another.

In the end the blood sisters show much more solidarity other than the gang "sisters" do. As such, the blood sisters survive the massacre, whereas the gang is hacked apart. This comparison between real sisterhood and a sisterhood that is imploding, because it has lost its sense of solidarity, is in a sense the moral of the story. It's interesting too that not one of the male characters lives. So if the girls are being punished for lapses in sisterly feelings, the boys are being punished because they're male. Amy Jones says that the high male body count is no coincidence. She also acknowledges that the men die a much gorier, more violent death than the women.

It is generally acknowledged that the underlying thematic of the classic slasher film resides in the close relationship between sex and death. The crux of the action almost always involves the stalking and murder of the female characters, because, in psycho-analytic terms, it is they who pose the threat of castration that underpins the male gaze.[4] In **The Slumber Party Massacre** the castration anxiety at the heart of the slasher film, is adapted to accord with a female point of view. As Amy Jones has observed: "I think the fears are basically female fears of a man outside in the night, and actually, the primal fear involved is the fear of losing your virginity. I hate to put it this way but it's about a man with a drill who comes and gets these girls. Rita Mae Brown wrote it obviously, and I think it's a little bit about 'oh my god, he's going to get me with that big thing!'".[5]

COMIC MOMENTS IN "THE SLUMBER PARTY MASSACRE"

Laughter is not an uncommon response to a scary film but it normally derives from the audience's reaction to terror. There is a qualitative difference between this anxious laughter and the laughter that comes from seeing something funny or hearing something witty. It's generally acknowledged that Wes Craven's **Scream** (1998) blurred this line between the fearful and the funny, by deliberately playing on the audience's very sophisticated knowledge of the codes of the horror film. There are also some extremely funny moments in **The Slumber Party Massacre**. Some are created by the reversal of normal gender codes in the film and by some imaginative play with the iconography of horror. These too depend upon a knowing audience. It could be argued that in this sense **The Slumber Party Massacre** is a precursor of **Scream**.

The film's first comic reversal occurs with the first death. The telephone repair-man is a woman, who brushes off the nerdish chat-up lines from the two boys, Jeff and Neil. Having dispensed with their adolescent sexism, she then falls victim to the homicidal maniac, who murders her in the van and steals her power tools. At other points of the movie the boys get beaten up by the girls. Diane wrestles her boyfriend to the floor on one occasion. Jeff is similarly roughed-up for playing a stupid practical joke. The boys are also more spooked than the girls once the massacre begins; Jackie, who admits to an insatiable hunger, calmly tears off a slice of pizza from the box resting on the body of the dead delivery boy.

Next door Valerie and her kid sister, Courtney, can hear weird noises coming from the party. Bored with gazing at the centrefold pin-up in *Playgirl*, Courtney is restless; "I bet they're having a blast over there," she complains. Later she chats on the phone to a friend about french-kissing; "It was all slimy and everything... I just wanted to die!" Finally, realising something is wrong the sisters go next door to join Trish, who's the only one of the gang left alive. In an extremely grizzly denouement the three remaining girls hack at the psychopath with a variety of implements. There's blood everywhere. Then comes the film's defining castrating moment; first they cut off his hand, then they cut off the end of his power drill. One of the girls holds a dagger aloft; the psycho falls on to it and dies.

THE SLUMBER PARTY MASSACRE

THE LOWS AND THE HIGHS

The Slumber Party Massacre is an impressive first feature for Amy Jones. It's a tightly structured film with some memorable visuals and some great dialogue. In spite of being a slasher, Jones does not objectify her female characters, except for the school shower scene, which she clearly feels regretful about: "That particular scene is shot from a very male point of view. There's no reason for it except staring at those girls' bodies in the shower and I find it offensive."[6]

This is one of the problems of working in exploitation cinema that Stephanie Rothman also encountered. Nudity was an absolute requirement. Amy Jones confesses to having a much bigger problem with the nudity in the film than with the violence. She talks about one of the bloodiest murders as a scene she's especially proud of. This is a beautifully constructed sequence, which involves cross-cutting between Valerie inside watching a horror movie on TV and one of the boys being stabbed outside. For the film on television, she uses a sequence from **Hollywood Boulevard** (1977) that she had cut for

Joe Dante. It is perhaps **The Slumber Party Massacre**'s eeriest and most fascinating moment.

All in all, the film has a pace and humour that continues to appeal to the video rental crowd[7]. Its feminist credentials do not compromise the horror but give a unique spin to a genre that is almost synonymous with a male point of view and it's great to have a different story. Although the gang has been massacred, we are left at the end of the film with a new and tougher gang. Trish has survived precisely because she's held out the hand of friendship to Valerie. In return Valerie, with the help of her sister Courtney, saves Trish. This is a leaner gang, but they've been through the bloodiest initiation imaginable, and surely nothing now can stand in their way.

"THE VIRGIN SUICIDES": ELEGY TO THE GIRL GANG

WHY? WHY? WHY?

At the opening of **The Virgin Suicides**, Cecilia, the youngest of the five Lisbon sisters, who has attempted suicide by slitting her wrists, is confronted in the hospital by a bemused middle-aged male doctor, who remarks that she's not old enough to know how bad life can get. Cecilia's reply resonates through the film: "Obviously Doctor, you've never been a thirteen year old girl!".

Her reply is the clue to solving the movie's perceived mystery. Cultural theorists have observed that meaning tends to reside at the borders of the artwork and in this respect what happens at the beginning and ending of a film is crucial. Cecilia's suicide attempt and her explanation for it at the opening of **The Virgin Suicides** is the key to understanding it, presented as it is in a pre-title sequence, with all the portentousness of the prologue of a tragedy. Yet the real enigma of this film is not why the sisters kill themselves, but why so many critics don't get it.

For example, in spite of the film's obvious debt to magic realism, its achingly lyrical visuals and its dream-like pace, a number of critics have approached the film as though it were posing a sociological question; namely why five beautiful teenage girls should commit suicide. In realist terms there is no logical answer to this question, so the suicides are treated as an enigma. Another critical approach has been to read the film as a fairy tale, where the wicked witch locks her daughters in the tower, and they waste away, because the knights turn up too late. Although this is a more convincing interpretation, in my view both these approaches miss the point.

The Virgin Suicides is neither realism nor romance; it is a parable. As such the ostensible narrative points to a set of meanings that, for reasons of ideology, are generally concealed. The function of the parable is to shift people's habitual perceptions and so encourage them to look behind the veil that conceals the truth at the heart of purdah. **The Virgin Suicides** is structured like an investigative narrative – the story is told from a male point-of-view, using the flashback device – that appears to be dedicated to piecing together the mystery of the Lisbon girls. But throughout the film there are points when the identification with the boys' point of view is ruptured. Such moments generally occur when the girls, who are typically represented as objects of the male gaze, actually speak and as a result, are able to be perceived as "active" subjects. It is this perception that brings into focus the other story, the *girls'* story. The heroine of their story is also the heroine of the film. This is Lux, who provides the motor for the narrative development and the film's visual fascination. Of all the sisters, she's the most active, and as such, the most transgressive.

In terms of the film's structure, the boys are decentred – outside looking in – only seeing the girls from a distance and then, covertly. They gaze, as it were, through a glass darkly and are doomed never to understand what they see, being the victims, as much as the girls are, of a social ordering that precludes the possibility of gender mutuality. The boys, with an innate sense of their limitations, struggle to understand the "other" of sexual difference. But try as they may, the girls seem strange and exotic, distant and difficult. As noted above, the film's narrative point of view invites the spectator to identify with this perception and to view the girls' as unknowable objects whose behaviour is incoherent. Only by seeing through the film's structures of identification is it possible to reach an understanding of the girls' position and arrive at the perspective from which their actions make perfect sense. From time to time the film makes us aware that the boys' point-of view is not reliable; they even realise this themselves: "We knew that they knew everything about us and that we couldn't fathom them at all."

It is this realisation that is central to understanding the film. The boys' voyeurism reveals a truth that can be shown but is rarely spoken. It is what attracts and excludes them from the world of the teenage girls. The sexual difference that defines and divides them, leads to the obsession that will eventually blight their lives. Like the conspiracy of laughter between the women, at the end of the film **A Question Of Silence** (see Chapter 5) the collective deaths in **The Virgin Suicides** serve both to mystify and defy the laws of the state, the church and the family. The girls' suicides speak much louder than the few banal lines they're given, in a film that is no less repressed than the world it depicts. It is no surprise, therefore, that the sisters literally retreat into the wild zone of female reality, which in their case is the interior world of the bedroom, where they construct a fantasy world to escape into.[8] By glimpsing this exclusively female world (Lux's bedroom provides the perfect visualisation of it) **The Virgin Suicides,** like **A Question Of Silence** shows us the subversive potential of female conspiracy and the price it exacts.

THE BOYS WATCH THE GIRLS WHO WATCH THE BOYS

From the point of view of patriarchy (the law of the father) the female is traditionally construed as mysterious and enigmatic as a dark continent that must be conquered and controlled. Cecilia's first, and almost only, utterance makes the film's agenda very clear. It's about growing up a girl in a society whose values and aspirations repress and thwart the needs and development of its female subjects. The unquestioned difference in the status of the boys and the girls and the fact that they inhabit different universes is shown through the contrasting fate of the two groups. While the boys are free to

THE VIRGIN SUICIDES

roam, the girls retreat to the sanctuary of their bedroom. Their confinement is construed as a safe place but it is also a prison. The girls' bedrooms are the site of fascination for the boys, who peer through spy-glasses at them and it is the place, where like The Lady of Shallot in Tennyson's poem, the girls live a vicarious life through the looking glass of fantasy and falsity.

BACKGROUND

Dealing as it does with girls growing up, **The Virgin Suicides** has been compared to **Picnic At Hanging Rock** (Peter Weir, Australia 1975) and it is telling, that critics have had to cross three decades and a couple of continents to find another film that attempts to capture the spirit of female adolescence. Peter Weir's film was made in the '70s but set in the previous century; Sofia Coppola's film was made in the late '90s and set in the '70s. It seems that in order to express the enigmatic and ephemeral nature of budding female sexuality it is necessary to put some distance between the narrative and the time of its telling.

Like **Picnic At Hanging Rock**, **The Virgin Suicides** is a dreamy evocation of the life of teenage girls. The setting is a suburb, just outside Detroit; the style a feathery, fragile *mise-en-scène* that constructs a world of magic realism – all pinks and rainbows and scent bottles – using slow motion and time-lapse photography. The soundtrack too enhances the sense of the intensity of heightened teenage emotions with music by Air, as well as (memorably)

"Magic Man" by Heart (at the film's first sighting of the most beautiful boy, Trip Fontaine) and "Strange Magic" by ELO, when the slow-motion silver and blue balloons float down and the disco-lights twinkle at the Homecoming Dance.

Contrasting with the excited mood of teenage hyperventilation upstairs in the girls' bedrooms, downstairs is a zone of repression and hysteria, where the girls are overseen by their mad mother and dislocated father. Outside in the neatly ordered suburban street a line of diseased elms are being condemned, and soon the stench of decay from the polluted neighbourhood will spread throughout the whole area.

Against this backdrop, the Lisbon girls, Cecilia (13), Lux (14), Bonnie (15), Mary (16) and Therese (17) decorate their diaries with rainbows and sprinkle their drawings with silver glitter, listen to their records and cut out pictures from glossy catalogues. As the narrator observes "...they were happier with dreams than lives". In this gang of teenage sisters, the most desiring and desired is Lux, whose wanton flouting of the rules of curfew on the night of the Homecoming dance, staying out and losing her virginity to Trip Fontaine, proves the beginning of the end. In fact, the rot had already set in with the death of Cecilia, who impales herself on the garden railings during an excruciatingly embarrasing party presided over by her mother. After Lux's transgression, the sisters are taken out of school and confined to their rooms. Here they proceed to implode, the three older sisters retreating ever further into fantasy, while Lux entertains a stream of men to casual sex on the roof.

Confined to their rooms, the girls communicate with the boys by playing records over the phone and leaving carefully placed, artistic little notes for them to find. In this way, the sisters seduce the boys into believing they can liberate them, but it's only a tease. This is a girl gang that can no longer bare the burdens placed upon it, and as they have lived together, so they will die together, leaving behind a community that is in denial.

In many ways it's no surprise that post-feminist images of young women are negative ones. In contemporary terms, the heady days of the Women's Liberation Movement, are a distant memory, and today the prospects for the majority of (young) women in the world are no better now than they've ever been. Sofia Coppola's film is a reminder of why girls continue to be casualties.

NOTES

1. All quotations by Amy Jones taken from a filmed interview with Jane Root in conversation with Amy Jones and Penelope Spheeris. Presented by I.C.A. Video in conjunction with *Trilion*, I.C.A. London, 1986.

2. Quotation taken from I.C.A. Video. See above.

3. Quotation taken from I.C.A. Video.

4. See "Visual Pleasure And Narrative Cinema" by Laura Mulvey, in *Screen* #2, 1976, p122–127.

5. Quotation taken from I.C.A. Video. See above.

6. Quotation taken from I.C.A. Video.

7. The film actually led to two Corman-produced, women-directed sequels: **Slumber Party Massacre II** (Deborah Brock, 1987) and **Slumber Party Massacre 3** (Sally Mattison, 1990).

8. See "A Jury Of Their Peers" by Linda Williams in *Multiple Voices In Feminist Film Criticism,* Ed: Carson et al. Op cit. The idea of a "wild zone" of exclusively female knowledge and experience is referred to in the Introduction on p8 of *Renegade Sisters.*

CHAPTER THIRTEEN

CHARLIE'S ANGELS 2000

Charlie's Angels, released in the year 2000, is a fine example of the exploitation movie taking on the mantle of the blockbuster. Based on the '70s television series of the same name, it boasts an invincible girl gang, lots of high-octane action sequences and a minimal plot. The big-budget, however, gives the film an interesting spin, so that while in many respects the movie is faithful to the spirit of the '70s, it's also indebted to films like **The Matrix** and the Bond movies. In this respect its always on the edge of parody, having a jokey tongue-in cheek feel, and using cliché'd dialogue and comic-strip violence to please its audience. When it was released in the States it grossed $40m on the first weekend, proving that the public's insatiable appetite for '70s retro is far from satiated. In Britain it's also done well, but was unfortunately released the same time (January 2001) as **Crouching Tiger, Hidden Dragon**, which over-shadowed it – at least as far as getting the critical attention it deserved. In fact in most respects, especially in terms of its female protagonists, **Charlie's Angels** is a much better film – but that's another story!

THE ANGELS

The idea to make a feature film based on the series was Drew Barrymore's and she has a producer's credit as well as a starring role. Barrymore is no stranger to strong-girl roles and her appearance in the girl-gang western, **Bad Girls** (see Chapter 5) is particularly memorable. The first time director, McG directs with panache (he brings his experiences with television commercials and music videos to bear) making the film fast and fresh, characterised by pacey action sequences and a pumping soundtrack. The girl-gang is a stylish trio with Drew Barrymore as Dylan, Cameron Diaz as Natalie and Lucy Liu as Alex. Like the original "A" team Angels from the TV show, the girls are principally distinguished by physical characteristics and hair colour, a strategy adopted by the "girl-power" vocal groups of recent years, particularly the Spice Girls[1]. In the original show Sabrina (Kate Jackson) is brunette and brainy, with a tendency to tweeds and polo-neck sweaters; Jill (Farrah Fawcett-Majors) is the blonde, sexy one, with big hair and a great physique; and Kelly (Jaclyn Smith) has chestnut brown hair and (even though she is a less obvious sex bomb than Jill) was for many considered to be the real beauty of the show. Kelly has big hair as well and a tendency to wear jump-suits. Obviously, they're all gorgeous!

CHARLIE'S ANGELS (THE MOVIE)

The other reason for the girls' success is that they work together as a team, a rare quality in film and TV drama even today. Something else that made these gals different was the fact that they could all handle guns and complete dizzying karate moves without messing up their hair and makeup! And they always managed to escape. **Charlie's Angels** the film, takes its cue from these enduringly popular elements. In terms of distinguishing features, Alex (Lucy Liu) is the clever one – a rich, brainy techno-wizard and an oriental bomb-shell, with a lithe physique and straight black shiny hair. Natalie (Cameron Diaz) is the sexy blonde one, who at the beginning of the film is seen dancing in her underwear in a sequence of mutual joy (hers and ours!). And to complete the team, there's Dylan (Drew Barrymore) an endearing and curvaceous red-head, who having lived through the fog of a stoned adolescence, is sharp and laid-back all at the same time.

Like their prototypes, the girls are all sensational and work together in a smoothly co-ordinated way; their fight sequences are sheer choreography. They are all living undercover, passing as typically flaky young women, two of them with boyfriends neither one of whom has a clue that their girlfriend is part of an elite crime fighting team, backed by an anonymous millionaire. It was not unusual in the TV series for one or other of the Angels to get off with a hunky guy, but they'd always lost him by the next episode. In the film,

CHARLIE'S ANGELS (TV)

in a similar spirit the boyfriends are present but ultimately peripheral. Men are, in general, a source of trouble or betrayal and for our savvy sisters, the only man who really counts is Charlie, who is after all not really a man but a disembodied voice. It is the voice of Charlie (John Forsythe) that provides the nostalgic link between show and film and keeps alive the sense of an "homage", by the film, to the spirit of the '70s.

THE TELEVISION SHOW

The original *Charlie's Angels*, Kate, Farrah and Jaclyn, lasted from 1976–78. So popular was the series that in its very first year the girls had their photograph on the cover of *Time* magazine. The show was finally cancelled in 1981, having survived 109 episodes and a number of personnel changes. The earlier episodes, generally held to be the classics of the series, while relatively anodyne do borrow from exploitation cinema, and it is precisely the exploitation elements – even watered down – that give the show its frisson. Apart from slipping into bathing suits whenever possible, the girls frequently find their assignment to be somewhat risqué. For example in "Angels In Chains", an episode in the first season, they are undercover as inmates on a prison farm, which is not a million miles away from Roger Corman's New World WIP movies. There is a lesbian guard, a sadist warden and a corrupt and brutalised regime, where the prison staff are operating a prostitution racket and killing off uncooperative female inmates. Lacking the nudity and violence of Corman's WIP productions this episode is still fairly close to the bone by the standards of the networks of the day.

During their search for a missing girl, our heroines are subjected to the usual indignities of prison life including a shower scene and some heavy-duty manual work sweating in the fields under the hot sun in very skimpy outfits. When they jump free of the chain gang the Angels find themselves escaping across country chained together, jiving, driving and diving their way out of trouble; shades of **Black Mama, White Mama** (see Chapter 1).

Such spicy situations were not untypical of the early seasons of the series. Another episode entitled "Lady Killer" involves a dangerous assignment at a playboy-type club, in which Farrah gets a job as a waitress, dressed in – you guessed it – a bathing suit and kitten ears and tail. This was another episode that threw more than a passing glance to exploitation cinema. In fact there was always plenty of (semi-) nudity and violence in the show, but looking back on the action sequences, they appear really tame compared to the slick scenarios of the movie, which just goes to show that retro is all very well, but sometimes it's nice to have state of the art film and digital technology working to create sublimely exciting fight sequences. In respect of the effects, the big budget for **Charlie's Angels** really pays off.

THE SPECIAL EFFECTS

Some of the film's best moments are the fight sequences, with their **Matrix**-like virtual effects, their cool choreography, the slow motion, the fast cuts and the static tableaux which punctuate them, where the Angels strike their characteristic pose and draw breath for the next round of high kung-fu kicks and leaps. The film is full of adrenaline-charged stunts, including the mind-blowing opening sky-jack sequence, which is by way of introduction to the new trio, the knuckle-biting racing-car chase and head-on collision between Natalie and the thin man, and the all-singing all dancing scene at Red Star Systems, that mixes cross-dressing and bondage with bravura acrobatics.

While the special effects take your breath away, the photography and art direction are pure eye-candy. The set designs are wonderfully lavish with groovy '70s colours, blues and pinks, predominating throughout the interiors. The camp aspect of the '70s revival is here played to perfection and summed-up by the final scene, where on an exotic beach, the girls, clad only in bikinis and skimpy sarongs, sip rainbow-coloured cocktails and soak up the sun, their glistening brown limbs a pleasure to behold. Many of the scenes have that groovy '70s texture; particularly evocative is the race track sequence and the use of split screen and multiple screen image. It's not all glam though and there are some seriously hard-edged bondage sequences. Lucy Liu at Red Star, is kitted out in leather, high heels and whips, giving the film a more contemporary feel and bringing to mind the soft-core version of a Britney Spears music video. The girls also cross-dress as security guards, referencing the implicit female on female desire of the series. Desire is inevitably a strong element of the film, and in terms of the audience's desire for the characters, Cameron Diaz's erotic dance sequences have not gone unnoticed. Kelly Lynch as the scheming seductress is equally memorable.

The baddies are also very '70s. *Charlie's Angels* on television featured male characters who were either villains or fools. Business magnate, Roger Corwin, tech-head, Eric Knox and the "thin man" are classic "Angels" fare. There's also a dash of exploitation in there, with the presence of evil dominatrix, Vivien Wood (Kelly Lynch) who's cleverer than all the men put together – cue all those larger-than-life scheming boss-bitches that we love to hate, from the blaxploitation and the Bond movies.[2] There are also a few good men. There's Bosley, Charlie's intermediary, as well as a sprinkling of romantic male interest. Pete the barman falls for Natalie and there's an amusing sequence where we see her trying to talk to him on her mobile phone between bouts of kung-fu action, as she fights off an attacker.

COMIC ROLE REVERSAL

Throughout the film the role reversal elements that go with the Angels being a top fighting unit are played for laughs. When Dylan is supposed to be minding Knox, she gives him a panic button in case he needs her to defend him. When the bad men fail to deliver, Vivien, their leader remarks ironically: "Never send a man to do a woman's job!".

Alex, who is an electronics genius spends her spare time trying to cook a decent meal and failing miserably. The women expend a lot of their energy trying to reassure their men that things are OK. It's the opposite of the Hollywood norm; the guys seem very needy and the gals seem very independent. Of course, it's all totally tongue-in-cheek, but never fails to amuse and inspire. There are still so few films that celebrate women's talent, that when there's an image of a gang of talented women, working, thinking and fighting together as sisters, although it's played for laughs, it's still special. Part of the pleasure of this film is in the deliberately comic episodes, where the Angels dress up to defeat the opposition. From the sublime to the ridiculous, they are sexy belly-dancers one minute, a group of alpine maidens singing harmony, the next. There are plenty of belly laughs in the film, in the best tradition of the big budget action thriller. In this sense we are miles away from the TV series, but somehow the spirit of the original shines through. In the same way as the series was, **Charlie's Angels**, the film, manages to be extremely popular and yet still pack a political punch – the iron fist in the velvet glove, so to speak!

CONCLUSION

Julie Burchill writing about the original *Charlie's Angels*, attributes the vast popularity of the '70s show to its dual appeal. She argues that for boys, the sight of gorgeous women in bikinis was the hook, whereas, for girls it was the trio's glamour, power and solidarity in the face of adverse conditions that gave the show its edge. Speaking from personal experience, Burchill claims, that for adolescent girls, growing up at the time, *Charlie's Angels* provided strong role-models and a sense of self-image and style. Although the series was far from feminist it was better than everything else that was on offer[3]. Today, thirty years on, there's still a dearth of strong female representations in popular culture (the Pamela Anderson vehicle *VIP*, with its trio of fighting girls, is a pale shadow of the original *Angels*). In fact, these days you're more likely to find interesting images of young women in the Hollywood genre film than in the supposedly more serious indie/art-house production. Looking at the critically celebrated films directed by the likes of Todd Solondz or the Dogme group, its easy to uncover a strand of vicious misogyny concealed under their oh-so-cool veneer.[4] On the other hand, the less "artistic", more commercial Hollywood genre movie, while hardly radical, does not pretend to be anything other than it is; does not pretend, that is, to be deep and meaningful just because it's full of stereotypical damaged women and women-hating men.

At the start of this chapter, the critical phenomenon that is **Crouching Tiger, Hidden Dragon** was alluded to, and in the context of the discussion it is a case in point. This art-house kung-fu movie, with its special effects and its sub-titles has wowed the critics. But consider the female characters; they all hate each other and as such pose no real threat to the male power-base they exist within, because they're so distracted by jealousies and rivalries. By the end of the film of the three central female characters, the old woman (Jade Fox) has been killed, the young woman (Jen) has committed suicide and the middle-aged woman (Yu Shu Lien) is left alone in deep despair. In **Charlie's Angels**, on the other hand, the women not only *like* each other but work as a team and look out for one another; their kung-fu isn't bad either. As such **Charlie's Angels** is a genuine girl-gang movie, whereas **Crouching Tiger, Hidden Dragon** is an *anti*-girl gang film – no wonder it's won so many awards! In the BAFTA (British Academy of Film & Television) awards **Crouching Tiger, Hidden Dragon** was nominated by a panel of critics, for fourteen awards, but when it came to the public's choice, they nominated **Charlie's Angels** for the special "audience" award and **Crouching Tiger** wasn't even short-listed.

It seems that within the hybrid notion of "popular culture", "popular" is one thing, and "culture" is certainly another. Because **Charlie's Angels** the film is linked to a television series, which owes a substantial debt to exploitation cinema it has, in spite of its big-budget credentials and its fine production values been left out in the critical cold. Serious critics have no time for exploitation films[5] even though the best ones provide a range of female roles that are much more powerful than those that "respectable" films have on offer. The trouble is, they're just *too* popular!

NOTES

1. The original line up for The Spice Girls was Ginger Spice (Geri Halliwell) Posh Spice (Victoria Adams) Scary Spice (Mel B.) Sporty Spice (Mel C.) and Baby Spice (Emma Bunton), and each one of the "girls" was individualised in terms of hair – colour & style – and style of dress.

2. The scheming female boss (castrating bitch who was probably a dyke) was a popular stereotype in exploitation and big-budget films alike. See for example Col. Rosa Kleb in **From Russia With Love** (Terence Young 1963) and Katherine Wall in **Foxy Brown** (Jack Hill 1974).

3. See "Why I Fell In Love With Charlie's Angels" by Julie Burchill, in *The Guardian, Friday Review*, November 17th 2000.

4. There was a spate of independent features in the late '90s, including **Welcome To The Doll House** (Todd Solondz, '95) and the first two Dogme films, **Festen** (Thomas Vinterberg) and **The Idiots** (Lars von Trier) that were able to conceal a vicious misogyny beneath the veneer of social critique.

5. See ageing film critic Alexander Walker's craven diatribe against **Switchblade Sisters** in *The Evening Standard* 11th Feb. 1999. He writes: "Yet this month the British Board of Film Classification issues a new licence for a film that glamorises them [knives] and brazenly plays to the emerging trend of violence among teen and under-age girls. It is a public disgrace".

Note: *Where relevant information is available sources are fully referenced, however given the nature of various cuttings, archives and sources this has not always been possible.*

Acker, Alli: *Reel Women: Pioneers Of The Cinema 1896 To The Present*, B T Batsford, London, 1991.

Anger, Kenneth: *Hollywood Babylon*, Straight Arrow Books, New York, 1975.

Anger, Kenneth: *Hollywood Babylon II*, E P Dutton, New York, 1984.

Babuscio, Jack: "Camp And The Gay Sensibility" in Dyer Richard (ed): *Gays And Film*, London, 1984.

Barr, Charles (ed): *All Our Yesterdays: 90 Years Of British Cinema*, British Film Institute, London 1986.

Becker, Edith., Citron, Michelle., Lesage, Julia and Rich, Ruby B: "Lesbians And Film" in Steven, P (ed): *Jump Cut: Hollywood, Politics And Counter-Cinema*, Praeger, New York, 1985.

Bell-Metereau, Rebecca: *Hollywood Androgyny*, Columbia University Press, 1993.

Betrock, Alan: *The I Was A Teenaged Juvenile Delinquent, Rock'n'Roll, Horror, Beach Party Movie Book. A Complete Guide To The Teen Exploitation Film 1954–69*, Plexus, London, 1986.

Biskind, P: *Seeing Is Believing: How Hollywood Taught Us To Stop Worrying And Love The Fifties*, Pantheon, New York, 1983.

Black Film Bulletin, Great Britain, January, 1997.

Black, Andy (ed): *Necronomicon: Book One. The Journal Of Horror And Erotic Cinema*, Creation Books, London, 1996.

Boffin, Tessa and Fraser, Jean (eds): *Stolen Glances: Lesbians Take Photographs*, Pandora, London, 1991.

Bogle, Donald: *Blacks In American Film And Television*, Garland Press, New York, 1988.

Bonnr, Francis, et al, (eds): *Imagining Women: Cultural Representations And Gender*, Open University, Cambridge, 1992.

Brosnan, John: *The Primal Screen. A History Of Science fiction Film*, Orbit, London, 1991.

Brown, Geoff: *Launder And Gilliat*, British Film Institute, London, 1977.

Brunsdon, Charlotte (ed): *Films For Women*, British Film Institute, London 1986.

Burana, Lily and Due, Roxie Linnea. (eds): *Dagger: On Butch Women*, Cleis Press, San Francisco, 1994.

Carson, Ditmar and Welsch (eds): *Multiple Voices In Feminist Film Criticism*, University of Minnesota Press, Minneapolis.

Clover, Carol J: *Men, Women And Chainsaws: Gender In The Modern Horror Film*, British Film Institute, London, 1992.

Cohen, Steven and Hark, Ina Rae (eds): *Screening The Male: Exploring Masculinities In Hollywood Cinema*, Routledge, London, 1993.

Cook, Pam and Dodd, Phillip (eds): *The Sight And Sound Reader*, Scarlet Press, London, 1993.

Cook, Pam: " 'Exploitation' Films And Feminism" in *Screen*, 17:2, p112–127, 1976.

Cook, Pam: *The Cinema Book*, British Film Institute, London, 1982.

Core, Phillip: *Camp: The Lie That Tells The Truth*, Delilah Books, New York, 1984.

Craig, Patricia and Cadogan, Mary: *The Lady Investigates: Detectives And Spies In Fiction*, Oxford University Press, Oxford, 1986.

Creed, Barbara: *The Monstrous Feminine: Film, Feminism, Psychoanalysis*, Routledge, London, 1993.

Crowther, Bruce: *Captured On Film: The Prison Movie*, B T Batsford, London, 1989.

Dash, Julie: *Daughters Of The Dust*, The New Press, New York, 1992.

Debord, Guy: *Society Of The Spectacle*, Black and Red, London, 1970.

Deyan, Sudjic: *Cult Heroes: How To Be Famous For More Than Fifteen Minutes*, Andre Deutsch, London, 1989.

Diawara, Manthia (ed): *Black American Cinema*, American Film Institute, New York, 1993.

Dickens, Homer: *What A Drag: Men As Women And Women As Men In The Movies*, Quill, New York, 1984.

Donald, James(ed): *Fantasy And The Cinema*, British Film Institute, London, 1989.

Dowell, Pat et al: "Should We Go Along For The Ride?: A Critical Symposium On 'Thelma And Louise'" in *Cineaste*, 18:4, pp 28–36, 1991.

Dyer, Richard: *Now You See It: Studies On Lesbian And Gay Film*, Routledge, London, 1990.

Dyer, Richard: *The Matter Of Images: Essays On Representations*, Routledge, London, 1993.

Gaines, Jane and Herzog, Charlotte(eds): *Fabrications: Costume And The Female Body*, American Institute Film Reader, New York, 1990.

Garr, Gillian G: *She's A Rebel: The History Of Women In Rock'n'Roll*, Landford, London, 1993.

Gelder, Ken and Thornton, Sarah: *The Subculture Reader*, Routledge, London, 1977.

Gever, Martha et al(eds): *Queer Looks: Perspectives On Lesbian And Gay Film And Video*, Routledge, London, 1993.

Gledhill, Christine (ed): *Home Is Where The Heart Is: Studies In Melodrama And The Woman's Film*, British Film Institute, London, 1986.

Greig, Charlotte: *Will You Still Love Me Tomorrow: Girl Groups From The 50s On...*, Virago, London, 1989.

Hadleigh, Boze: *The Lavender Screen: The Gay And Lesbian Films: Their Stars, Makers, Characters And Critics*, Citadel Press, New York, 1993.

Hamer, Diane and Budge, Belinda (eds): *The Good, The Bad And The Gorgeous: Popular Culture's Romance With Lesbianism*, Pandora, London, 1994.

Hardy, Phil: *The Encyclopedia Of Science Fiction*, Octopus Books, London, 1984.

Hart, Lynda: *Fatal Women: Lesbian Sexuality And The Mark Of Aggression*, Routledge, London, 1994.

Haskell, Molly: *From Reverence To Rape: The Treatment Of Women In The Movies*, Holt, Rhinehart and Winston Inc, New York, 1973.

Hebdige, Dick: *Hiding In The Light*, Comedia, London, 1988.

Hogan, David J: *Dark Romance: Sex And Death In The Horror Film*, MacFarland and Co, Jefferson, North Carolina, 1986.

Horan, James D and Sann, Paul: *Pictorial History Of The Wild West*, Hamlyn, London, 1961.

Johnston, Claire (ed): *Notes On Women's Cinema: Screen Pamphlet 2*, Society for Education in Film and Television, London, 1973.

Johnston, Claire (ed): *The Work Of Dorothy Azner*, BFI, London, 1975.

Karyn, K and Peary, Gerard (eds): *Women And Cinema: A Critical Anthology*, E P Dutton, New York, 1977.

Kirkham, Pat and Thumin, Janet (eds): *You Tarzan: Masculinity, Movies And Men*, Lawrence and Wishart, London, 1993.

Kuhn, Annette: *Women's Pictures; Feminism And Cinema*, Routledge, London, 1982.

Landy, Marcia: *British Genres: Cinema And Society 1930–1960*, Princeton University Press, 1991.

Launder, Frank: *The Wildcats Of St Trinians*, Fontana, London, 1980.

Lloyd, Ann (ed): *Movies Of The Fifities*, Orbis, London, 1982.

Lloyd, Ann(ed): *Movies Of The Sixties*, Orbis, London, 1983.

Lovell, Alan: *Don Siegel: American Cinema*, British Film Institute, London, 1975.

Lyon, Christopher (ed): *The International Dictionary Of Films And Filmmakers: Directors*, MacMillan, London, 1984.

Mayne, Judith: *Cinema And Spectatorship*, Routledge, London, 1993.

McGuigan, Jim: *Cultural Populism*, Routledge, London, 1992.

Morse, L A: *Video Trash And Treasures*, Harper Collins, Toronto, 1990.

Newman, Kim: *Nightmare Movies: A Critical History Of The Horror Movie From 1968*, Bloomsbury, London, 1984.

O' Pray, Michael (ed): *Andy Warhol: Film Factory*, British Film Institute, London, 1989.

Parish, James Robert: *Prison Pictures From Hollywood: Plots, Critiques, Casts And Credits For 293 Theatrical And Made-For-Television Releases*, MacFarland, North Carolina, 1991.

Parker, Roszika and Pollock, Griselda (eds): *Framing Feminism: Art And The Women's Movement 1970–1985*, Pandora Press, London, 1987.

Peary, Danny: *Cult Movies*, Delta, New York, 1986.

Peary, Danny: *Guide Of The Film Fanatic*, Simon and Schuster, New York, 1986.

Penley, Constance (ed): *Feminism And Film Theory*, Routledge/BFI, London, 1988.

Perry, George: *The Great British Picture Show*, Paladin, St Albans, 1974.

Pilling, Jayne and O'Pray Mike (eds): *Into The Pleasure Dome: The Films Of Kenneth Anger*, British Film Institute, London, 1989.

Pirie, David: *The Vampire Cinema*, Galley Press, Leicester, 1977.

Pribram, E, Dierdra: *Female Spectators: Looking At Film And Television*, Verso, London, 1988.

Psychotronic #16, Fall, 1993, USA.

Quart, Barbara Koenig: *Women Directors: The Emergence Of A New Cinema*, Praeger, New York, 1988.

Redeemer, 1:1, Winter, 1992, GB.

Ross, Jonathan: *The Incredibly Strange Film Book: An Alternative History Of Cinema*, Simon & Schuster, London, 1993.

Russo, Vito: *The Celluloid Closet: Homosexuality In The Movies*, Harper & Row, New York, 1985.

Ryan, Alan (ed): *The Penguin Book Of Vampire Stories*, Penguin, Reading, 1988.

Sargeant, Jack: *Deathtripping: The Cinema Of Transgression*, Creation Books, London, 1995.

Savage, Candice: *Cowgirls*, Bloomsbury, London, 1996.

Screen 16:3, Autumn, 1975, GB.

Shock Xpress, 2:5, Winter, 1988/9, USA.

Sight And Sound, February, 1994, GB.

Sight And Sound, March, 1977, GB.

Something Weird: Video Catalogue #1, 1995/6, USA.

Sontag, Susan: *Styles Of Radical Will*, Dell Publishing, New York, 1966.

Stevenson, Jack: *Desperate Visions 1: Camp America, John Waters, George And Mike Kuchar*, Creation Books, London, 1996.

Stoker, Bram: *Dracula*, Wordsworth Classics, Herts.

Strang, Mrs Herbert (ed): *The Great Book Of School Stories For Girls*, The Humphrey Milford OU Press, London, 1932.

Tasker, Yvonne: *Spectacular Bodies: Gender, Genre And The Action Cinema*, Comedia, London, 1993.

Telotte, J P (ed): *The Cult Film Experience: Beyond All Reason*, University of Texas Press, Austin, 1991.

Thumin, Janet: *Celluloid Sisters: Women And Popular Cinema*, MacMillan, London,1992.

Tyler, Parker: *Screening The Sexes: Homosexuality In The Movies*, Rhinehart and Winston, New York, 1972.

Tyler, Parker: *Underground Film: A Critical History*, De Capo Press, New York, 1972.

Vale, V and Juno, Andrea (eds): *Angry Women*, Re-Search, SF, 1991.

Vale, V and Juno, Andrea (eds): *Incredibly Strange Films,* Plexus, London, 1986.

Video Watchdog: The Perfectionist's Guide To Fantastic Video, #31, 1996, USA.

Videooze, Winter, 1991, USA.

Vogel, Amos: *Film As A Subversive Art*, Random House, New York, 1974.

Waters, John: *Shock Value*, Delta, New York, 1981.

Weiss, Andrea: *Vampires And Violets: Lesbians In The Cinema*, Jonathan Cape, London, 1992.

Weldon, Michael: *A Psychotronic Encyclopedia Of Film*, Plexus, London, 1983.

Wilton, Tamsin (ed): *Immortal, Invisible: Lesbians And The Moving Image*, Routledge, London, 1995.

Wollen, Peter: *Signs And Meaning In The Cinema*, British Film Institute, London, 1969.

INDEX OF FILMS

Page numbers in bold indicate an illustration

www.creationbooks.com